# PSAT Prep 2017

# Table of Contents

# FREE Test Taking Tips DVD Offer

To help us better serve you, we have developed a Test Taking Tips DVD that we would like to give you for <u>FREE</u>. **This DVD covers world-class test taking tips that you can use to be even more successful when you are taking your test.**

All that we ask is that you email us your feedback about your study guide. Please let us know what you thought about it – whether that is good, bad or indifferent.

To get your **FREE Test Taking Tips DVD**, email <u>freedvd@studyguideteam.com</u> with "FREE DVD" in the subject line and the following information in the body of the email:

    a.   The title of your study guide.

    b.   Your product rating on a scale of 1-5, with 5 being the highest rating.

    c.   Your feedback about the study guide. What did you think of it?

    d.   Your full name and shipping address to send your free DVD.

If you have any questions or concerns, please don't hesitate to contact us at <u>freedvd@studyguideteam.com</u>.

Thanks again!

# Quick Overview

As you draw closer to taking your exam, preparing becomes more and more important. Thankfully, you have this study guide to help you get ready. Use this guide to help keep your studying on track and refer to it often.

This study guide contains several key sections that will help you be successful on your exam. The guide contains tips for what you should do the night before and the day of the test. Also included are test-taking tips. Knowing the right information is not always enough. Many well-prepared test takers struggle with exams. These tips will help equip you to accurately read, assess, and answer test questions.

A large part of the guide is devoted to showing you what content to expect on the exam and to helping you better understand that content. Near the end of this guide is a practice test so that you can see how well you have grasped the content. Then, answers explanations are provided so that you can understand why you missed certain questions.

Don't try to cram the night before you take your exam. This is not a wise strategy for a few reasons. First, your retention of the information will be low. Your time would be better used by reviewing information you already know rather than trying to learn lots of new information. Second, you will likely become stressed as you try to gain large amount of knowledge in a short amount of time. Third, you will be depriving yourself of sleep. So be sure to go to bed at a reasonable time the night before. Being well-rested helps you focus and remain calm.

Be sure to eat a substantial breakfast the morning of the exam. If you are taking the exam in the afternoon, be sure to have a good lunch as well. Being hungry is distracting and can make it difficult to focus. You have hopefully spent lots of time preparing for the exam. Don't let an empty stomach get in the way of success!

When travelling to the testing center, leave earlier than needed. That way, you have a buffer in case you experience any delays. This will help you remain calm and will keep you from missing your appointment time at the testing center.

Be sure to pace yourself during the exam. Don't try to rush through the exam. There is no need to risk performing poorly on the exam just so you can leave the testing center early. Allow yourself to use all of the allotted time if needed.

Remain positive while taking the exam even if you feel like you are performing poorly. Thinking about the content you should have mastered will not help you perform better on the exam.

Once the exam is complete, take some time to relax. Even if you feel that you need to take the exam again, you will be well served by some down time before you begin studying again. It's often easier to convince yourself to study if you know that it will come with a reward!

# *Test-Taking Strategies*

## 1. Predicting the Answer

When you feel confident in your preparation for a multiple-choice test, try predicting the answer before reading the answer choices. This is especially useful on questions that test objective factual knowledge or that ask you to fill in a blank. By predicting the answer before reading the available choices, you eliminate the possibility that you will be distracted or led astray by an incorrect answer choice. You will feel much more confident in your selection if you read the question, predict the answer, and then find your prediction among the answer choices. After using this strategy, be sure to still read all of the answer choices carefully and completely. If you feel unprepared, you should not attempt to predict the answers. This would be a waste of time and an opportunity for your mind to wander in the wrong direction.

## 2. Reading the Whole Question

Too often, test takers scan a multiple-choice question, recognize a few familiar words, and immediately jump to the answer choices. Test authors are aware of this common impatience, and they will sometimes prey upon it. For instance, a test author might subtly turn the question into a negative, or he or she might redirect the focus of the question right at the end. The only way to avoid falling into these traps is to read the entirety of the question carefully before reading the answer choices.

## 3. Looking for Wrong Answers

Long and complicated multiple-choice questions can be intimidating. One way to simplify a difficult multiple-choice question is to eliminate all of the answer choices that are clearly wrong. In most sets of answers, there will be at least one selection that can be dismissed right away. If the test is administered on paper, the test taker could draw a line through it to indicate that it may be ignored; otherwise, the test taker will have to perform this operation mentally or on scratch paper. In either case, once the obviously incorrect answers have been eliminated, the remaining choices may be considered. Sometimes identifying the clearly wrong answers will give the test taker some information about the correct answer. For instance, if one of the remaining answer choices is a direct opposite of one of the eliminated answer choices, it may well be the correct answer. The opposite of obviously wrong is obviously right! Of course, this is not always the case. Some answers are obviously incorrect simply because they are irrelevant to the question being asked. Still, identifying and eliminating some incorrect answer choices is a good way to simplify a multiple-choice question.

## 4. Don't Overanalyze

Anxious test takers often overanalyze questions. When you are nervous, your brain will often run wild causing you to make associations and discover clues that don't actually exist. If you feel that this may be a problem for you, do whatever you can to slow down during the test. Try taking a deep breath or counting to ten. As you read and consider the question, restrict yourself to the particular words used by the author. Avoid thought tangents about what the author *really* meant, or what he or she was *trying* to say. The only things that matter on a multiple-choice test are the words that are actually in the question. You must avoid reading too much into a multiple-choice question, or supposing that the writer meant something other than what he or she wrote.

## 5. No Need for Panic

It is wise to learn as many strategies as possible before taking a multiple-choice test, but it is likely that you will come across a few questions for which you simply don't know the answer. In this situation, avoid panicking. Because most multiple-choice tests include dozens of questions, the relative value of a single wrong answer is small. Moreover, your failure on one question has no effect on your success elsewhere on the test. As much as possible, you should compartmentalize each question on a multiple-choice test. In other words, you should not allow your feelings about one question to affect your success on the others. When you find a question that you either don't understand or don't know how to answer, just take a deep breath and do your best. Read the entire question slowly and carefully. Try rephrasing the question a couple of different ways. Then, read all of the answer choices carefully. After eliminating obviously wrong answers, make a selection and move on to the next question.

## 6. Confusing Answer Choices

When working on a difficult multiple-choice question, there may be a tendency to focus on the answer choices that are the easiest to understand. Many people, whether consciously or not, gravitate to the answer choices that require the least concentration, knowledge, and memory. This is a mistake. When you come across an answer choice that is confusing, you need to give it extra attention. A question might be confusing because you do not know the subject matter to which it refers. If this is the case, don't eliminate the answer before you have affirmatively settled on another. When you come across an answer choice of this type, set it aside as you look at the remaining choices. If you can confidently assert that one of the other choices is correct, you can leave the confusing answer aside. Otherwise, you will need to take a moment to try to better understand the confusing answer choice. Rephrasing is one way to tease out the sense of a confusing answer choice.

## 7. Your First Instinct

Many people struggle with multiple-choice tests because they overthink the questions. If you have studied sufficiently for the test, you should be prepared to trust your first instinct once you have carefully and completely read the question and all of the answer choices. There is a great deal of research to suggest that the mind can come to the correct conclusion very quickly once it has obtained all of the relevant information. At times, it may seem to you as if your intuition is working faster even than your reasoning mind. This may in fact be true. The knowledge you obtain while studying may be retrieved from your subconscious before you have a chance to work out the associations that support it. Verify your instinct by working out the reasons that it should be trusted.

## 8. Key Words

Many test takers struggle with multiple-choice questions because they have poor reading comprehension skills. Quickly reading and understanding a multiple-choice question requires a mixture of skill and experience. To help with this, try jotting down a few key words and phrases on a piece of scrap paper. Doing this concentrates the process of reading and forces the mind to weigh the relative importance of the question's parts. In selecting words and phrases to write down, the test taker thinks about the question more deeply and carefully. This is especially true for multiple-choice questions that are preceded by a long prompt.

## 9. Subtle Negatives

One of the oldest tricks in the multiple-choice test writer's book is to subtly reverse the meaning of a question with a word like *not* or *except*. If you are not paying attention to each word in the question, you can easily be led astray by this trick. For instance, a common question format is, "Which of the following is...?" Obviously, if the question instead is, "Which of the following is not....?," then the answer will be quite different. Even worse, the test makers are aware of the potential for this mistake and will include one answer choice that would be correct if the question were not negated or reversed. A test taker who misses the reversal will find what he or she believes to be a correct answer and will be so confident that he or she will fail to reread the question and discover the original error. The only way to avoid this is to practice a wide variety of multiple-choice questions and to pay close attention to each and every word.

## 10. Reading Every Answer Choice

It may seem obvious, but you should always read every one of the answer choices! Too many test takers fall into the habit of scanning the question and assuming that they understand the question because they recognize a few key words. From there, they pick the first answer choice that answers the question they believe they have read. Test takers who read all of the answer choices might discover that one of the latter answer choices is actually *more* correct. Moreover, reading all of the answer choices can remind you of facts related to the question that can help you arrive at the correct answer. Sometimes, a misstatement or incorrect detail in one of the latter answer choices will trigger your memory of the subject and will enable you to find the right answer. Failing to read all of the answer choices is like not reading all of the items on a restaurant menu. You might miss out on the perfect choice.

## 11. Spot the Hedges

One of the keys to success on multiple-choice tests is paying close attention to every word. This is never more true than with words like *almost*, *most*, *some*, and *sometimes*. These words are called "hedges", because they indicate that a statement is not totally true or not true in every place and time. An absolute statement will contain no hedges, but in many subjects, like literature and history, the answers are not always straightforward. There are always exceptions to the rules in these subjects. For this reason, you should favor those multiple-choice questions that contain hedging language. The presence of qualifying words indicates that the author is taking special care with his or her words, which is certainly important when composing the right answer. After all, there are many ways to be wrong, but there is only one way to be right! For this reason, it is wise when taking a multiple-choice test to avoid answers that are absolute. An absolute answer is one that says things are either all one way or all another. They often include words like *every*, *always*, *best*, and *never*. If you are taking a multiple-choice test in a subject that doesn't lend itself to absolute answers, be on your guard if you see any of these words.

## 12. Long Answers

In many subject areas, the answers are not simple. As already mentioned, the right answer often requires hedges. Another common feature of the answers to a complex or subjective question are qualifying clauses, which are groups of words that subtly modify the meaning of the sentence. If the question or answer choice describes a rule to which there are exceptions or the subject matter is complicated, ambiguous, or confusing, the correct answer will require many words in order to be expressed clearly and accurately. In essence, you should not be deterred by answer choices that seem excessively long. Oftentimes, the author of the text will not be able to write the correct answer without offering some qualifications and modifications. As a test taker, your job is to read the answer choices thoroughly and completely and to select the one that most accurately and precisely answers the question.

### 13. Restating to Understand

Sometimes, a question on a multiple-choice test is difficult not because of what it asks but because of how it is written. If this is the case, restate the question or answer choice in different words. This process serves a couple of important purposes. First, it forces you to concentrate on the core of the question. In order to rephrase the question accurately, you have to understand it well. Rephrasing the question will concentrate your mind on the key words and ideas. Second, it will present the information to your mind in a fresh way. This process may trigger your memory of some useful scrap of information picked up while studying.

### 14. True Statements

Sometimes an answer choice will be true in itself, but it does not answer the question. This is one of the main reasons why it is essential to read the question carefully and completely before proceeding to the answer choices. Too often, test takers skip ahead to the answer choices and look for true statements. Having found one of these, they are content to select it without reference to the question above. Obviously, this provides an easy way for test makers to play tricks. The savvy test taker will always read the entire question before turning to the answer choices. Then, having settled on a correct answer choice, he or she will refer to the original question and ensure that the selected answer is relevant. The mistake of choosing a correct-but-irrelevant answer choice is especially common on questions related to specific pieces of objective knowledge, like historical or scientific facts. A prepared test taker will have a wealth of factual knowledge at his or her disposal, but may be careless in its application.

### 15. No Patterns

One of the more dangerous ideas that circulate about multiple-choice tests is that the correct answers tend to fall into patterns. These erroneous ideas range from a belief that B and C are the most common right answers, to the idea that an unprepared test-taker should answer "A-B-A-C-A-D-A-B-A." It cannot be emphasized enough that pattern-seeking of this type is exactly the WRONG way to approach a multiple-choice test. To begin with, it is highly unlikely that the test maker will plot the correct answers according to some predetermined pattern. The questions are scrambled and delivered in a random order. Furthermore, even if the test maker was following a pattern in the assignation of correct answers, there is no reason why the test maker would know which pattern he or she was using. Any attempt to discern a pattern in the answer choices is a waste of time and a distraction from the real work of taking the test. A test taker would be much better served by extra preparation before the test than by reliance on a pattern in the answers.

## FREE DVD OFFER

Don't forget that doing well on your exam includes both understanding the test content and understanding how to use what you know to do well on the test. We offer a completely FREE Test Taking Tips DVD that covers world class test taking tips that you can use to be even more successful when you are taking your test.

All that we ask is that you email us your feedback about your study guide. To get your **FREE Test Taking Tips DVD**, email freedvd@studyguideteam.com with "FREE DVD" in the subject line and the following information in the body of the email:
- The title of your study guide.
- Your product rating on a scale of 1-5, with 5 being the highest rating.
- Your feedback about the study guide. What did you think of it?
- Your full name and shipping address to send your free DVD.

# Evidence-Based Reading Test

The reading portion of the PSAT consists of one 60-minute section. It will contain 5 single passages or passage pairs. There will be a total of 47 questions relating to these passages. The breakdown of passages and questions is in the table below.

| U.S and World Literature | 1 passage; 9 questions | 20% |
|---|---|---|
| History/Social Studies | 2 passages, or 1 passage and 1 pair; 9-10 questions each | 40% |
| Science | 2 passages, or 1 passage and 1 pair; 9-10 questions each | 40% |

The PSAT Reading Test will contain a range of text complexities from grades 9-10 and post secondary entry. The passages will cover U.S. and World Literature, History/Social Studies, and Science. The test will also contain 1-2 graphical representations. These may include tables, graphs, and charts. They will vary in level of difficulty as well as data density, and number of variables.

## Information and Ideas

The questions tested in this section will focus on the informational content contained in the text.

## Reading Closely

These questions will focus on the student's ability to read a passage and extrapolate beyond the information presented. They will look at both the explicit and implicit meanings of the text.

Explicitly stated information
Identifying information stated explicitly in text means locating facts or opinions stated outright in the text and not requiring reader inference or interpretation. For example, when including factual information, an author might give specific names of people, places, or events; specific numbers; specific days of the week, names of months, or dates including the month, date, and year. In informational text, the author might state numerical measurements, e.g., the size of a room or object; the distance between places; how many people live in a certain locality; how many people die annually from a certain cause; or the date, time, and/or place a certain event occurred. Abraham Lincoln began his Gettysburg Address, "Four score and seven years ago," which today is archaic language but does not require inference or interpretation; even a reader unfamiliar with the meaning of "score" can easily look up and find it. In a fictional novel, the author might state how many people are invited to, or were in attendance at, a party or other event.

Drawing inferences from text
Some meanings in text are implicit rather than explicit; in other words, they are not directly stated (explicit), but implied (implicit). This means the reader needs to make an assumption or draw an inference based on what is actually stated. Inferring meaning is often described by the saying "reading between the lines," i.e., determining what is unsaid through carefully observing what is said. For example, if an author writes, "Considering recent economic changes, what were once necessities are now luxuries for many businesses," the reader can infer that the "recent economic changes" the author refers to involve recession, not recovery or prosperity. Describing things formerly viewed as necessary but now as unnecessary implies worse, not better changes. Or a novelist might write, "Trembling and flushing, she asked breathlessly, 'You saw him? How is he? Did he ask how I am? Did he mention me at all?'" From the author's description of the character, the reader can infer she feels love/attraction for "'him'."

**Determining Explicit Meanings**

These questions will require the student to identify information explicitly stated in the text.

Explicit descriptors
Writers explicitly state not only factual information in their texts; they also explicitly state other kinds of information. For example, authors use description to give readers a better idea of the characteristics of whatever they are describing. If an author writes, "This sarcophagus is decorated with a vivid color illustration," the word "vivid" is more descriptive than factual. It communicates to the reader that the color illustration described is especially bright, vibrant, or intense visually. This is very helpful when there are no visual images of the object being described to accompany the text. Explicit descriptive words also apply to abstract concepts. For example, the author might write that the vivid color illustration depicts a famous figure's "brave actions." The word "brave" describes the actions of the person using an abstract concept. It communicates to the reader that the person's actions are considered brave or courageous by the author, and usually by other people as well.

Explicitly stated opinions
An essayist might state an opinion; for example, "These people were not treated fairly." Since readers are expected to be able to distinguish opinion from fact, the essayist need not write, "In my opinion, these people were not treated fairly." It is a common practice of authors, especially those writing argumentative or persuasive types of text, to state opinions the same as facts. Even though not proven factual, opinions are stated just as explicitly as facts in these instances. Writers state ideas explicitly in text as well. For example, an author might write about how people historically believed that the Earth was flat, or that the Sun revolved around the Earth. These are not factual, but not simply opinions either; they were the prevailing beliefs at the time, i.e., commonly held ideas. When an author explicitly states his or her *main* idea, he or she typically makes it the topic sentence of the paragraph, chapter, or piece. Topic sentences are also examples of explicitly stating ideas, i.e., expressing them directly in text rather than implying them.

**Determining Implicit Meanings**

The questions in this section will require the student to read the text and then draw inferences from the text and form logical conclusions.

Inferences
Inferences are educated guesses that can be drawn from the facts and information available to a reader. Inferences are usually based upon a reader's own assumptions and beliefs. The ability to make inferences is often called reading between the lines. There are three basic types of inference: deductive reasoning, abductive reasoning, and inductive reasoning. Deductive reasoning is the ability to find an effect when given a cause and a rule. Abductive reasoning is the ability to find a cause when given a rule and an effect. Inductive reasoning is the ability to find a rule when given the cause and effect. Each type of reasoning can be used to make logical inferences from a piece of writing.

Drawing conclusions
An essayist might state an opinion; for example, "These people were not treated fairly." Since readers are expected to be able to distinguish opinion from fact, the essayist need not write, "In my opinion, these people were not treated fairly." It is a common practice of authors, especially those writing argumentative or persuasive types of text, to state opinions the same as facts. Even though not proven factual, opinions are stated just as explicitly as facts in these instances. Writers state ideas explicitly in text as well. For example, an author might write about how people historically believed that the Earth was flat, or that the Sun revolved around the Earth. These are not factual, but not simply opinions either; they were the prevailing beliefs at the time, i.e.,

commonly held ideas. When an author explicitly states his or her *main* idea, he or she typically makes it the topic sentence of the paragraph, chapter, or piece. Topic sentences are also examples of explicitly stating ideas, i.e., expressing them directly in text rather than implying them.

<u>Ways that drawing inferences are tested</u>
One way a test might ask you to draw inferences or conclusions is asking what a character in text would likely react to a given event/circumstance based on a text passage. You would need to read closely for clues on which to base your inference. You might see a description of an earlier incident wherein this character reacted a certain way. For example, the author wrote, "The last time somebody hit her, she ran away." Based on this, you could infer she would do the same thing. Or one character says, "If he finds out what you did, he'll kill you," and the passage includes explicit description of the referenced character having killed people. You could then conclude if the third character finds out what the second character did, he will kill him or her. Some works, rather than providing a neat conclusion, seem to end in mid-action; yet readers can predict much from it. An excellent example of such a midstream ending inviting readers to infer conclusions is in Joyce Maynard's novel *Baby Love* (1981).

**Using Analogical Reasoning**

The student will be required to extrapolate information and idea from the text in order to answer these questions. They will also need to be able to this information and ideas to new, analogous situations.

<u>Using analogical reasoning</u>
Using analogical reasoning as described above involves thinking about situations that are comparable to one in the text and applying information from the text to those other parallel situations. For example, suppose a student reads that colonial Americans, dissatisfied with British laws and influenced by Enlightenment philosophy, wanted freedom to govern themselves instead of being ruled by the British monarchy, so they started the American Revolution to fight for their freedom and won, forming a democratic government. Suppose the student then further reads that the French, strongly influenced both by the same Enlightenment philosophy and by the Americans' success, started the French Revolution, also fighting for their freedom from an unfair monarchy, winning, and forming a democratic government. Then suppose the same student reads about people in other countries being ruled unfairly by a tyrannical monarchy. The student could reasonably apply the information about America and France to these other countries and expect revolutionary wars to break out in some of these other countries.

<u>Extrapolate from text</u>
Even fictional text can be applied to analogous situations, particularly when the author's knowledge of human nature is sound and some of the text elements can be applied across settings. For example, reading William Shakespeare's tragedy *Romeo and Juliet,* one might first observe differences from today's real world: It is set centuries ago, in another country, and involves a family feud, which is rare today. However, one could then observe similarities: The main characters are teenagers; they fall madly in love; their families prohibit their seeing each other; and their families dislike each other, which is commoner today than actual feuds. Teen suicide and teen suicide pacts occur today. Thus the student could extrapolate from this play, albeit fictional, that two teens today as fervently in love as Romeo and Juliet whose parents kept them apart, feeling there were no better options, might take the same actions. Despite today's technology, the chance/accidental element (lack of timely information) causing the double tragedy could equally occur today.

*Example:*

Consider that a student reads in a biology text that mitosis is an asexual type of reproduction in which cells divide to produce more identical cells. The student reads further that mitosis takes place in all living organisms. From this information, the student can extrapolate that since mitosis occurs in all living organisms, mitosis must therefore occur in human beings. Since mitosis is an asexual type of reproduction, the student can further infer that mitosis is not the way in which humans reproduce sexually. By process of elimination, the student can then deduce that mitosis in humans must involve only the reproduction of cells within each individual human body. The student can further deduce that sexual reproduction in human beings must not be mitosis. The student cannot know that human sexual reproduction involves meiosis, or how this differs from mitosis, without reading about meiosis; however, he or she can determine all the aforementioned things just from reading about mitosis alone.

## Citing Textual Evidence

These questions will ask the student to support their answer with evidence from the text. The student should be able to specifically identify the information in the text and be able to properly cite it.

### Citing supporting evidence

Citing evidence from text that supports a point or claim in that text involves identifying which information is most directly related to that point or claim. As an example, if a writer makes the claim that the world population is increasing, that author might provide evidence to support this claim, such as census statistics from the past several consecutive years, decades, or centuries that give world population numbers larger than they were previously. In the same text, the author may also provide figures measuring poverty, hunger, and other ills related to overpopulation in certain parts of the world to make a case for the argument that population growth is bad and should be controlled. However, the student would be mistaken to cite those figures as evidence supporting the claim that the population is increasing; they are, rather, evidence supporting the claim that population growth is bad and should be controlled.

### Citing information that is not informational or argumentative

Whereas informational and argumentative text may often use facts and/or figures as evidence to support various points or claims, fictional narration or description may use more descriptive details as supporting evidence. Moreover, the points or claims in such works may not be stated explicitly in words, but instead may be demonstrated through the actions or responses of characters. For example, an author of a play or novel may establish that a character is highly emotional by portraying or describing behaviors demonstrating this—e.g., flying into a rage, crying easily, becoming overjoyed readily, etc. The playwright or novelist need not write in another character's dialogue that this character is passionate or has mood swings; it is demonstrated through actions/behaviors. Subsequently in the play or novel, the character may do something which is not surprising but expected based on this established character trait. The character's previous actions are evidence supporting the credibility of the later action—i.e., it was "in character."

### Steps to cite textual evidence

To cite evidence explicitly stated in text to support what they think about the text, students can take several steps. First, students should state their idea regarding the text. When answering a test question, students should also ensure his or her idea is or includes a restatement of the question. Then, to cite textual evidence supporting that idea, students can either paraphrase the evidence, i.e., restate or describe it in their own words; or quote part of the text directly, enclosing it in quotation marks and introducing it by referencing the paragraph or portion where it appears. Then students need to explain how the evidence they cited supports their idea about the text. For example, students might write that the evidence illustrates a similarity or difference between things, gives a reason for something, demonstrates a cause-and-effect relationship, explains what something means or how something works, etc. Students should also identify how the evidence cited contributed to their formulation of the idea answering the question. Students should cite at least two pieces of textual evidence per idea/question.

## Determining Central Ideas and Themes

For these questions the student should be able to identify central ideas and themes that are explicitly stated in the text. They will also need to be able to determine implicit central ideas and themes from the text.

### Determining the central ideas of a passage
Central ideas are what a passage is mainly about. They are why the passage is written. The main idea is often found in a topic sentence or even a concluding sentence, and there are supporting details found in the passage that expand upon the main idea. There can, however, be more than one central idea, and these main ideas can be related and intertwined. For instance, the main or central idea of a passage may be that rainforests are drying out. A related main idea might be that the result of rainforest destruction is a loss of wildlife. These two central ideas are obviously related, and the passage may present both of them by focusing on one in one part of the passage and the other in another part of the passage. Another way they could be related is in a cause and effect relationship, with the loss of rainforests being the reason for losses of wildlife. It is important to always check to see if there is more than one central idea in a passage.

*Read the excerpt below. Identify and discuss the main idea.*

> Students who have jobs while attending high school tend not to have as much time to complete their homework as other students. They also do not have time for other activities. We should try to persuade our young people to concentrate on doing well in school, not to concentrate on making money. Having a job while you are a student is harmful.

The main idea of the excerpt is actually the last sentence: "Having a job while you are a student is harmful." This is what the excerpt is mostly about. The other sentences contain supporting information: students who have jobs don't have as much time for homework; students with jobs don't have time for as many activities. These are both supporting details that tell more about the main idea. The third sentence deals with a persuasive argument; it is another kind of detail. Only the last sentence tells what the excerpt is mostly about. Main ideas are sometimes found in a topic sentence at the start of a text or in the concluding sentence, which is the case in this excerpt.

### Theme
As opposed to a main idea, themes are seldom expressed directly in a text, so they can be difficult to identify. A theme is an issue, an idea, or a question raised by the text. For instance, a theme of William Shakespeare's *Hamlet* is indecision, as the title character explores his own psyche and the results of his failure to make bold choices. A great work of literature may have many themes, and the reader is justified in identifying any for which he or she can find support. One common characteristic of themes is that they raise more questions than they answer. In a good piece of fiction, the author is not always trying to convince the reader, but is instead trying to elevate the reader's perspective and encourage him to consider the themes more deeply.

### 5 Steps to identify the main idea or theme
As with all learning and development, reading should begin with concrete and gradually progress to abstract. Students must identify and understand literal information before they can make inferences. The first step is to identify the most important nouns and verbs in a sentence and define what the sentence is about. The second step is to identify the most important nouns, verbs, and adjectives in a whole paragraph, and define what that paragraph is about. The third step is to read brief passages, all of which use topic sentences with literal meanings. Students should be able to identify topic sentences not only at the beginning, but also anywhere else in a

paragraph. In the fourth step, students can begin to make inferences by reading a single paragraph and then determining and articulating what the main idea is that the paragraph implies. The fifth step involves reading passages with more than one paragraph, gradually and slowly increasing the length of passages and identifying the implicit main idea each time. Students should be able to infer the main idea in shorter texts before proceeding to longer ones.

## Summarizing

These questions will test the student's ability to identify a summary of a text after reading the text. The student should be able to identify a reasonable summary of the text or of key information presented in the text.

### Summarizing

It is also helpful to summarize the information you have read in a paragraph or passage format. This process is similar to creating an effective outline. To begin with, a summary should accurately define the main idea of the passage, though it does not need to explain this main idea in exhaustive detail. It should continue by laying out the most important supporting details or arguments from the passage. All of the significant supporting details should be included, and none of the details included should be irrelevant or insignificant. Also, the summary should accurately report all of these details. Too often, the desire for brevity in a summary leads to the sacrifice of clarity or veracity. Summaries are often difficult to read, because they omit all of graceful language, digressions, and asides that distinguish great writing. However, if the summary is effective, it should contain much the same message as the original text.

### Activities to help students learn to summarize

For students to be able to identify good summaries of text or its key information, it will help if they learn how to summarize these themselves. Although they will find recognizing good summaries easier than making their own summaries, both processes require identifying subject matter through locating representative words and recalling significant information. One activity in which students can practice summarizing skills and teachers can provide scaffolding and guidance is using an ABC Chart. This is a simple square grid containing smaller squares, each labeled A, B, C, etc. through Z. Students read a passage; the teacher guides them to recall important phrases and words in the text, write each one on a Post-it Note, and attach it to the square labeled with the first letter of the phrase/word. Students should try to recall as many details, facts, etc. as possible. Then they remove the Post-it Notes from the chart and stick them randomly on the board. The teacher helps them arrange the notes in some pattern—e.g., into a web, by ideas; or chronologically along a timeline, etc. This helps students organize their thoughts.

## Understanding Relationships

Texts will contain many different relationships between individuals, events, and ideas. These questions will test the student's ability to identify explicitly stated relationships as well as determine implicit ones.

### Textual features that help identify relationships

Authors use various relationships as ways of organizing, presenting, and explaining information. For example, describing cause-and-effect relationships is a common technique in expository/informational text. The author describes some event(s), and then either explicitly states or implicitly establishes factors causing them. When authors use comparison-contrast, they typically compare similarities between/among ideas/things using similes (stated comparisons), metaphors (implied comparisons), and analogies (comparisons of similarities in two unrelated things). Authors identify contrasts by describing opposing qualities/characteristics in things/ideas. One example of using sequence or order is arranging events chronologically, beginning to end. Students can recognize sequential organization by observing specific dates, times, and signal words including "first," "before," "next," "then," "following," "after," "subsequently," "finally," etc. Sequence can also be spatial or by order of importance. Authors introduce some problem, describe its characteristics, and then offer solutions in problem-solution relationships. Descriptive writing provides sensory details to make information realer and easier for readers to imagine. How-to/instructional texts use serial directions to provide information.

<u>Compare and Contrast</u>
Authors will use different stylistic and writing devices to make their meaning more clearly understood. One of those devices is comparison and contrast. When an author describes the ways in which two things are alike, he or she is comparing them. When the author describes the ways in which two things are different, he or she is contrasting them. The "compare and contrast" essay is one of the most common forms in nonfiction. It is often signaled with certain words: a comparison may be indicated with such words as *both*, *same*, *like*, *too*, and *as well*; while a contrast may be indicated by words like *but*, *however*, *on the other hand*, *instead*, and *yet*. Of course, comparisons and contrasts may be implicit without using any such signaling language. A single sentence may both compare and contrast. Consider the sentence *Brian and Sheila love ice cream, but Brian prefers vanilla and Sheila prefers strawberry*. In one sentence, the author has described both a similarity (love of ice cream) and a difference (favorite flavor).

<u>Cause and effect</u>
One of the most common text structures is cause and effect. A cause is an act or event that makes something happen, and an effect is the thing that happens as a result of that cause. A cause-and-effect relationship is not always explicit, but there are some words in English that signal causality, such as *since*, *because*, and *as a result*. As an example, consider the sentence *Because the sky was clear, Ron did not bring an umbrella*. The cause is the clear sky, and the effect is that Ron did not bring an umbrella. However, sometimes the cause-and-effect relationship will not be clearly noted. For instance, the sentence *He was late and missed the meeting* does not contain any signaling words, but it still contains a cause (he was late) and an effect (he missed the meeting). It is possible for a single cause to have multiple effects, or for a single effect to have multiple causes. Also, an effect can in turn be the cause of another effect, in what is known as a cause-and-effect chain.

<u>Text sequence</u>
A reader must be able to identify a text's sequence, or the order in which things happen. Often, and especially when the sequence is very important to the author, it is indicated with signal words like first, then, next, and last. However, sometimes a sequence is merely implied and must be noted by the reader. Consider the sentence He walked in the front door and switched on the hall lamp. Clearly, the man did not turn the lamp on before he walked in the door, so the implied sequence is that he first walked in the door and then turned on the lamp. Texts do not always proceed in an orderly sequence from first to last: sometimes, they begin at the end and then start over at the beginning. As a reader, it can be useful to make brief notes to clarify the sequence.

**Interpreting Words and Phrases in Context**

These questions will ask the student to determine the meaning of words and phrases from the text. The student must use context clues to help determine the meaning of these words and phrases.

<u>Contextual clues</u>
Look for contextual clues. An answer can be right but not correct. The contextual clues will help you find the answer that is most right and is correct. Understand the context in which a phrase is stated.

When asked for the implied meaning of a statement made in the passage, immediately go find the statement and read the context. Also, look for an answer choice that has a similar phrase to the statement in question.
*Example:*

In the passage, what is implied by the phrase "Churches have become more or less part of the furniture"?

Find an answer choice that is similar or describes the phrase "part of the furniture" as that is the key phrase in the question. "Part of the furniture" is a saying that means something is fixed, immovable, or set in their ways. Those are all similar ways of saying "part of the furniture." As such, the correct answer choice will probably include a similar rewording of the expression.
*Example:*

Why was John described as "morally desperate"?

The answer will probably have some sort of definition of morals in it. "Morals" refers to a code of right and wrong behavior, so the correct answer choice will likely have words that mean something like that.

Using word meaning

Paying attention to the phrase, sentence, paragraph, or larger context surrounding a word gives students two distinct advantages: One, it can help figure out the meaning of a new or unfamiliar vocabulary word by the information its context provides; and two, it can help distinguish between/among different meanings of the same word according to which meaning makes sense within context. For example, when reading words like "nickelback" and "bootleg," if the surrounding context is football, these refer to an additional, fifth defensive back position played by a safety or cornerback and a play run by the quarterback, respectively; but if the surrounding context is rock music, "Nickelback" refers to the name of a Canadian band, and "bootleg" to unofficial or unauthorized recordings of musical performances. Students can look for contextual synonyms for unknown words; for example, a reader unfamiliar with the meaning of "prudent" may observe the words "careful," "cautious," "judicious," etc. Antonyms also help; e.g., if text says, "Smug? On the contrary, he's the most self-critical person I know." This informs defining "smug" as self-congratulatory/overly self-satisfied.

**Rhetoric**

The questions in this section will focus on the rhetorical analysis of a text.

**Analyzing Word Choice**

Authors use specific words, phrases, and patterns of words in their writing. The student will be asked to determine how these help to shape the meaning and tone in the text.

Rhetorical Analysis

When analyzing the rhetoric a text uses, students should aim to reveal the purpose of the text or the author's purpose in writing it; who the author's intended audience was; the decisions that the author made, and how these decisions may have influenced the final result of the text. Identifying the intended purpose and audience of a text is identifying two main components of its rhetorical situation, i.e., the circumstances wherein communication occurs, which serves as a major basis for rhetorical analysis. The third main component is the context. Context can include many factors, e.g., the occasion of the work; the exigency, i.e., what motivated the author to write the text; the media and/or venue of its original appearance; the historical background and even the state of the world relative to the text's topic. As an example, texts written respectively before and after 9/11/2001 on the topic of air travel would have some marked differences.

## Word choice or diction in rhetoric

Word choice or diction affects the tone of a text and how readers perceive its meaning. Writers inform their diction in part by considering their intended audience and selecting words that will be understood by and appeal to this audience. For instance, language with more denotative meanings (i.e., straightforward dictionary definitions) is more suitable for informational texts, whereas language with more connotative meanings (i.e., words that carry implied associated meanings) is more suitable for descriptive and narrative texts to evoke images and emotions. As examples, describing a sound or noise as "extremely loud" or "at a volume of 100 dB" is more factual and denotative; describing it as "thunderous," "deafening," or in specific reference to a speaker's voice, "stentorian," is more descriptive, connotative, and evocative. Audience also influences the relative formality of diction. For example, more formal text appropriate for an adult professional academic audience might describe size as "massive," whereas more informal language appropriate for high school and younger students might use the blending neologism "ginormous."

## How word choice or diction influence meaning and understanding

When writers use good judgment in word choice, they communicate their messages more effectively for readers to understand. Poor word choice, as well as not considering the intended audience in one's diction, can distract readers to the point that they miss the message. Readers can consider the denotations (dictionary definition meanings) and connotations (implied associated meanings) of words used in text, as well as the rhythm and force of words and whether the author uses words concisely, includes verbiage, or appears to have logorrhea. When analyzing word choice in a text, students can consider whether the author has selected words that are comprehensible to the identified reading audience; whether words are chosen with precision and specificity; whether the author selected strong words to express meaning; whether the author placed more emphasis on positive than negative words in text; whether/how often the author included words that are overused, making the language cliché or trite; and whether the text incorporates words that are obsolete today, which readers may not recognize or understand.

## Analyzing Text Structure

For these questions students will be asked to answer questions about why the author structured the text a certain way. They will also be asked about the relationship between a particular part of the text and the whole text.

## Elements to consider in analyzing text structure

Text structure is how a text is organized. In analyzing the overall structure of a text, the reader can consider its order, e.g., what is written first, what follows, and how it ends; and how its sections and chapters are divided. The genre or type of text is another consideration. For example, consider whether the text is fictional or nonfictional; prose, poetry, drama, or oratory; in fictional prose, whether a novel is a romantic, adventure, action, graphic, historical, fantasy, science fiction novel, etc.; in nonfiction, whether it is an essay; research article, journalistic article, opinion-editorial article; how-to manual; travelogue; etc. The relationship or pattern organizing the text may be a timeline sequence, logical sequence, a priority sequence, or spatial sequence; an analysis of the balance of forces; an analysis of similarities and differences/comparison-contrast; a process of problem, solution, and resolution; simply a list of items; or a piece that seems to jump around without order. Consider also what tone the language establishes; vocabulary and imagery used; and the accuracy of text mechanics (grammar, punctuation, spelling, etc.).

## Organizational methods to structure text

Authors organize their writing based on the purpose of their text. Common organizational methods that authors use include: cause and effect, compare and contrast, inductive presentation of ideas, deductive presentation of ideas, and chronological order. Cause and effect is used to present the reasons that something happened. Compare and contrast is used to discuss the similarities and differences between two things. Inductive presentation of ideas starts with specific examples and moves to a general conclusion. Deductive presentation of ideas starts with a conclusion and then explains the examples used to arrive at the conclusion. Chronological order presents information in the order that it occurred.

Cause and effect and chronological order
Authors have to organize information logically so the reader can follow what is being said and locate information in the text. Two common organizational structures are cause and effect and chronological order. In cause and effect, an author presents one thing that makes something else happen. For example, if you go to bed very late, you will be tired. The cause is going to bed late. The effect is being tired the next day. When using chronological order, the author presents information in the order that it happened. Biographies are written in chronological order. The subject's birth and childhood are presented first, followed by adult life, and then by events leading up to the person's death.

Compare and contrast example
Read the following thesis statement and discuss the organizational pattern that the author will most likely use:

> Among people who are current on the latest technologies, there is a debate over whether DVD or Blu-ray Disc is a better choice for watching and recording video.

From the thesis statement the reader can assume that the author is most likely going to use a compare and contrast organizational structure. The compare and contrast structure is best used to discuss the similarities and differences of two things. The author mentions two options for watching and recording video: DVD and Blu-ray Disc. During the rest of the essay, the author will most likely describe the two technologies, giving specific examples of how they are similar and different. The author may discuss the pros and cons of each technology.

Chronological example
Read the following thesis statement and discuss the organizational pattern that the author will most likely use:

> Throughout his life, Thomas Edison used his questioning and creative mind to become one of America's greatest inventors.

Based on the thesis statement, the reader can assume that the author is most likely going to use chronological order to organize the information in the rest of the essay. Chronological order presents information in the order that it occurred. It is often used as the organizational structure in biographies as a way to logically present the important events in a person's life. The words "throughout his life" clue in the reader to the chronological organizational structure. The author will probably discuss Edison's childhood and initial inventions first and then move on to his later queries and inventions.

> Todd is writing an editorial on the need for more bus stops in his town. Discuss the type of organization he should use for his editorial and what each might look like.

Todd could organize the information in his editorial in a few different ways. An editorial is a persuasive text so Todd will want to keep that in mind. First, he could organize the information by making his most important points first, following with his lesser points towards the end. Alternatively, Todd could use a cause and effect structure. He could discuss the reasons that his town needs more bus stops and the effects they would have for the people living there. Finally, Todd could discuss the pros and cons of adding the bus stops, using a compare and contrast structure. The organizational structure Todd chooses will depend on the information he wants to write and the method he thinks will be most persuasive.

## Part-whole relationships

Students should be able to recognize and explain how a portion of a text is related to the overall text to demonstrate they understand part-to-whole relationships when analyzing text. Every part of a text must serve essential purposes, including setting up/establishing the text at the beginning; fitting together logically with all other parts of the text; remaining focused on the point; supporting the overall text through introducing its topic, establishing evidence, supporting or countering a claim, outlining subtopics, aspects, or components, describing a characteristic or feature, etc.; and informing the reader—about the setting of the text, a character in it, a relationship between/among characters, a research study, an opinion, or something else relevant to the text. Test questions may ask about how words function within sentences, as these examples address; or sentence-to-paragraph relationships, which also include setup or setting the tone, logic, focus or point, including shifts in focus, and evidence supporting claims as functions; or paragraph-to-whole-text relationships, wherein paragraphs should establish a claim/situation; support or refute a claim; maintain focus; and/or inform readers.

## Analyzing Point of View

These questions will make the student to determine from which point of view a text was written. They will also need to determine the influence that that this point of view has on the content and style of the text.

### Point of view

The point of view of a text is the perspective from which it is told. Every literary text has a narrator or person who tells the story. The two main points of view that authors use are first person and third person. If a narrator is also the main character, or protagonist, the text is written in first-person point of view. In first person, the author writes with the word *I*. Third-person point of view is probably the most common point of view that authors use. Using third person, authors refer to each character using the words *he* or *she*. In third-person omniscient, the narrator is not a character in the story and tells the story of all of the characters at the same time.

### Example

Read the following excerpt from Jane Austen's *Emma* and discuss the point of view:
"Doing just what she liked; highly esteeming Miss Taylor's judgments, but directed chiefly by her own. The real evils, indeed, of Emma's situation were the power of having rather too much her own way, and a disposition to think a little too well of herself...."

To determine the point of view, you should first look at the pronouns used in the passage. If the passage has the pronoun "I" it is probably written in first-person point of view. In first-person point of view, the protagonist is the narrator. In the case of this excerpt, a narrator who is not the protagonist is telling the story. The pronouns used are "she" and "her," which are clues that someone is talking about the character rather than the character speaking for herself. This excerpt is written in the third-person point of view. An outside narrator is telling the story *about* Emma. Emma is not telling the story about herself.

### How to determine point of view

In expository text, authors apply various strategies for communicating their points of view about specific topics. As readers, students can identify author point of view readily in some texts; however, they will have to analyze other texts closely to determine point of view. To discern author viewpoint, students can ask themselves four questions: (1) The author is writing to persuade readers to agree with what main idea? (2) How does the author's word choice influence the reader perceptions about the topic? (3) How does the author's selection of examples and/or facts as supporting evidence influence reader thinking about the topic? And (4) What purpose does the author wish to achieve through the text? Students may find the main idea stated directly, as in a topic sentence found in the text, often somewhere in the first paragraph; or they may need to infer it by carefully reading to identify sentences or paragraphs implying it. Students can assess influences of word choice by identifying words/phrases with positive or negative connotations rather than only objective denotations, emphasis through repetition, etc. Examples/facts should illustrate the main idea/point. Author purpose coincides with point of view.

## Analyzing Purpose

These questions will ask the student to determine the purpose of a text or a piece of a text. The pieces of text are typically one particular paragraph of the text.

### Author's purpose
An author writes with four main purposes: to inform, to entertain, to describe, or to persuade. These purposes play into an author's motivation to craft a text. If the author wants to entertain, he or she may write a novel or short story that has humorous elements and/or dramatic elements. Remember, entertainment does not have to mean comedy or humor; it can just as easily be drama. To determine an author's motives, think about the author's purpose. If the text is fiction, the author's purpose is most likely to entertain or describe. If the text is nonfiction, the author's purpose is most likely to inform. If the text is an editorial or advertisement, the author's purpose is most likely to persuade. Once you identify the author's purpose, you can determine the author's motives.

### Determining author's purpose by looking for context clues
To determine the author's purpose in writing text, students can look for certain words as clues to various purposes. For example, if the author's purpose was to compare similarities between/among ideas, look for "clue words" including "like," "similar(ly)," "same," "in the same way," and "just as." If the author's purpose was to contrast differences between/among ideas, clue words include "but," "however," "on the other hand," "dissimilar(ly)," and "in contrast/contrastingly." If the author's purpose was to criticize an idea, clue words connoting judgment/negative opinion include "poor," "bad," "inadequate," "insufficient," "lacking," "excessive," "wasteful," "harmful," "deleterious," "disserve," "unfair," etc. If the purpose was to paint a picture illustrating an idea, descriptive clue words include "morose," "crestfallen," "lusty," "glittering," "exuberant," etc. Explanatory purposes involve using simpler words to describe or explain more complex/abstract ideas. Identification purposes entail listing series of ideas without much accompanying opinion or description. To intensify an idea, authors add superlative ("-est") adjectives, more specific details; and enlarge concepts. To suggest or propose an idea, authors typically express positive opinions and provide supporting evidence for points to convince readers to agree.

## Analyzing Arguments

Students will need to be able to analyze arguments in a text for their structure and content.

### Introducing an argument in a persuasive passage
The best way to introduce an argument in a persuasive passage and to structure it is to begin by organizing your thoughts and researching the evidence carefully. You should write everything down in outline format to start. Make sure you put the claim at the beginning of the passage. Then, list the reasons and the evidence that you have to support the claim. It is important that you provide enough evidence. Reasons and evidence should follow each other in a logical order. Write the passage so that you hold the reader's attention; use a strong tone and choose words carefully for maximum effect. If you can get the reader to understand your claim, he or she will be more likely to agree with your argument. Restate your claim in the concluding paragraph to maximize the impact on the reader.

## Analyzing Claims and Counterclaims

These questions will ask the student to identify explicitly stated claims and counter claims made in a text. They will also need to be able determine implicit claims and counterclaims made in a text.

## Defining and supporting claims

A claim/argument/proposition/thesis is anything a writer asserts in that is not a known/proven/accepted fact. As such, it is the author's opinion or at least includes an element of opinion. The writer usually will, or should, provide evidence to back up this claim. Some writers make claims without supporting them, but these are not as effective in convincing readers to believe or agree with them. Some may attempt to provide evidence but choose it poorly; if they cite evidence that is not related directly enough to the claim, or the "evidence" is information from untrustworthy sources or not verified as accurate, this is also less effective. Writers sometimes state their claims directly and clearly; in other instances, they may discuss a number of related topics from which the reader must infer the claims implied in the discussion. For example, suppose two writers take opposing positions, one that immigration to the USA is bad and the other that it is good. Rather than explicitly stating these claims, both may present information supporting negative/positive aspects/views of immigration. Critical readers can infer these claims from the information's negativity/positivity.

## Making claims

A persuasive essay will likely focus on one central argument, but it may make many smaller claims along the way. These are subordinate arguments with which the reader must agree if he or she is going to agree with the central argument. The central argument will only be as strong as the subordinate claims. These claims should be rooted in fact and observation, rather than subjective judgment. The best persuasive essays provide enough supporting detail to justify claims without overwhelming the reader. Remember that a fact must be susceptible to independent verification: that is, it must be something the reader could confirm. Also, statistics are only effective when they take into account possible objections. For instance, a statistic on the number of foreclosed houses would only be useful if it was taken over a defined interval and in a defined area. Most readers are wary of statistics, because they are so often misleading. If possible, a persuasive essay should always include references so that the reader can obtain more information. Of course, this means that the writer's accuracy and fairness may be judged by the inquiring reader.

## Compare counterclaims to claims

Whereas a claim represents a text's main argument, a counterclaim represents an argument that opposes that claim. Writers actually use counterclaims to support their claims. They do this by presenting their claim; introducing a counterclaim to it; and then definitively refuting the counterclaim. Rather than only promoting and supporting the claim, which leaves the text open to being refuted or attacked by other writers who present their own counterclaims, authors who present both claim and counterclaim have anticipated opposing arguments before others can raise them; have given a voice to the opposition to their claim, and then discredited that voice; and, when they do this effectively, show that their ability to do so indicates how familiar and competent they are with respect to the topic they are discussing in their text. Words such as "but," "yet," "however," "nevertheless," "nonetheless," "notwithstanding," "despite," "in spite of," "on the contrary," "contrastingly," etc. indicating contrast/difference/disagreement signal counterclaims. If readers/students cannot locate a claim in text, they may identify a counterclaim by signal words and work backwards to discover what claim the counterclaim opposes.

## Discrediting a counterclaim

When writers present a claim, i.e., a central argument in text, they may also introduce a counterclaim opposing that claim. When journalists do this, by presenting the other side to their argument they can demonstrate their objectivity. In a different use, writers of argumentative/persuasive text may find that furnishing evidence to support a claim, appealing to various reader responses, and other rhetorical devices may still not lend their claim as much strength as they would like. In such cases, another rhetorical technique they may use is presenting a counterclaim. This enables writers not only to anticipate opposing arguments to their claim, but also to rebut these opposing arguments, which in turn lends additional strength to their original claim. As an example, one might claim that using a dentist-approved mouthwash regularly can prevent gingivitis. A counterclaim might be that in a recent survey, dentists questioned the effectiveness of mouthwash. When the next sentence states that this survey included only three dentists, all of whose dental studies were incomplete, the writer has effectively discredited the counterclaim and opposition, reinforcing the original claim.

Example:
> While referencing and refuting counterclaims are rhetorical devices we often consider tools of serious argument, they can also be used humorously. In a real-life example, addressing the April 2015 annual White House Correspondents' Association Dinner, President Barack Obama drew many laughs from his audience while rebutting political and journalistic attacks by using the technique of presenting counterclaims and then rejecting them to strengthen his own claims, but with sarcastic humor. A central tactic, replayed repeatedly since on various news programs, was Obama's "bucket" joke. A bucket list is a list of things someone wants to do before he or she dies, i.e., "kicks the bucket," hence its name. The president said he had made a "bucket list" of things he wanted to do before his second term ends in 2017. Taking advantage of the fact that "bucket" rhymes with a profane expression, Obama created a euphemism to address criticisms: "Take executive action on immigration? Bucket. New climate regulations? Bucket. It's the right thing to do," implying what he thought of these criticisms without directly cursing them.

## Assessing Reasoning

### Assessing a claims soundness
In addition to identifying claims and counterclaims that authors present in their texts, students must be able to evaluate whether those claims and counterclaims are sound. The PSAT, SAT, and other standardized tests ask questions that require students to assess the soundness of an author's reasoning in text. A valid argument is logical, i.e., each premise/statement follows and/or builds upon the previous one. However, test questions are not limited to requiring students to assess text logic/validity; they moreover require students to assess soundness, meaning whether the argument is true. Students will likely not have thorough knowledge of all text content on tests. They should assume the content of unfamiliar text is true, since the test will not try to trick students by providing false material. To assess a text argument, the student must first identify its central claim. The remainder of the argument should both answer why the central claim is true, and also prove or support that claim.

### How to approach these types of test questions
Some text-based test questions may ask students not only what central claim or argument an author makes in a passage, but also what the author's reasoning behind that claim is. To help select the correct answer from among multiple choices on such questions, the student will need to follow the reasoning that the author uses in the text and relate it to the answer choices. The student can do this by reading each answer choice and then asking himself/herself whether this choice answers the question of why the author's central claim is true. For the student to be able to assess the author's reasoning for soundness, he or she must have the ability to cite evidence with accuracy to support that assessment of reasoning and its soundness or lack thereof. The best and also easiest way of justifying one's assessment of reasoning and its relative soundness by citing evidence is to ask oneself whether why the author makes the claim; how the author justifies the claim; and whether evidence supports the claim and answers the question of why.

### Four levels of critical reading
Experts (cf. Elder and Paul, 2004) identify four levels of critical reading. The first level is paraphrasing the text one sentence at a time, which develops and demonstrates understanding. The second level is identifying and explicating a text paragraph's main idea. The third level is analyzing the author's logic and reasoning, including the main purpose, question, information, inferences, concepts, assumptions, implications, and viewpoints. The fourth level is assessing logic or reasoning. Since text quality varies among authors and texts, readers must assess author reasoning. Paraphrasing author meaning accurately on the first level is a prerequisite. To assess

reasoning, consider whether the author states his or her meaning clearly; whether the author's claims are accurate; whether he or she offers specifics and/or details with enough precision when these are relevant; whether the author strays from his or her purpose by introducing irrelevant information; whether the text is written superficially or addresses the topic's inherent complexities; whether the author's perspective is narrow or considers other pertinent perspectives; whether the text has internal contradictions or is consistent; whether the text addresses the topic in a trivial or significant way; and whether the author's attitude is narrow/unilateral or fair.

**Analyzing Evidence**

For these questions the student will be asked to determine how the author uses evidence to support his claims and counterclaims.

Presenting Evidence
When in a focused discussion, be prepared to present your claims, findings, and supporting evidence in a clear and distinct manner. This means being prepared. When compiling your data, make sure to create an outline that has the main ideas and then the supporting evidence, including graphics that you want to present. Attention to details will result in a successful presentation, one in which the diverse individuals in the group will come away with a feeling of having been part of something meaningful. Facts and examples should be stressed. Repetition creates retention. It is important for the speaker to choose the right words, and to build momentum by gradually building up to the strongest argument(s). Graphics are important, because participants will be more convinced if they can see evidence as well as hear it. By breaking up the flow of the discussion and introducing pauses before and after pertinent arguments, the speaker will make the presentation of facts more interesting.

Identifying evidence
In order to assess claims an author makes in text, the reader must be able to analyze the evidence the author supplies to support those claims and evaluate whether the evidence is convincing or not. Students should ask themselves why the author makes a given claim; how the author justifies that claim; and whether the evidence the author uses to justify the claim convincingly and thoroughly answers the "why" question, which means the evidence is effective. If the student can easily come up with counterclaims to the author's claims, the author's reasoning and/or evidence used to support it may not be as convincing as they could be. When answering text-based multiple-choice questions asking them to identify evidence supporting a central claim, students can determine the correct choice by identifying and eliminating choices citing text that extends the argument rather than supporting it because it does not answer why; and text that is related but not the main source of support, in addition to completely incorrect choices.

Strategies for supporting evidence
Test questions will not only ask students to identify what evidence an author uses in text to support his or her claims; they will also ask students to evaluate an author's strategy for using evidence to support his or her argument. For example, a passage of text might be an author's review of a book, film, or other work. A review most commonly makes the main point that the work is either good or bad, or sometimes a combination of both. A review might also make, argue, and support the point that a movie or book demonstrates a particular central trait (e.g., a movie identified in the romantic comedy genre is actually "anti-romantic"). In order to support his or her main point, the reviewer could use various tactics, such as comparing the work to others as evidence supporting the claim; stating and then effectively addressing a counterclaim to support the claim; or giving a number of examples from the work which can all be used to serve as support for the claim. Some reviewers combine all of these strategies, which when done well can be most effective.

<u>Essential considerations and questions when analyzing evidence</u>
When analyzing the evidence that an author presents in a text to organize and back up his or her argument, as he or she reads, the student should remember to focus not only on what the author's central claim or point is, but also on what the actual content of that evidence is; how the author uses the evidence to prove the point or claim that he or she is making; and whether or not the evidence that the author provides is effective in supporting that central claim or point. A good way to evaluate whether or not a piece of evidence that an author uses is supportive of that author's central claim is whether or not that evidence answers the question of why the author is making that claim. The reader should also consider the questions of how the author justifies this claim and whether the evidence the author has presented to justify the claim is convincing or not.

**Synthesis**

The questions in this section will focus on synthesizing across multiple sources of information.

**Analyzing Multiple Texts**

The student will be required to synthesize information and ideas across multiple texts. This means that they will need to apply all of the other skills above to analyze paired passages.

<u>Define synthesis with respect to analyzing multiple texts</u>
Synthesizing, i.e., understanding and integrating, information from multiple texts can at times be among the most challenging skills for some students to succeed with on tests and in school, and yet it is also among the most important. Students who read at the highest cognitive levels can select related material from different text sources and construct coherent arguments that account for these varied information sources. Synthesizing ideas and information from multiple texts actually combines other reading skills that students should have mastered previously in reading one text at a time, and applies them in the context of reading more than one text. For example, students are required to read texts closely, including identifying explicit and implicit meanings; use critical thinking and reading; draw inferences; assess author reasoning; analyze supporting evidence; and formulate opinions they can justify, based on more passages than one. When two paired texts represent opposing sides of the same argument, students can find analyzing them easier; but this is not always the case.

<u>Similarities in texts</u>
When students are called upon to compare things two texts share in common, the most obvious commonality might be the same subject matter or specific topic. However, two texts need not be about the same thing to compare them. Some other features texts can share include structural characteristics. For example, they may both be written using a sequential format, such as narrating events or giving instructions in chronological order; listing and/or discussing subtopics by order of importance; or describing a place spatially in sequence from each point to the next. They may both use a comparison-contrast structure, identifying similarities and differences between, among, or within topics. They might both organize information by identifying cause-and-effect relationships. Texts can be similar in type, e.g., description, narration, persuasion, or exposition. They can be similar in using technical vocabulary or using formal or informal language. They may share similar tones and/or styles, e.g., humorous, satirical, serious, etc. They can share similar purposes, e.g., to alarm audiences, incite them to action, reassure them, inspire them, provoke strong emotional responses, etc.

<u>Contrasts in texts</u>
When analyzing paired or multiple texts, students might observe differences in tone; for example, one text might take a serious approach while another uses a humorous one. Even within approaches or treatments, style can differ: one text may be humorous in a witty, sophisticated, clever way while another may exercise broad, "lowbrow" humor; another may employ mordant sarcasm; another may use satire, couching outrageous suggestions in a "deadpan" logical voice to lampoon social attitudes and behaviors as Jonathan Swift did in *A Modest Proposal.* Serious

writing can range from darkly pessimistic to alarmist to objective and unemotional. Texts might have similar information, yet organize it using different structures. One text may support points or ideas using logical arguments, while another may seek to persuade its audience by appealing to their emotions. A very obvious difference in text is genre: for example, the same mythological or traditional stories have been told as oral folk tales, written dramas, written novels, etc.; and/or set in different times and places (e.g., Shakespeare's *Romeo and Juliet* vs. Laurents, Bernstein, and Sondheim's *West Side Story*).

## Analyzing Quantitative Information

These questions will test the student's ability to analyze quantitative information. This information may be presented in graphs, tables, and charts and may relate to other information presented in the text.

### Analyzing quantitative information
When students read text, particularly informational text, authors may include graphs, charts, and/or tables to illustrate the written information under discussion. Students need to be able to understand these representations and how they are related to the text they supplement. For example, a line graph can show how some numerical value—like number or percentage of items, people, groups, dollars, births, deaths, cases of specific illnesses, etc. or amount of rainfall, products, waste matter, etc.—has increased, decreased, or stayed the same over designated periods of time. A bar graph may be used like a line graph to show the same chronological change; or to compare different numbers or proportions of things side by side without reference to time. A pie chart visualizes distribution and proportion by depicting percentages or fractions of a whole occupied by different categories, e.g., how much money is allocated or spent for each division among services or products, what percentages or proportions of a population has certain characteristics, etc. Tables and charts often list numbers by category; students must be able to identify largest and smallest quantities, order by quantity, etc.

### Interpreting information from graphics
It is important to be able to interpret information presented in graphics and be able to translate it to text. These graphics can include maps, charts, illustrations, graphs, timelines, and tables. Each of these different graphics is used to present a different type of quantitative or technical information. Maps show a visual representation of a certain area. A map may contain a legend which helps to identify certain geographic features on the map. A graph or chart will usually contain two axes that show the relationship between two variables. A table can also be similar to this but may show the relationship between any number of variables. So no matter how the information is presented it is important to be able to interpret it and explain what it means.

### Charts and graphs
An author may organize information in a chart, a graph, in paragraph format, or as a list. Information may also be presented in a picture or a diagram. The information may be arranged according to the order in which it occurred over time, placed in categories, or it may be arranged in a cause-and-effect relationship. Information can also be presented according to where it occurs in a given space (spatial order), or organized through description. The way an author chooses to organize information is often based on the purpose of information that is being presented, the best way to present given information, and the audience that the information is meant to reach.

## Sentence Completions

Read each sentence, inserting the answer choices in the blanks. Don't stop at the first answer choice if you think it is right, but read them all. What may seem like the best choice, at first, may not be after you have had time to read all of the choices.

**Adjectives Give it Away**

Words mean things and are added to the sentence for a reason. Adjectives in particular may be the clue to determining which answer choice is correct.

*Example:*
   The brilliant scientist made several _____ discoveries.
      A. dull
      B. dazzling

Look at the adjectives first to help determine what makes sense. A "brilliant" or smart scientist would make dazzling, rather than dull discoveries. Without that simple adjective, no answer choice is clear.

**Use logic**

Ask yourself questions about each answer choice to see if they are logical.

*Example:*
   The deep pounding resonance of the drums could be _____ far off in the distance.
      A. seen
      B. heard

Would resonating poundings be "seen"? or Would resonating pounding be "heard"?

**Multiple Blanks Are an Opportunity**

Some sentence completion questions may have multiple blanks. It may be easier to focus on only one of the blanks and try to determine which answer choices could logically fit. This may allow you to eliminate some of the answer choices and concentrate only upon the ones that remain.

**Transitional words**

Watch out for key transitional words! This can include however, but, yet, although, so, because, etc. These may change the meaning of a sentence and the context of the missing word.

*Example:*
   He is an excellent marksman, but surprisingly, he _____ comes home empty handed from a hunting trip.
      A. often
      B. never
      C. rarely

A good shot or marksman would be expected to be a successful hunter. Watch out though for the transition phrase "but surprisingly". It indicates the opposite of what you would expect, which means this particular marksman must not be a successful hunter. A successful hunter would either never or rarely come home empty handed from a hunt, but an unsuccessful hunter would "often" come home empty handed, making "a" the correct answer.

**The Trap of Familiarity**

Don't just choose a word because you recognize it. On difficult questions, you may only recognize one or two words. PSAT doesn't put "make-believe words" on the test, so don't think that just because you only recognize one word means that word must be correct. If you don't recognize four words, then focus on the one that you do recognize. Is it correct? Try your best to determine if it fits the sentence. If it does, that is great, but if it doesn't, eliminate it.

## Reading Passages

Some questions will be concerning sentence insertions. In those cases, do not look for the ones that simply restate what was in the previous sentence. New sentences should contain new information and new insights into the subject of the text. If asked for the paragraph to which a sentence would most naturally be added, find a key noun or word in that new sentence. Then find the paragraph containing exactly or another word closely related to that key noun or word. That is the paragraph that should include the new sentence.

Some questions will ask what purpose a phrase fulfilled in a particular text. It depends upon the subject of the text. If the text is dramatic, then the phrase was probably used to show drama. If the text is comedic, then the phrase was probably to show comedy.

In related cases, you may be asked to provide a sentence that summarizes the text, or to reorganize a paragraph. Simple sentences, without wordy phrases, are usually best. If asked for a succinct answer, then the shorter the answer, the more likely it is correct.

## Skimming

Your first task when you begin reading is to answer the question "What is the topic of the selection?" This can best be answered by quickly skimming the passage for the general idea, stopping to read only the first sentence of each paragraph. A paragraph's first is usually the main topic sentence, and it gives you a summary of the content of the paragraph.

Once you've skimmed the passage, stopping to read only the first sentences, you will have a general idea about what it is about, as well as what is the expected topic in each paragraph.

Each question will contain clues as to where to find the answer in the passage. Do not just randomly search through the passage for the correct answer to each question. Search scientifically. Find key word(s) or ideas in the question that are going to either contain or be near the correct answer. These are typically nouns, verbs, numbers, or phrases in the question that will probably be duplicated in the passage. Once you have identified those key word(s) or idea, skim the passage quickly to find where those key word(s) or idea appears. The correct answer choice will be nearby.

*Example:*
>    What caused Martin to suddenly return to Paris?

The key word is Paris. Skim the passage quickly to find where this word appears. The answer will be close by that word.

However, sometimes key words in the question are not repeated in the passage. In those cases, search for the general idea of the question.

*Example:*
>    Which of the following was the psychological impact of the author's childhood upon the
>    remainder of his life?

Key words are "childhood" or "psychology". While searching for those words, be alert for other words or phrases that have similar meaning, such as "emotional effect" or "mentally" which could be used in the passage, rather than the exact word "psychology".

Numbers or years can be particularly good key words to skim for, as they stand out from the rest of the text.

*Example:*
> Which of the following best describes the influence of Monet's work in the 20th century?

20th contains numbers and will easily stand out from the rest of the text. Use 20th as the key word to skim for in the passage.

Other good key word(s) may be in quotation marks. These identify a word or phrase that is copied directly from the passage. In those cases, the word(s) in quotation marks are exactly duplicated in the passage.

*Example:*
> In her college years, what was meant by Margaret's "drive for excellence"?

"Drive for excellence" is a direct quote from the passage and should be easy to find.

## Beware of Directly Quoted Answers

Once you've quickly found the correct section of the passage to find the answer, focus upon the answer choices. Sometimes a choice will repeat word for word a portion of the passage near the answer. However, beware of such duplication – it may be a trap! More than likely, the correct choice will paraphrase or summarize the related portion of the passage, rather than being exactly the same wording.

## Truth does not equal correctness

For the answers that you think are correct, read them carefully and make sure that they answer the question. An answer can be factually correct, but it MUST answer the question asked. Additionally, two answers can both be seemingly correct, so be sure to read all of the answer choices, and make sure that you get the one that BEST answers the question.

## When there's no key word

Some questions will not have a key word.

*Example:*
> Which of the following would the author of this passage likely agree with?

In these cases, look for key words in the answer choices. Then skim the passage to find where the answer choice occurs. By skimming to find where to look, you can minimize the time required.

Sometimes it may be difficult to identify a good key word in the question to skim for in the passage. In those cases, look for a key word in one of the answer choices to skim for. Often the answer choices can all be found in the same paragraph, which can quickly narrow your search.

## Paragraph focus

Focus upon the first sentence of each paragraph, which is the most important. The main topic of the paragraph is usually there.

Once you've read the first sentence in the paragraph, you have a general idea about what each paragraph will be about. As you read the questions, try to determine which paragraph will have the answer. Paragraphs have a concise topic. The answer should either obviously be there or obviously not. It will save time if you can jump straight to the paragraph, so try to remember what you learned from the first sentences.

Example: The first paragraph is about poets; the second is about poetry. If a question asks about poetry, where will the answer be? The second paragraph.

The main idea of a passage is typically spread across all or most of its paragraphs. Whereas the main idea of a paragraph may be completely different than the main idea of the very next paragraph, a main idea for a passage affects all of the paragraphs in one form or another.

*Example:*
What is the main idea of the passage?

For each answer choice, try to see how many paragraphs are related. It can help to count how many sentences are affected by each choice, but it is best to see how many paragraphs are affected by the choice. Typically the answer choices will include incorrect choices that are main ideas of individual paragraphs, but not the entire passage. That is why it is crucial to choose ideas that are supported by the most paragraphs possible.

## Eliminate choices

Some choices can quickly be eliminated. "Andy Warhol lived there." Is Andy Warhol even mentioned in the article? If not, quickly eliminate it.

When trying to answer a question such as "the passage indicates all of the following EXCEPT" quickly skim the paragraph searching for references to each choice. If the reference exists, scratch it off as a choice. Similar choices may be crossed off simultaneously if they are close enough.

Watch for answers that are similarly worded. Since only one answer can be correct, if there are two answers that appear to mean the same thing, they must BOTH be incorrect, and can be eliminated.

Example Answer Choices:
A.    changing values and attitudes
B.    a large population of mobile or uprooted people

These answer choices are similar; they both describe a fluid culture. Because of their similarity, they can be linked together. Since the answer can have only one choice, they can also be eliminated together.

## Fact/opinion

Remember that answer choices that are facts will typically have no ambiguous words. For example, how long is a long time? What defines an ordinary person? These ambiguous words of "long" and "ordinary" should not be in a factual statement. However, if all of the choices have ambiguous words, go to the context of the passage. Often a factual statement may be set out as a research finding.

*Example:*
"The scientist found that the eye reacts quickly to change in light."

Opinions may be set out in the context of words like thought, believed, understood, or wished.

*Example:*
"He thought the Yankees should win the World Series."

**Time Management**

In technical passages, do not get lost on the technical terms. Skip them and move on. You want a general understanding of what is going on, not a mastery of the passage.

When you encounter material in the selection that seems difficult to understand, bracket it. It often may not be necessary and can be skipped. Only spend time trying to understand it if it is going to be relevant for a question. Understand difficult phrases only as a last resort.

Answer general questions before detail questions. A reader with a good understanding of the whole passage can often answer general questions without rereading a word. Get the easier questions out of the way before tackling the more time consuming ones.

Identify each question by type. Usually the wording of a question will tell you whether you can find the answer by referring directly to the passage or by using your reasoning powers. You alone know which question types you customarily handle with ease and which give you trouble and will require more time. Save the difficult questions for last.

**Final Warnings**

Hedge phrases revisited
Once again, watch out for critical "hedge" phrases, such as likely, may, can, will often, mostly, usually, generally, rarely, sometimes, etc. Question writers insert these hedge phrases, to cover every possibility. Often an answer will be wrong simply because it leaves no room for exception.

*Example:*
    Animals live longer in cold places than animals in warm places.

This answer choice is wrong, because there are exceptions in which certain warm climate animals live longer. This answer choice leaves no possibility of exception. It states that every animal species in cold places live longer than animal species in warm places. Correct answer choices will typically have a key hedge word to leave room for exceptions.

*Example:*
    In severe cold, a polar bear cub is likely to survive longer than an adult polar bear.

This answer choice is correct, because not only does the passage imply that younger animals survive better in the cold, it also allows for exceptions to exist. The use of the word "likely" leaves room for cases in which a polar bear cub might not survive longer than the adult polar bear.

Word usage questions
When asked how a word is used in the passage, don't use your existing knowledge of the word. The question is being asked precisely because there is some strange or unusual usage of the word in the passage. Go to the passage and use contextual clues to determine the answer. Don't simply use the popular definition you already know.

Switchback words
Stay alert for "switchbacks". These are the words and phrases frequently used to alert you to shifts in thought. The most common switchback word is "but". Others include although, however, nevertheless, on the other hand, even though, while, in spite of, despite, regardless of.

Avoid "fact traps"
Once you know which paragraph the answer will be in, focus on that paragraph. However, don't get distracted by a choice that is factually true about the paragraph. Your search is for the

answer that answers the question, which may be about a tiny aspect in the paragraph.  Stay focused and don't fall for an answer that describes the larger picture of the paragraph. Always go back to the question and make sure you're choosing an answer that actually answers the question and is not just a true statement.

# Writing and Language Test

The writing and language portion of the PSAT consists of one 35-minute section. It will contain 4 passages and there will be a total of 44 questions relating to these passages. The breakdown of passages and questions is shown in the table below.

| Careers | 1 passage; 11 questions | 25% |
|---|---|---|
| History/Social Studies | 1 passage; 11 questions | 25% |
| Humanities | 1 passage; 11 questions | 25% |
| Science | 1 passage; 11 questions | 25% |

The PSAT Writing and Language Test will contain a range of text complexities from grades 9-10 to post secondary entry. The passages will cover the subjects from the table above. The test will also contain one or more graphics in one or more sets of questions. These may include tables, graphs, and charts. They will vary in level of difficulty as well as data density, and number of variables.

## Expression of Ideas

The questions in this section will focus on the revision of text. They will ask the student to revise for topic development, accuracy, logic, cohesion, rhetorically effective use of language.

## Proposition

For these questions the student will add, revise, or retain central ideas, main claims, counterclaims, and topic sentences. These revisions should be made to convey arguments, information, and ideas more clearly and effectively.

### Writing propositions

Students need to read and review their own writing critically and make revisions accordingly to ensure it informs its reading/listening audience with clarity and argues points effectively to convince its audience. For example, a short essay needs a topic sentence; longer pieces may need one topic sentence per paragraph. A topic sentence must clearly summarize the main point or idea that the rest of the paragraph or piece addresses. Therefore, a sentence that is overly long and complex is not a good topic sentence; the student must revise it to be shorter, simpler, and clearer. In the same vein as a topic sentence, the main claim in a piece of expository or argumentative writing must also be stated clearly and simply so that the audience both notices and understands it. It should be concise, attention-getting, and unambiguously stated. Any counterclaim, which the writer introduces to present both sides of an argument or to refute as a way of strengthening the original claim that it presumes to oppose, must be stated just as clearly and simply as the claim itself.

### Main Idea

The main idea of a passage is what the passage is mostly about. It is the main point of the passage. Sometimes the main idea is stated in a passage by the use of a topic sentence either at the beginning of the passage or elsewhere. Sometimes the main idea may be found in the title of the passage. Oftentimes the main idea is not stated in the passage; the reader needs to determine it from the information or details in the passage. The main idea will become more and more obvious to a reader as detail after detail supports it. Some information in the passage may not be supporting, but most ideas and details will support the main idea. The main idea is filled out by the supporting details in a passage.

## Making a claim

When making a claim, it is important to first think about the arguments that support that claim. While researching, try to anticipate what readers might say; this will help you thoroughly develop your claim. It is not enough to research a claim on the Internet, because many sources are dubious at best. Look for sites that are objective. Find authorities that you can quote, and use statistics. Present counterclaims using ample evidence. Mention both the strengths and weaknesses without any prejudice. Divide each counterclaim into a separate paragraph with supporting evidence. Make sure to present everything in a logical manner so that the information will be easily understood by the reader. Most importantly, one needs to separate opinions from facts.

## Support

These questions will ask students to add, revise, or retain information and ideas with the intention of supporting claims in the text.

## Text evidence

The term text evidence refers to information included in a text that supports the main point of the paper, from which a reader can draw conclusions or generalizations. The author will deliberately include key points that serve as supporting details for the main point of a paper. For example, the main point of a paper may state: The average yearly rainfall in the city has risen by 2 inches per year since 1999. The paper would go on to include the amount of rainfall for each month or season and any contributing factors that may be causing an increase in yearly rainfall. Additional facts, or text evidence to support the point that yearly rainfall is rising in the city would help to prove that the author's main point is correct.

## Supporting details

Supporting details are crucial to a story. These details allow the reader to "see" a character or scene in their mind. Supporting details may include descriptions of the weather, the color of a character's eyes or hair, or the sounds that a character hears. All of these details help readers understand the character as a person. Supporting details also add interest to a story. Readers must be able to distinguish between a main idea and supporting details. Supporting details are usually mentioned only once; they help create or develop the main idea.

## How supporting information strengthens a text

Anytime a writer wants to convince readers/listeners to believe or agree with his or her opinion or position, he or she should provide factual information that proves or supports it. As an example, by now most people are aware that smoking tobacco can damage health. However, making the written assertion that "Smoking is unhealthy" with no accompanying information does not carry as much weight as saying the same thing and then citing statistics such as how many people die from smoking-related illnesses each year; how many cases of lung and other cancers, emphysema, etc. are caused annually by smoking, etc. Citing a highly reputable source(s) for such statistics lends additional weight to their credibility. This principle can be extended to apply to other assertions that are less obviously true or accepted. In fact, when writers argue opposing sides of some debate or controversy, each can present different facts, statistics, or other details that support one side or the other. Thus, with good supporting evidence and good writing, two authors or students can present equally convincing cases for diametrically opposed arguments about the same subject.

**Focus**

For these questions students will be asked to add, revise, retain, or delete information for the sake of relevance. These revisions should be made to make the text more relevant and focused.

Maintaining clarity and relevance
One situation wherein students need to add information and ideas to text is if they have stated a main point, but not developed it sufficiently. They may assert a position or opinion—even a fact—in broad and/or simple terms, but not elaborate in enough detail to explain specifically what it means; give examples illustrating it; or anticipate and rebut counterclaims. If the main idea is an abstract concept, providing an analogy with something concrete could illustrate it for better understanding. Students also need to add information if they have asserted some claim without any proof or support. Students especially need to delete text when their writing wanders off topic. If they include too much information that is irrelevant, their topic and main point become unclear and readers become confused. Even when on topic, if sentences discussing it are written unclearly, students must revise them. Feedback from teachers, peers, and/or the actual reading/listening audience is helpful to determine clarity. Students should also develop judgment and conviction and confidence in their writing to retain material they find essential.

Relevant information
Before information is sought, a list of guiding questions should be developed to help determine whether information found is adequate, relevant, and consistent. These questions should be based on the research goals, which should be laid out in an outline or concept map. For example, a student writing a report on Navajo social structure might begin with questions concerning the general lifestyle and location of Navajos, and follow with questions about how Navajo society was organized. While researching his questions, he will come up with pieces of information. This information can be compared to his research questions to determine whether it is relevant to his report. Information from several sources should be compared to determine whether information is consistent. Information that is adequate helps answer specific questions that are part of the research goals. Inadequate information for this particular student might be a statement such as "Navajos had a strong societal structure," because the student is probably seeking more specific information.

**Quantitative Information**

These questions will ask the student to relate information presented quantitatively to information presented in the text. The quantitative information may be in the form of graphs, charts, and tables.

Quantitative Information
When they include graphs, tables, or charts to illustrate numerical or quantitative information that proves or supports their textual claims; or write text about existing graphical presentations of quantitative information, students should be able to explain clearly how material in a graph/table/chart is related to verbal information in text and vice versa. For example, in a bar graph, higher/taller bars indicate larger numbers/quantities, lower/shorter bars smaller numbers/amounts. These numbers may also be percentages. In a line graph, higher points represent larger numbers; lower points, smaller quantities. If the line connecting points ascends steadily, this depicts some quantity increasing steadily; a descending line indicates an ongoing decrease. Line graphs whose points yo-yo up and down repeatedly indicate instability; flat lines show no change. In pie charts, larger and smaller "slices" or sections equal larger and smaller proportions of the whole, typically percentages. Tables may list numbers in ascending/descending order of quantity, or by order of category without numerical patterns. With the latter, students must be able to read, create, and explain greater/smaller quantities and relationships in tables.

<u>Interpreting information from graphics</u>
It is important to be able to interpret information presented in graphics and be able to translate it to text. These graphics can include maps, charts, illustrations, graphs, timelines, and tables. Each of these different graphics is used to present a different type of quantitative or technical information. Maps show a visual representation of a certain area. A map may contain a legend which helps to identify certain geographic features on the map. A graph or chart will usually contain two axes that show the relationship between two variables. A table can also be similar to this but may show the relationship between any number of variables. So no matter how the information is presented it is important to be able to interpret it and explain what it means.

## Organization

These questions will have the student revise the text to improve logic and cohesion at the sentence, paragraph, and whole-text levels.

<u>Transition words</u>
The use of appropriate transition words helps to clarify the relationships between ideas and concepts and creates a more cohesive passage. A good writer knows that such words and phrases serve to indicate the relationship between ideas and concepts. Words or phrases that show causality between ideas include "as a result," "consequently" and "therefore." Words that show a compare-and-contrast relationship include "however," "on the other hand," "in contrast" and "but." When introducing examples of different concepts, words such as "namely," "for example" and "for instance" act as transition words. Transition words such as "foremost," "primarily," "secondly," "former" and "latter" can be used when showing the order of importance of ideas or concepts.

## Logical Sequence

For these questions the student should revise the text with the intention of improving the logical order that the information is presented in.

<u>Importance of presenting information logically</u>
Including all of the necessary information in a paragraph is not enough if that information is not presented in the most logical order. The first sentence in the first paragraph of a piece of writing should introduce that paragraph, and sometimes introduce the entire text as well. It should also get the readers' attention and interest and make them want to continue reading. After introducing the main idea, students should present evidence supporting it. They must include transitional language from the first sentence and paragraph to the next, and introduce the evidence by quoting, citing, or paraphrasing. They should then analyze the evidence so readers understand why they chose it and how it connects to their argument. Each sentence should lead to or connect to the next; each succeeding sentence should build upon or extend from the previous one; and all sentences should proceed in a linear fashion to the conclusion. If students write sentences that jump around rather than following a logical sequence, the result will be unclear and confuse readers.

<u>Logical sequence</u>
Students can convince their readers to believe or agree with the points and arguments in their text not only by presenting supportive evidence, but moreover by ordering their ideas in the most compelling sequence. Since writing is a process, any written piece may be regarded as never finite but capable of continually evolving further. If students discover new evidence during their writing process, they may need to assume a different position than they originally had; or use the same argument, but structure it differently; or substitute different transitional language between sentences and/or paragraphs, etc. Some challenges that students face include allowing for complexity in their text while still maintaining clarity and firmness in their textual structure, yet also avoiding having the text read like a "laundry list" or seem mechanical in its execution. Rather than merely repeating their main point, student writers must move their argument and readers forward.

Since ideas must follow a logical sequence in text, the transitions or "stitching" connecting them must be transparent to readers.

### Revision of text for logic

There are many ways to revise writing. It is important to check for the logic of ideas and make sure the text has cohesion and belongs together. There must also be a progression of ideas that a reader can follow. The ideas should fit naturally with one another. After the writing is done, there are other ways to revise it. Sometimes sentences need to be rearranged or even deleted. Sometimes sentences need to be added to put more information into the text. Sometimes sentences need to be combined so that the sentences are more varied. The best way to revise a text is by rereading it carefully to see if the writing makes sense and flows well and then to make the appropriate changes.

### Importance of strong transitions in logical sequence

When they are writing academically, students need to connect their sentences and paragraphs with transitions that make the logical progression of their argument or discussion clear to their readers so they can follow it. Readers should never have to try to figure out why the writer selected certain supporting evidence, what that evidence signifies, or specifically how it backs up the writer's point. Good transitions serve as guides to lead readers from one idea to the next. One element required for strong transitions is using strong verbs. These function as signals to the reader how a new sentence or paragraph (or section or chapter) proceeds logically from the one before. Strong verbs should be active verbs; single words are usually preferable over two-word phrases that combine verbs with prepositions. For example, rather than "set up," students can write "establish." Instead of "go up," they could better write "increase." And rather than writing "help out," they can use a verb like "assist," "aid," or just "help" without the preposition.

## Introductions, Conclusions, and Transitions

These questions will have the student revise the beginning or ending of full texts and paragraphs. They should make sure that transition words, phrases, or sentences are used effectively to connect information and ideas.

### General guidelines for beginning, transitioning, and concluding a text

Before starting to write, students must ascertain their purposes for writing. Their general purpose might be to inform, convince, or entertain readers; they can determine their specific purpose by finishing the sentence, "After reading my paper (/speech), people will...." While the introduction and conclusion may be shorter than the rest, they are critically important. The introduction gets audience attention; enables readers/listeners to form impressions sooner; and make the impressions they form indelible. To get reader/listener attention, cite a startling opinion/fact; ask a rhetorical question; relate a short anecdote; present a quotation; relate a pertinent joke; or refer to something familiar. State the main idea/proposition/thesis in one clear, direct sentence. Then establish credibility, e.g., by identifying experience with/research into the topic; the reason for topic choice; and/or reasons for writer authority regarding the topic. Briefly preview the main points by listing them in the same order they will be discussed. Connect all discussion ideas and information with transitional words/phrases (e.g., "next," "moreover," "furthermore," "notwithstanding," "however," "for example," "therefore," "similarly/conversely," etc. as applicable), including to the conclusion, which should summarize the main points and restate the main idea differently.

### Introduction

An introduction announces the main point of the work. It will usually be a paragraph of 50 to 150 words, opening with a few sentences to engage the reader, and concluding with the essay's main point. The sentence stating the main point is called the thesis sentence. If possible, the sentences leading to the thesis should attract the reader's attention with a provocative question, vivid image, description, paradoxical statement, quotation, or anecdote. The thesis sentence could also appear at the beginning of the introduction. Some types of writing do not lend themselves to stating a thesis in one sentence. Personal narratives and some types of business writing may be better served by conveying an overriding purpose of the text, which may or may not be stated directly. The important point is to impress the audience with the rationale for the writing.

Conclusion
The conclusion of a text is typically found in the last one or two paragraphs of the text. A conclusion wraps-up the text and reminds the reader of the main point of the text. The conclusion is the author's way of leaving the reader with a final note to remember about the paper and comes after all the supporting points of the text have been presented. For example, a paper about the importance of avoiding too much sunlight may have a conclusion that reads: By limiting sun exposure to 15 minutes a day and wearing sunscreen of at least SPF 15, a person can reduce their risk of getting skin cancer later in life.

Transitional words and phrases
A good writer will use transitional words and phrases to guide the reader through the text. You are no doubt familiar with the common transitions, though you may never have considered how they operate. Some transitional phrases (*after, before, during, in the middle of*) give information about time. Some indicate that an example is about to be given (*for example, in fact, for instance*). Writers use them to compare (*also, likewise*) and contrast (*however, but, yet*). Transitional words and phrases can suggest addition (*and, also, furthermore, moreover*) and logical relationships (*if, then, therefore, as a result, since*). Finally, transitional words and phrases can demarcate the steps in a process (*first, second, last*). You should incorporate transitional words and phrases where they will orient your reader and illuminate the structure of your composition.

**Effective Language Use**

These questions have the student revise the text for the purpose of improving the use of language to accomplish particular rhetorical purposes.

Figure of speech
A figure of speech, sometimes termed a rhetorical figure or device, is a word or phrase that departs from straightforward, literal language. Figures of speech are often used and crafted for emphasis, freshness of expression, or clarity. However, clarity may suffer from their use.

As an example of the figurative use of a word, consider the following sentence: I am going to crown you.

It may mean:
- I am going to place a literal crown on your head.
- I am going to symbolically exalt you to the place of kingship.
- I am going to punch you in the head with my clenched fist.
- I am going to put a second checker on top of your checker to signify that it has become a king.

Rhetorical fallacy
A rhetorical fallacy, or a fallacy of argument, does not allow the open, two-way exchange of ideas upon which meaningful conversations exist. They try to distract the reader with various appeals instead of using logic. Examples of a rhetorical fallacy include, ad hominem, exaggeration, stereotyping, and categorical claims. Ad hominem is an attack on a person's character or personal traits in an attempt to undermine their argument. An exaggeration is the representation of something in an obviously excessive manner. Stereotyping is the thought that all people in a certain group have a certain characteristics or tendencies. A categorical claim is a universal statement about a particular type of thing or person. A categorical claim can be thought of as the verbalization of a stereotype.

<u>Figurative language</u>
Figurative language is language that goes beyond the literal meaning of the words. Descriptive language that evokes imagery in the reader's mind is one type of figurative language. Exaggeration is also one type of figurative language. Also, when you compare two things, you are using figurative language. Similes and metaphors are ways of comparing things, and both are types of figurative language commonly found in poetry. An example of figurative language (a simile in this case) is: The child howled like a coyote when her mother told her to pick up the toys. In this example, the child's howling is compared to that of a coyote. Figurative language is descriptive in nature and helps the reader understand the sound being made in this sentence.

**Precision**

For these questions students will revise the text to improve the exactness or content appropriateness of word choice.

<u>Precise word choice</u>
Consider that a student wants to convey in a text the idea that an innovative composer had deviated from a number of musical traditions (for example, the rhythms that Igor Stravinsky used in *The Firebird*, 1910). The student is looking for a word that means "moved away from" or "left" (tradition) and is most appropriate in the context of the sentence and surrounding text. Using a thesaurus, classmate suggestions, or simply his or her own vocabulary knowledge, the student considers the synonyms "evacuated," "vacated," "retired," and "departed." These words can be synonyms in the sense that they indicate leaving or going away from something. However, they are not all appropriate in this context. "Evacuate" means leaving/going away in the sense of physically exiting/being made to exit a location, as when people must evacuate buildings/towns/cities or a nurse digitally evacuates a patient's bowel. "Vacate" means leaving/going away from a place or role, e.g., vacating the premises or a job position. "Retire" means leaving a job/position/career, or leaving company/waking activity as in going to bed. Only "depart" can mean literally leaving a place OR figuratively diverging from traditions, usual practices, etc.

<u>Examples of strong and precise word choice</u>
Students need to consider whether they choose nouns and verbs that are both strong and accurate. For example, "This book tells about the Civil War" is neither as strong nor as accurate as it could be because the subject noun and verb are not as precise as they could be. If the student instead writes, "This novel describes a Confederate soldier's experiences during the Civil War," the subject noun "novel" specifies what kind of book it is, whereas "book" could mean many different types of books; and the verb "describes" more specifically identifies how the novel communicates its subject matter than "tells," which could mean narrates, informs, entertains, ridicules, etc. rather than—or as well as—describes. Words not mindfully chosen can have unintended connotations, e.g., "We will attack them in their private spots" vs. "We will attack them where they hide." Technical terminology/jargon should only be used as necessary within a discipline, not to impress at the expense of understanding; e.g., "dialogue" is clearer than "dialectical interface."

<u>Examples of poor word choice</u>
Student writers may select words whose precise meaning is inappropriate to the sentence context. The fact that many adults do the same in their speech makes it all too easy for students to fall prey to this type of error. For example, describing a house that she admired, a woman said, "That house positively reeks of charm." Another responded enthusiastically about a performance she had just attended, "Oh, it was horribly good!" (These are both real-life examples.) In both cases, the connotation of a word was inconsistent with sentence meaning and context; word meaning was precise but incorrect. Another type of error is simply lack of precision. Vague, imprecise words/phrases are not descriptive. For instance, contrast the impact of "A bad smell came from the apartment" with "A stench of putrefaction emanated from the apartment." Visual details add precision: contrast "Her pretty dress was shiny" with "Her sequin-encrusted dress

sparkled with reflected light." Sensory details evoke emotions: contrast "He was sad" with "His reddened eyes and tear-stained face betrayed him." Precise adjectives and verbs are stronger: contrast "The hungry dog ate the food" with "The famished dog devoured the food."

## Concision

For these questions the student will revise the text to improve the economy of word choice. This means they should cut out wordiness and redundancy.

### Redundant phrases

In an effort to write as clearly as possible to ensure direct communication and correct reader understanding, student writers may err on the side of excess by using redundant wording. For example, a student might describe something as "the current design of the school building as it stands right now." This is triply redundant: "current," "as it stands," and "right now" all have the same meaning. Therefore the student need not use all three. He or she can write EITHER "the current design of the school building" OR "the design of the school building as it stands" OR "the design of the school building right now." Some common redundancy errors by students and others include "In addition, there is also..."/"adding an additional..."; "advance planning"; "ask the question"; "a brief moment"; "component parts"; "completely destroy," "crisis situation"; "could possibly"; "fellow classmates," etc. Common redundant spoken expressions have become so accepted/taken for granted that these too can invade writing, e.g., "ATM machine" or "PIN number." While calculated repetition can be an effective rhetorical device, redundancy is *unnecessary* repetition. (Classic joke = "Department of Redundancy Department.")

### Eliminating wordiness

Edit the following sentence so that it expresses ideas precisely and concisely, and wordiness and redundancy are eliminated.

"If you go to the library on Sunday, you will find the library doors are locked and that the facility is closed on Sunday."

Here is one possible revision:

> If you go to the library on Sunday, you will find the library doors are locked and that the facility is closed on Sunday.

## Style and Tone

These questions will have the student revise the style and tone of the text. These revisions will be made to ensure consistency of style and tone as well as improve the match of style and tone to purpose.

### Style, tone, and mood

An author can vary the feel of a text by changing the style, tone, and mood of each sentence. The style of a text refers to whether the author uses long, flowing sentences, short, choppy sentences, or something in-between. The text may be organized in short lines, short paragraphs, or long paragraphs. The tone of a paper helps to establish the mood of the text. Tone involves the attitude that the author displays in the paper. For example, the author may feel exuberant about a sunny day, but feel down on a gloomy day. The words that the author uses to describe the scene and situation in the story help to define its tone. The mood of a story may be uplifting, down, scared, or excited, again, depending upon the words the author uses. All of these elements: style, tone, and mood, can affect how the reader feels about the story.

### Effect on purpose

Authors use language and word choice to convey a certain style, tone, and mood in a piece of literature. When an author writes, he or she uses a style appropriate to the purpose of the text, but also uses language in a way that sets him or her apart. Tone is the author's attitude toward the subject and mood is the feeling the work invokes in the reader. Authors use their own personal style, their attitude toward the subject, and the mood they create to help craft their stories. Style, tone, and mood all contribute to the effect of a text. As readers, we know there is a difference between a serious or humorous piece, for example.

<u>Impact of words on tone</u>
Words can have a large impact on the tone of a passage. Tone is a result of the choice of language. For instance, when talking about or suggesting the mood of a person or a setting, it is vital to choose the right language to describe it. Is a person ecstatic, or is the person simply content? Is a room barren, or is it just empty? Similarly, using strong action verbs can create a tone that is forceful and remembered easily. The verb buttress, for instance, has a much stronger impact than the verb strengthen. Even though both words have basically the same meaning, the first one creates a more vivid image in the mind of the reader. It is important to use words that will be understood by the audience and will have the desired effect.

<u>Relate style and tone</u>
Although content is what we write and style is how we write it, the two are very closely interrelated because writing style influences reader perception of content. Style encompasses diction (word choice) and tone. Tone reflects how the writing expresses the writer's attitude overall. For example, a writer can use an informative tone, for objectively providing factual information; or an affective tone, for persuading readers to believe or agree with the writing by appealing to their emotions. In addition to objective or subjective, a writer can use a tone that is formal or informal; calm or excited, etc. Just as we behave differently at school, at work, at a party, at a religious service, etc., tone in writing varies with context and purpose. To establish tone, student writers can ask themselves about their purpose and audience, i.e., why they are writing a text; to/for whom they are writing it; and what they want readers to consider, understand, or learn. Developing tone involves as many qualitative as technical factors and is a subjective choice, particularly in creative writing, including literary techniques like metaphor, symbolism, imagery, allusion, etc. as well as usage, grammar and other mechanics.

**Syntax**

These questions will require the student to use various sentence structures to achieve the needed rhetorical structure.

<u>Syntax</u>
Syntax is the order of the words in a sentence. When writing, it is important to make sure not only that the syntax is correct, but also that it is not repetitive. There is nothing worse than reading a passage that has sentences that are all alike: noun, verb, object. These need to be interspersed with sentences that use a variety of clause constructions. This will lend a musicality to the writing, and will allow for greater flow of language and ideas. Make sure to reread any written material to ensure that the syntax is correct and engaging. Otherwise, you may end up with something that comes off as confused rather than well-written.

*Rewrite the following sentences by varying their syntax.*

Marilyn and Rosemary worked together. They were having a party. They had to get all the food done first. They cleaned the house and decorated. They invited about 20 people. The people were all work associates. They were having the party in Marilyn's backyard. This is where she had many similar parties. They were always fun.

*This is one way to rewrite the sentences so that the syntax is varied:*

Marilyn and Rosemary, who worked together, were going to have a party. But before they could do that, they had to get all the food ready for it, as well as clean the house and decorate. They invited about 20 people, who were all work associates, and were holding the party in Marilyn's backyard, where there had been many other parties that were always fun.

The rewritten sentences provide a greater variety of syntax, and consequently, greater rhythm. The language is more engaging as a result. Remember to make use of clauses to introduce information and create sentences that are complex. In addition, remember to reread any work you rewrite to make sure it makes sense.

Rhetorical devices that use syntax

One way to emphasize an idea is through repetition. For example, **anadiplosis**, a literary/rhetorical device meaning literally to double back, repeats the last word in one sentence, clause, or phrase at the beginning of the next. In *The Caine Mutiny* (1951), author Herman Wouk uses this technique writing Captain Queeg's dialogue, "'Aboard my ship, excellent performance is standard. Standard performance is sub-standard. Sub-standard performance is not permitted to exist.'" Or in a lyric (1979) from Frank Zappa, "Information is not knowledge. Knowledge is not wisdom. Wisdom is not truth. Truth is not beauty. Beauty is not love. Love is not music. Music is the best." Contrasts, particularly subtle ones, can be emphasized or clarified via **antithesis**, i.e., juxtaposition, as in Alexander Pope's famous line from his poem *An Essay on Criticism* (1711), "To err is human; to forgive, divine." While redundancy generally should be avoided, it may be used deliberately to emphasize, as Shakespeare did in *Julius Caesar* (1599): "This was the most unkindest cut of all." The term for this literary device is **pleonasm**.

**Standard English Conventions**

The questions in this section focus on editing text to make sure that it conforms to the conventions of standard written English. This includes the editing of sentences, usage, and punctuation.

**Sentence Structure**

These questions will focus on editing text for sentence formation and sentence structure. The main focus will be on inappropriate shifts in construction within and between sentences.

Types of sentence structures

The four major types of sentence structure are:
1. Simple sentences: Simple sentences have one independent clause with no subordinate clauses. A simple sentence may contain compound elements—a compound subject, verb, or object, for example—but does not contain more than one full sentence pattern.
2. Compound sentences: Compound sentences are composed of two or more independent clauses with no subordinate clauses. The independent clauses are usually joined with a comma and a coordinating conjunction or with a semicolon.
3. Complex sentences: A complex sentence is composed of one independent clause with one or more dependent clauses.
4. Compound-complex sentences: A compound-complex sentence contains at least two independent clauses and at least one subordinate clause. Sometimes they contain two full sentence patterns that can stand alone. When each independent clause contains a subordinate clause, this makes the sentence both compound and complex.

**Sentence Boundaries**

For these questions the student will need to recognize and correct grammatically incorrect sentences. This includes rhetorically inappropriate fragments and run-ons.

Fragments

A fragment is an incomplete sentence or thought that cannot stand on its own. Fragments are missing either nouns or verbs and are very confusing to the reader because the thought is not complete. When revising their writing, the author needs to read carefully to be sure to catch any fragments and revise them, making sure to read each word on the page and only the words on the page. The author will want to identify whether the fragment is missing a noun or verb and replace it. Sometimes, a fragment is the beginning part of the next sentence. In this case, you can combine it with the following sentence in order to make one complete thought.

## Run-on
A run-on sentence is a sentence that should be written as two, or more, sentences. It contains too much information for a single sentence. When reading a run-on sentence, a reader would be out of breath, or very confused. When revising their writing, the author needs to read carefully to be sure to catch any run-ons and revise them. Usually, the easiest way to revise a run-on sentence is to split it up into two or more complete sentences. Figure out where to put the period to make the first part a complete sentence, then, read the second part. You may have to tweak it a bit to make the second part a complete sentence as well.

## Correcting incomplete sentences
Complete sentences need not be long, but require a subject and predicate. For instance, "I see" or "He lives," albeit only two words apiece, are complete sentences. Sentence fragments are missing subject, verb, or both. For example, "While I was walking down the street one day" is a fragment though it seems to have a subject ("I") and predicate ("was walking") because the conjunction "While" makes it a dependent clause needing an independent clause to complete it—e.g., "While I was walking down the street one day, I met a man." The added clause actually contains the subject ("I") and verb ("met"). Run-on sentences lack divisions like punctuation/conjunctions separating clauses and phrases. For example, "We went to the party we had a good time" is a run-on with two independent clauses, which should be separated one of several ways: into two sentences by a period, "We went to the party. We had a good time"; within one sentence by a semicolon, "We went to the party; we had a good time"; by a conjunction, "We went to the party and we had a good time," or "We went to the party, where we had a good time."

## Subordination and Coordination

These questions will require the student to recognize and correct problem with coordination and subordination in a sentence.

## Subordination vs coordination
Coordination connects clauses that are equal in importance and type, demonstrating relationships between ideas and preventing repetitious writing. According equal importance or emphasis to unrelated or unequal clauses is a coordination error. For example, "This author won the Pulitzer Prize for fiction, and she resides in Columbia, South Carolina." This sentence connects two unrelated clauses. It can be corrected by making one clause dependent, e.g., "This author, who resides in Columbia, South Carolina, won the Pulitzer Prize for fiction"; or by changing one clause to a modifying phrase, e.g., "This author, a Columbia, South Carolina resident, won the Pulitzer Prize for fiction"; or by changing it to an appositive phrase: "This author, a Columbia, South Carolina resident, won the Pulitzer Prize for fiction." Subordination makes one clause less important than/subordinate to another. Reversing their importance is a subordination error. In a piece about American jobs, "American consumers like Japanese cars, though importing them threaten American jobs" emphasizes the wrong clause. Reversing the subordinating clause's position corrects it: "Though American consumers like Japanese cars, importing threatens American jobs."

<u>Subordinating conjunctions</u>
Subordinating conjunctions introduce adverbial clauses. They join a dependent adverb clause to an independent clause.

Cause: as, because, since
Comparison: more than, as...as
Conditional: even if, if, unless
Contrast: although, even though, though
Manner: as, as if, as though
Place: where, wherever
Purpose: in order that, so that
Result: so...that
Time: after, before, since, until, when

<u>Coordinating and correlative conjunctions</u>
Conjunctions join words, phrases, and clauses, showing the relationship between them.

The categories of conjunctions are coordinating, correlative, and subordinating. Conjunctive adverbs or transition words are another type of conjunction.

Coordinating conjunctions join grammatically equal words, phrases, or clauses (two pronouns, two prepositional phrases, two independent clauses, etc.) The coordinating conjunctions are and, but, or, nor.

Correlative conjunctions are used in pairs to join two or more words, phrases, or clauses that are grammatically equal.

*Examples:*
        both...and; not only...but also; either...or; whether...or; neither...no

**Parallel Structure**

For these questions the student will need to recognize and correct problems dealing with parallel structure in sentences.

<u>Parallel structure</u>
Parallel structure is keeping grammatical elements consistent with one another within the same sentence. As an example, "She likes skiing, skating, and snowboarding" is correct because the three gerunds (i.e., verbs functioning as nouns—in this case, the participial forms of *to ski, to skate,* and *to snowboard*) are all in the same progressive participle ("-ing participle") form of the verbs. However, the sentence "She likes to ski, skate, and snowboarding" is incorrect by mixing two infinitives with one gerund. Similarly, "She likes skiing, skating, and to snowboard" is also wrong. Parts of speech should also not be mixed/inconsistent within the same clause, comparing unlike items. For example, "We have openings in software development, engineering management, sales trainees, and service technicians." Departments and occupations like software development and engineering management are incorrectly equated here with people like sales trainees and service technicians. These can be corrected to "sales and technical services" to make all items consistent/parallel. Or the reverse, i.e., "We have openings for software developers, engineering managers, sales trainees, and service technicians."

**Modifier Placement**

These questions will require the student to recognize and correct problems with modifier placement such as misplaced or dangling modifiers.

Placing phrases and clauses
Modifying phrases or clauses should be placed as closely as possible to the words they modify to ensure that the meaning of the sentence is clear. A misplaced modifier makes the meaning of a sentence murky. For instance, the meaning of Walt barely missed the dog speeding down the street becomes evident when the phrase is moved: Speeding down the street, Walt barely missed the dog. A dangling modifier doesn't have a word that it is modifying, so a word must be put into the sentence in order to complete its meaning. Having arrived late for assembly, a written excuse was needed. This sentence makes it sound as though the written excuse was late for assembly, so something needs to be added to the sentence. The meaning is clear when the name Jessica is added. Having arrived late for assembly, Jessica needed a written excuse. Here the phrase modifies Jessica.

Misplaced and dangling modifiers
Misplaced and dangling modifiers, especially dangling participles, are among the most common grammatical and syntactic errors made in English writing—and students are not necessarily the primary culprits. A modifier should precede or follow the noun, verb, clause/phrase or other target that it modifies. When separated from its target by intervening words, phrases, or clauses, it will appear to modify those incorrectly instead. For example, in the sentence, "She served him breakfast eggs glistening with mucus," the participial phrase "glistening..." modifies "eggs." However, if the syntax were different, e.g., "Glistening with mucus, she served him breakfast eggs" sounds as if she were glistening with mucus rather than the eggs. When the modifier is not just separated from its target but the target is missing altogether, this creates a dangling modifier—often a participle. An example is, "Walking down the street, the house was on fire." The house was not walking down the street. Correction would add a target in the independent clause: "Walking down the street, we saw that the house was on fire," or in the dependent clause: "As we were walking down the street, the house was on fire."

Word order can give a sentence completely different meanings just by changing the position of one modifier, e.g., an adverb, by one word. For example, consider the meanings of two sentences: (1) "I only ate produce." (2) "I ate only produce." Sentence (1) means I only ATE produce, i.e., I did not plant, grow, harvest, wash, chop, cook, or otherwise prepare the produce; I only ate it. Sentence (2) means I ate nothing other than produce, i.e., I did not eat meat, dairy products, etc.; I only ate PRODUCE. The order of the word "only" changes the meaning. Similarly, (1) "He failed nearly every English class he took" means he passed only one or a few English classes at most because he failed almost all of them; but (2) "He nearly failed every English class he took" means he passed every English class he took, though he came very close to failing all of them. In both sentences, the modifying adverb "nearly" affects the following word— the determiner "every" in (1) and the verb "failed" in (2).

Correct word order
When a modifying phrase, often a participle, begins a sentence and a comma follows it, whatever word(s) that phrase modifies should follow the comma immediately. However, many people frequently misplace such modifiers, following them with an object instead of the subject they modify. For example, this sentence has a misplaced modifier: "Falling down the mountain, Tom was afraid the boulders would hit the campgrounds." This placement means Tom was falling down the mountain. Some correction alternatives include: (1) "Falling down the mountain, the boulders seemed about to hit the campgrounds, scaring Tom." Or: (2) "Tom was afraid the boulders falling down the mountain would hit the campgrounds." Or: (3) "Tom was afraid the boulders, which were falling down the mountain, would hit the campgrounds." A squinting modifier (sometimes called a two-way modifier) is sandwiched between two words and could modify

either, confusing readers. For example, "Children who laugh seldom are shy" could mean children who seldom laugh are shy; or children who laugh are seldom shy. Either corrects it, depending on the meaning.

## Inappropriate Shifts in Construction

For these questions the student will need to edit text to correct inappropriate shifts in verb tense, voice, mood, pronoun person, and number.

<u>Verb tense</u>
Verb tenses are ways in which verbs show that an action takes place. Verbs change according to when an action occurs. An action can take place in the present tense, which means the action is happening right now. An action can take place in the past tense, which means the action has already happened and is in the past. An action can take place in the future, which means the action has not yet happened but will do so. A progressive tense shows that the action is ongoing and continuing to go on in the present

<u>Changes in verb tense</u>
Verbs change form to agree with the subject of the action and to indicate the time or tense of the action. Verb tenses can be categorized as simple or perfect. Each of these tenses has a continuous form.

Simple present tense expresses habitual or repeated actions, general truths, future actions, literary or historic present, and states or qualities of being. In statements, do/does expresses emphasis.  See examples below:

> Susie exercises on Thursdays and Fridays. (habitual action)
> Fred is a doctor.  (linking verb--state of being)

Simple past tense expresses finished actions. Did in statements expresses emphasis.  See examples below.

> World War II ended in 1945. (finished action)
> Benedict Arnold began as a loyal American, but later he did betray his country. (emphasis)

Future tense expresses actions or conditions occurring in the future. Simple present tense with an adverb of time can indicate future.

> She will see it next week.  (future tense)
> The insurance coverage ends next month. (simple present)

<u>Example of incorrect shift in voice</u>
Read the following sentence and correct it:

> When the doctor turned on the instrument, a strange sound was heard.

This sentence is an example of an incorrect shift in the voice of the verb, something that is very common in colloquial English. The sentence starts out with an active verb, "turned on," and then shifts to a passive voice with "was heard." It can be corrected by rewording the second part of the sentence; the correct sentence reads: "When the doctor turned on the instrument, he heard a strange sound." Now both verb forms are in the active voice. The pronoun "he" agrees with its precedent "doctor." The active voice is preferred because it is stronger and more direct than the passive voice.

<u>Noun-pronoun agreement in number</u>
A pronoun must agree with its antecedent in number.  If the antecedent is singular, the pronoun referring to it must be singular; if the antecedent is plural, the pronoun referring to it must be plural.

Use singular pronouns to refer to the singular indefinite pronouns: each, either, neither, one, everyone, everybody, no one, nobody, anyone, anybody, someone, somebody.

*Example:*
- Each of the students bought their own lunch.  (incorrect)
- Each of the students bought his own lunch.  (correct)

Use plural nouns to refer to the plural indefinite pronouns: both, few, several, many.

*Example:*
> Both were within their boundaries.

The indefinite pronouns some, any, none, all, most may be referred to by singular or plural pronouns, depending on the sense of the sentence.

*Example:*
- Some of the children have misplaced their toys. (plural)
- Some of the carpet has lost its nap. (singular)

Pronouns that refer to compound antecedents joined by and are usually plural.  Example: Bill and Joe cook their own meals.

<u>Examples of incorrect shifts</u>
Two verb tenses in one sentence are correct when one event occurs before/after another, e.g., "The class <u>will be</u> tested next week on the lessons they <u>completed</u> last week." However, tense should not shift when describing simultaneous/concurrent events, e.g., "This shirt didn't fit; it is too tight" is incorrect: it still does not fit. It should be, "This shirt doesn't fit; it is too tight." Similarly, "Although I admired her bravery, I cannot stand her rudeness" incorrectly implies I no longer admire her bravery; "admire" is correct. In "The wind abates and the waves rolled gently," coordinating conjunction "and" implies concurrent events; for consistency, it should be either "abated" or "roll." Shifts in voice switch between active and passive voice in one sentence. "After oversleeping, Marshall hurried to class, where <u>it was discovered</u> class was cancelled." The subject, Marshall, hurried in active voice, so the rest of the sentence should maintain this: "..<u>where he discovered</u> class was cancelled." Shifts in mood incorrectly change the conditional in conditional-subjunctive constructions to indicative: "If I <u>was</u> rich..." should be "If I <u>were</u> rich, I <u>would</u> buy you a mansion."

**Pronoun person and number**

The student will recognize and correct inappropriate shifts in pronoun person and number within and between sentences.

<u>Narrative voice</u>
Narrative voice can be first person "I" or "we"; second person "you"; or third person "he," "she," "it," "one," "anyone"; "they," "people," etc. Students often reproduce person shifts from spoken to written language, e.g., "We should leave early; you never know what could happen" shifts from first to second person. Correction: "We should leave early; we don't know what could happen." "If one reads the book, they will like it better than the movie" should be "If they read the book, they will...." Shifts in pronoun number are often the results when students begin sentences with indefinite pronouns like "all," "none," or "anyone" as subjects, but then incorrectly switch between singular and plural or vice versa. For example, "Every student is working their hardest" shifts from

singular to plural; "All of the students are working their hardest" correctly maintains consistent plural number. "Anyone can be captain since they are well trained" can be corrected to ."..since each of them is well trained."

## Conventions of Usage

For these questions the student should be able to edit sentences to conform to the conventions of standard written English.

### Conventions of written language
The conventions of written language include capitalizing words correctly. Proper names are capitalized. The first word of a sentence is capitalized. Titles are capitalized. The names of countries are capitalized. The names of rivers are capitalized. The conventions also include using proper punctuation. This means using end marks correctly. End marks include periods, question marks, and exclamation marks. It means using commas correctly. It means using apostrophes correctly. Good penmanship is also important. Good penmanship helps a reader to understand what has been written. It means that the handwriting is neat and well formed. Using these conventions will help the author communicate clearly.

## Pronouns

These questions will require the student to edit sentences for proper pronoun use. They should be able to recognize and correct pronouns that are unclear or have ambiguous antecedents.

### Pronoun use
Pronouns are used to replace nouns. They substitute for a person, place or thing. "Tommy is running home. He is running home." In these sentences the pronoun he takes the place of Tommy. Some pronouns are subject pronouns. They are: *I, you, he, she, it, we,* and *they*. There are also object pronouns. They are: *me, you, him, her, it, us,* and *them*. Possessive pronouns are used to show that someone or something owns something. Some possessive pronouns are used before a noun, such as *my, your, his, her, its, our,* and *their*. Some possessive pronouns stand alone. They are: mine, yours, his, hers, ours, and theirs. Pronouns must always agree with the noun that they refer to. "Peter and Lucy took their seats in the front row." In this sentence, the possessive pronoun *their* refers to the plural subject Peter and Lucy. A reflexive pronoun occurs when the pronoun is after the noun that is in the sentence. Reflexive pronouns are: *myself, herself, ourselves,* and *himself.*

### Objective pronoun
An objective pronoun is a pronoun that is the object of a verb. The objective pronouns are: me, you, him, her, it, us, and them. For example, in the sentence, "Monica invited us to her birthday party," *us* is the objective pronoun. It is the object of the verb *invited*. Objective pronouns can be used in compound sentences as well: "Monica invited Jane and us to her birthday party." Here the object of the verb is *Jane and us*. Objective pronouns can be used with a preposition: "His sister pulled the blanket over me." In this case *me* is the object of the preposition *over*.

### Pronoun referents
Pronoun referents or antecedents are the word or group of words that a pronoun refers to. All pronouns must agree with their antecedents in number, gender, and person. A pronoun antecedent may be a noun, another pronoun, or a phrase or clause acting as a noun. Read the following sentence. "Lawyers must research their cases thoroughly." In this example, the pronoun referent or antecedent is the noun lawyers. The pronoun *their* refers to lawyers. It agrees with its antecedent because it is a plural pronoun. "Marian loved her new bicycle." In this sentence the pronoun *her* refers to Marian. It is correct because it agrees with the subject, since it is a singular feminine pronoun.

**Pronoun clarity**

The student will recognize and correct pronouns with unclear or ambiguous antecedents.

<u>Ambiguous antecedents to pronouns</u>
When sentences describe more than one person, place, or thing, the pronouns referring to each noun must clearly indicate which for reader understanding. Students may write unclearly by using multiple pronouns in one sentence with ambiguous antecedents—i.e., pronouns could refer to more than one antecedent noun. In the sentence "My luggage was in that car, but now it is missing," either the luggage or the car could be missing. Depending on desired meaning, corrections could be either "My luggage was in that car, but now my luggage is missing" or "My luggage was in that car, but now the car is missing." In "The teacher told Helen it would take her a long time to correct all the errors in her essay," "her" could refer to either Helen or the teacher. The first "her" should be either "Helen" or "the teacher" and the second, either "Helen's" or "the teacher's," depending on meaning. Another way antecedents become unclear is by being too far from corresponding pronouns. For example, in "Buford espied Longstreet's troops advancing. Reynolds' unit came quickly to help; soon <u>he</u> was engaged in battle," "he" is unclear and should be the subject, "Buford."

**Possessive Determiners**

For these questions the student should recognize and correct cases in which possessive determiners, contractions, and adverbs are confused with each other. Examples of possessive determiners are "its, your, their", contractions "it's, you're, they're", and adverbs "there".

<u>Contractions</u>
A contraction is a word formed by combining two other words. Contractions are often used to make writing flow more easily. When the words are formed, letters are left out. An apostrophe is used in place of the letters that were left out. For example, can and not combine to become can't. The apostrophe is put in place of the omitted letter. Some contractions are used often. Learning them is useful. Aren't is a combination of are not; don't is a combination of do not, doesn't is a combination of does not and hasn't is a combination of has not.

<u>Adverbs</u>
An adverb modifies a verb, an adjective, or another adverb by answering such questions as how? how much? how long? when? and where? Adverbs also act as sentence modifiers.
1. He dressed handsomely. how?
2. She knows more than she thinks. how much?
3. He was gone a week. how long?
4. Last month they flew to Hawaii. when?
5. I went home. where?
6. Unfortunately, he revealed the story's surprise ending. Sentence modifier

Other Parts of Speech as Adverbs - Nouns, prepositions and adjectives sometimes act as adverbs.
1. I'll see you Friday. noun when?
2. He came outside. preposition where?
3. My brother Fred runs slow. adjective how?

Adverbs Formed by Adding 'LY' to Adjectives - An adverb is often formed by adding an 'ly' to an adjective

<u>Homophonous possessive determiners and contactors</u>
Common writing errors are confusing "its" with "it's," "your" with "you're," and "their" with "they're" and/or "there." The source of these errors is that in speech, these pairs are homophones, i.e., they sound alike. But in writing, they are spelled differently corresponding to different meanings

and grammatical functions. Possessive determiners "its," "your," and "their" do NOT have apostrophes—the same as "hers," "his," and "our." (The fact that possessive pronouns DO use apostrophes, e.g., "Mary's hat," "John's book," "the passenger's ticket," only adds to the confusion.) Contrasting from their homophones, "it's," "you're," and "they're" are all contractions of pronoun and verb—the verb *to be* specifically. Expanded, they mean "it is," "you are," and "they are," not indicating possession. "There" is an adverb indicating place, point, or manner; or an "existential" pronoun as in "There are people inside." The incorrect "This book is missing it's cover" should be "...its cover." "We know your confused" should be "...you're confused." "Sign you're name here" should be "...your name here." "There going their with they're friends" is triply incorrect; "They're going there with their friends" is correct.

## Agreement

These questions will require the student to ensure grammatical agreement. This will include agreement between pronoun and antecedent, subject and verb, and noun agreement.

## Pronoun-antecedent agreement

The student will recognize and correct lack of agreement between pronoun and antecedent.

### Pronoun-antecedent agreement

Pronoun-antecedent agreement means that the pronoun and the antecedent (the word that refers back to the pronoun) need to match in number and gender. A singular pronoun needs a singular antecedent, just as a plural pronoun needs a plural antecedent. Likewise, masculine pronouns need masculine antecedents, and feminine pronouns need feminine antecedents. Here is an example of a sentence with a mistake in pronoun-antecedent agreement: The bike rack is there for everyone to lock up their bikes. This is a very common error and one that people make in speaking and in writing all the time. In the sentence, the pronoun is *their*. This is a plural pronoun. In the sentence, the antecedent is everyone, which is singular. The sentence should have correct pronoun-antecedent agreement. Here is one correct revision of the sentence:

- The bike rack is there for everyone to lock up his bike.

### Lack of agreement

Excepting indefinite pronouns, other pronouns need referents, i.e., antecedents. Antecedents and pronouns should agree in number, person, and gender. "Every student must bring their permission slips" is incorrect because "every" and "student" are singular, whereas "their" and "permission slips" are plural. "All students must bring their permission slips" is correct. To correct the antecedent-pronoun number mismatch in "I never eat at that restaurant because they have stale bread," change "they have" to "it has." Differing number, person, and/or gender between antecedent and pronoun can also be called faulty co-reference. For example, "Politics is fun because they are such interesting people" is incorrect because (plural) "they" does not even refer to (singular) "politics." "Politics is fun because politicians are such interesting people" is correct. Faulty co-reference can also involve pronouns not replacing nouns or adverbs not replacing adverbial clauses/phrases. "He should know German well; he lived there for ten years" is incorrect because the second clause refers to the country, not the language from the first clause. "He should know German well; he lived in Germany for ten years" is correct.

## Subject-verb agreement

The student will recognize and correct lack of agreement between subject and verb.

### Subject-verb agreement

Subject-verb agreement means that the subject and verb in a sentence have to agree in number. A singular subject needs a singular verb, just as a plural subject needs a plural verb. Errors occur when people incorrectly match the number of the subject and the verb. Here is an example of an incorrect sentence: The dogs of the neighborhood was barking loudly. The sentence is incorrect because the subject, dogs, is plural. The sentence is referring to more than one dog. The verb, was, is singular. The subject and verb do not match. Here are two correct versions of the sentence, depending on the meaning the author wants to convey:

The dog of the neighborhood was barking loudly.
The dogs of the neighborhood were barking loud.

Subject-verb agreement errors

Common errors in subject-verb agreement involve singular vs. plural number, e.g., students (plural) write; a student (singular) writes. When prepositional phrases intervene between them, subject and verb should still agree regardless. A common error is mistaking the object of the preposition for the sentence subject. "Large <u>amounts</u> of mercury <u>are</u> found in some fish" is correct; "Large amounts of <u>mercury is</u> found in some fish" is incorrect. "<u>Water</u> in your fuel lines <u>makes</u> your car stall" is correct; "Water in your fuel <u>lines make</u> your car stall" is incorrect. Quantitative units, like "ten dollars" or "five miles" are considered singular units, e.g., "Five miles <u>is</u> a long walk" or "The price <u>is</u> ten dollars." Nouns with singular meanings, despite plural forms, take singular verbs: "<u>Mumps is</u> rare today in America." Most compound subjects joined by "and" are plural: "Dogs and cats <u>are</u> popular pets," not "is." Two exceptions are compound subjects that have become units through usage, like "corned beef and cabbage" or "bacon and eggs," which are singular; and compound subjects describing one person/thing: "He is the <u>founder and pioneer</u> of the discipline." Or "This is the <u>cause and solution</u> of our problem."

**Noun agreement**

The student will recognize and correct lack of agreement between nouns.

Just as verbs must agree with their subject nouns in sentences, and pronouns must agree with the nouns they reference, nouns referring to other nouns must agree in number. For example, "Bert and Ernie both got jobs as <u>a lifeguard</u> over the summer" is incorrect: the noun "jobs" is plural to agree with the compound subject "Bert and Ernie," i.e., two people; but "a lifeguard" is singular. It should be "Bert and Ernie both got jobs <u>as lifeguards</u> over the summer." Related nouns in the same sentence should agree in number, i.e., all singular or all plural. For example, "The teacher said she would give us answers to every question" is incorrect: "answers" is plural but "question" is singular. Two ways of correcting this sentence are making both nouns singular, e.g., "The teacher said she would give us an answer to every question"; or making both plural, e.g., "The teacher said she would give us answers to all questions." Exceptions include abstract and/or mass nouns that would become awkward if plural: "The <u>courage</u> of the soldiers..." is acceptable because "The <u>courages</u> of the soldiers" is illogical as well as awkward.

**Frequently Confused Words**

For these questions the student should be able to recognize and correct instances where one word is confused with another. An example would be the words, accept and except.

Contractions

All contractions, such as they're, it's, and who's are actually two words joined together by the use of an apostrophe to replace a missing letter or letters. Whenever a contraction is encountered, it can be broken down into the two distinct words that make it up.

*Example:*

I wouldn't eat in the cafeteria. = I would not eat in the cafeteria.

The apostrophe in the contraction is always located where the missing letter or letters should be. In the examples below, the apostrophe replaces the "o" in the word "not". The contraction "doesn't" actually stands for the two words "does not".

Incorrect Example: He does'nt live here.
Correct Example: He doesn't live here.

Whenever there is a contraction in an answer choice, it can always be replaced by the two words that make the contraction up. If necessary, scratch through the contractions in the choices, and replace them with the two words that make up the contraction. Otherwise the choices may be confusing. Alternatively, while reading the answer choices to yourself, instead of reading the contractions as a contraction, read them as the two separate words that make them up. Some contractions are especially confusing.

Its/it's
"It's" is actually a contraction for the two words "it is". Never confuse "it's" for the possessive pronoun "its". "It's" should only be used when the two words "it is" would make sense as a replacement. Use "its" in all other cases.
Example 1: It's going to rain later today. = It is going to rain later today.
Example 2: The dog chewed through its rope and ran away.

They're/their/there
"They're" is actually a contraction for "they are", and those two words should always be used to replace "they're" when it is encountered.

*Example:*
They're going to the movie with us. = They are going to the movie with us.

"Their" is an adjective used to show ownership.
Example 1: Their car is a red convertible.
Example 2: The students from each school sat in their own stands.

"There" should be used in all other cases.
Example 1: There exists an answer to every question.
Example 2: The man was over there.

Who's/whose
Who's is actually a contraction for "who is", and those two words should always be used to replace who's when it is encountered.

*Example:*
Who's going with me? = Who is going with me?

Whose would be used in all other cases, where "who is" does not fit.

*Example:*
Whose car is this?

Their/his
"Their" is a plural possessive pronoun, referring to multiple people or objects.

*Example:*
The men went to their cars.

"His" is a singular possessive, referring to an individual person or object.

*Example:*
The man went to his car.

<u>Which/that/who</u>
"Which" should be used to refer to things only.
>   John's dog, which was called Max, is large and fierce.

"That" may be used to refer to either persons or things.
>   Is this the only book that Louis L'Amour wrote?
>   Is Louis L'Amour the author that [or who] wrote Western novels?

"Who" should be used to refer to persons only.
>   Mozart was the composer who [or that] wrote those operas.

<u>Who/Whom or Whoever/Whomever</u>
Who/whom will be encountered in two forms, as an interrogative pronoun in a question, or as a relative pronoun not in a question.

*Interrogative pronoun in a question:* If the answer to the question would include the pronouns he, she, we, or they, then "who" is correct.

*Example:*
>   Who threw the ball?  He threw the ball.

If the answer to the question would include the pronouns him, her, us, or them, then "whom" is correct.

*Example:*
>   With whom did you play baseball?  I played baseball with him.

*Relative pronoun NOT in a question*:  If who/whom is followed by a verb, typically use "who".

*Example:*
>   Peter Jackson was an obscure director who became a celebrity overnight.

*If who/whom is followed by a noun, typically use "whom":*

*Example:*
>   Bob, whom we follow throughout his career, rose swiftly up the ladder of success.

However, beware of the insertion of phrases or expressions immediately following the use of who/whom.  Sometimes, the phrase can be skipped without the sentence losing its meaning.

*Example:*
>   This is the woman who, we believe, will win the race.

To determine the proper selection of who/whom, skip the phrase "we believe".  Thus, "who" would come before "will win", a verb, making the choice of "who" correct.

In other cases, the sentence should be rephrased in order to make the right decision.

*Example:*
>   I can't remember who the author of "War and Peace" is.

To determine the proper selection of who/whom, rephrase the sentence to state, "I can't remember who is the author of 'War and Peace'."

<u>Knowledge of word roots</u>

When words are both homophones, i.e., they sound alike, and *homographs*, i.e., they are spelled alike, students must rely on context to differentiate meaning, e.g., "I cannot <u>bear</u> to think how that <u>bear</u> and others will be unable to <u>bear</u> young because you have destroyed their habitat." However, when homophones are spelled differently, knowing their roots can inform their meaning. For example, the Latin root *cept* means "take" or "receive." Knowing this informs the meaning of "inception"; knowing also that *con* means "with" or "together" informs the meanings of "concept" and "conception." Knowing *ac-* means "to" or "toward" informs the meaning of "accept"; knowing *ex-* means "out of" (as in "exit") or "away from" informs the different meaning of "except." Similarly, knowing *al-* means "to," "toward," or "near" informs the meaning of *allusion;* also knowing *il-* means "not" helps differentiate it from *illusion.* Hence "allusion" means referring TO something whereas "illusion" means something NOT real. In both, the root *lūdere* means "to play." "Allusion" plays TO a referent; "illusion" plays an impression of reality that is false, NOT real.

## Logical Comparison

These questions will require the student to recognize and correct cases in which unlike terms are compared.

Incorrect vs correct comparison
To make effective comparisons in written text, writers need to compare terms that are alike rather than unlike ones. For example, if someone writes, "This artist's works have frequently been compared to much earlier portrait artists" or "This artist's works have frequently been compared to portrait painters from earlier historical eras," the writer has incorrectly compared the subject "works" to "artists" and "painters," respectively. To make it correct, the writer would either have to change the sentence to "This artist has frequently been compared to much earlier portrait artists" or "to portrait painters from earlier historical eras," which are both correct but change the meaning slightly; or to "This artist's works have frequently been compared to <u>those of</u> much older portrait artists" or "This artist's works have frequently been compared to portraits painted by much earlier artists" or "to portraits by painters from earlier historical eras," neither of which changes the meaning but both of which compare like nouns, rectifying the error of comparing unlike nouns.

Logically incorrect sentences
Items compared in sentences must be similar to be logically correct. For example, "Living in a city is very different from the country" is logically incorrect by comparing the subject, gerund phrase "Living in a city," to the object of the preposition ("to"), article and noun "the country." In other words, it compares dissimilar terms. "Living in a city is very different from living in the country" is logically correct by comparing like terms. In the same way, "More words in Spanish are pronounced as they are spelled than English" is logically incorrect. It can be corrected by changing the end to "...than words in English," or even "...than in English," to match "...words in Spanish" or "...in Spanish." To avoid always repeating the same/similar word/phrase/clause, writers can simplify sentences by replacing the first term(s) with "that" (singular) or "those" (plural) in the second instance: "The call of the cardinal is much prettier than <u>that of</u> the blue jay" instead of "the call of the blue jay"; "The landforms in Finland are similar to <u>those in</u> eastern Canada" instead of "the landforms in eastern Canada."

Effective comparisons
To make effective comparisons, writers must compare words/phrases representing things/concepts that can legitimately be compared. Some people forget what the sentence subject represents and compare it to something not representing the same kind/class of thing. For example, "Her wedding dress looked as fashionable as a celebrity appearing on the red carpet before an awards show" is a logically incorrect sentence because it compares a dress, the subject of the sentence, to a celebrity, the object of the preposition "as" and of the comparison. A dress is a thing; a celebrity is a person. Hence these are unlike terms. To correct this sentence, one option is to write, "Her wedding dress looked as fashionable as <u>a dress worn by</u> a celebrity appearing on the red carpet before an awards show"—i.e., repeating the noun "dress" on both

sides of the comparison. Another way is to refer to the dress, e.g., "as fashionable as that of a celebrity...." Another is to change the sentence subject: "In her wedding dress, she looked as fashionable as a celebrity...."

## Conventional Expression

For these questions the student will be required to recognize and correct situations where a given expression is inconsistent with standard written English.

### Examples of conventional expressions
Certain expressions have been used so often in speech and writing that speakers and writers may rely upon them as signals of their accepted meanings to clarify audience understanding. However, many people also unwittingly say and write them incorrectly. For example, an English idiomatic expression meaning you can't have it both ways is almost universally stated incorrectly as "You can't have your cake and eat it too." This is backwards; as expert Milton Friedman has pointed out, if you have your cake, of course you can eat it. The original correct saying is "You can't eat your cake and have it too." This means if you eat the cake up, you won't have it anymore; you can either eat it or still have it, not both. Another ubiquitous error involving reversal is "I could care less," literally meaning I care more than possible, i.e., I do care; the correct expression is "I couldn't care less," meaning I care as little as possible, i.e., I don't care.

### Common expressions becoming distorted
In typical language development, people learn to listen and speak before learning to read and write. Hence they become acquainted, eventually familiar, with commonly used expressions that have become English conventions. Without seeing correct spelling and exact word choice in print, many people mistake these expressions. Then they become incorrectly used so frequently by so many people that the incorrect form becomes common and taken for granted. Many people incorrectly say—and therefore write—"for all intensive purposes" when they really mean "for all intents and purposes." The latter means for all practical purposes or for all possible reasons; the former means for purposes that were extremely intense—almost undoubtedly NOT what the writer intended. Another expression is "Nip it in the bud." This metaphor compares a situation to a flower: cutting it while it is a bud will prevent its growing to full bloom. The implied comparison is that eliminating a situation/problem in an early stage will prevent its growing to be bigger/full-blown. The common error, "Nip it in the butt," means bite it in the hindquarters instead, inviting unintended humor.

### Knowledge of word roots
Some incorrect usages of Standard English words betray speaker and writer ignorance of the etymologies of words and word parts, and hence of the meanings of those parts. For example, the suffix –less means "without," as in speechless, childless, hopeless, reckless, etc. Therefore, the word "regardless" means "without regard." However, many people apparently do not know, pay attention to, or think about this meaning when they use the non-word "irregardless" in writing, which they have transferred from using it in their speech—also incorrectly. There is no such word; it would constitute a double negative, since both ir- and –less mean "without." Some people may confuse it with "irrespective," which is a correct word because it contains only one negative (ir-). But more have likely learned the incorrect usage from others. Another error involves a small yet important difference: instead of "one and the same," an expression meaning exactly alike, many people say/write "one in the same," meaning united inside of something called "the same"—whatever that is.

## Conventions of Punctuation

For these questions the student will edit sentences to ensure that they conform to the conventions of standard written English punctuation.

**End of sentence punctuation**

The student will recognize and correct inappropriate uses of ending punctuation in cases in which the context makes the intent clear.

<u>Most common sentence ending punctuation</u>
Most sentences are declarative, stating facts or opinions, other information, describing or explaining ideas, etc. A declarative sentence is always punctuated with a period at the end. For example: "Technology has advanced very rapidly in the last few years." Questions are not declarative, but interrogative: they do not tell, but ask. Writers and speakers sometimes convert declarative into interrogative by appending a question at the end of a statement; for example, using the sentence above: "Technology has advanced very rapidly in the last few years, am I right?" (In this case the question is rhetorical, emphasizing the preceding statement.) Exclamation points indicate heavy emphasis, excitement, or surprise. They also punctuate spoken, frequently monosyllabic exclamations, as in "Yikes! You scared me!" They can clarify or match meaning: Without additional contextual information, "That test was hard!" expresses a more intense degree of "hard" than "That test was hard." When context indicates intent, as in "I cannot believe how hard that test was!," the exclamation point matches the meaning. Some of these same examples with inappropriate punctuation include: "Technology has advanced very rapidly in the last few years?" "Technology...years, am I right!" "Yikes. You scared me."

**Within-sentence punctuation**

The student will correctly use and recognize and correct inappropriate uses of colons, semicolons, and dashes to indicate sharp breaks in thought within sentences.

<u>Ways to use colons, semicolons, hyphens, and dashes</u>
Use <u>semicolons</u> to separate two related independent clauses: "People are concerned about the environment; not conserving natural resources endangers our future." Commas, NOT semicolons, separate independent and dependent clauses: "Although he arrived late, Marshall enjoyed the class." Use <u>colons</u> to introduce lists, e.g., "The teacher gave me three choices: do the extra credit report, retake the test, or fail." Introduce new examples/ideas, e.g., "Only one person can remember that war: your grandfather." Separate titles and subtitles, e.g., "The Lord of the Rings: The Return of the King." Hyphenating when adding prefixes to some words avoids confusion; e.g., "I <u>re-sent</u> the message you did not receive" clarifies sending again; "resent" is a verb meaning begrudge/dislike. Use <u>hyphens</u> when creating compound words "up-to-date," "IBM-compatible," etc. Hyphenate spelled-out numbers, e.g., "twenty-four" or "one-hundredth," but NOT "one hundred" "(only hyphenate numbers over 100 as compound adjectives). When interrupting a sentence with a parenthetical but relevant statement, e.g., for clarification; an added comment/dramatic qualification/sudden change in thought, use a dash—singly, e.g., "This is the end of the story—or so we thought"; or paired, enclosing mid-sentence interruption: "Dashes mark an interruption —yes, you guessed it—in the middle of a sentence."

<u>Flow</u>
Commas break the flow of text. To test whether they are necessary, while reading the text to yourself, pause for a moment at each comma. If the pauses seem natural, then the commas are correct. If they are not, then the commas are not correct.

<u>Subjects and verbs</u>
Subjects and verbs must not be separated by commas.  However, a pair of commas setting off a nonessential phrase is allowed.

*Example:*
> The office, which closed today for the festival, was open on Thursday.

"Was" is the verb, while "office" is the subject.  The comma pair between them sets off a nonessential phrase, "which is allowed".  A single comma between them would not be allowed. If you are trying to find the subject, first find the verb and use it to fill in the blank in the following sentence. Who or what _____?

*Example:*
> The boy on the bicycle raced down the hill.

The verb is "raced".  If you can find "raced" and identify it as the verb, ask yourself, "Who or what raced down the hill?"  The answer to that question is the subject, in this case "boy".

<u>Independent clauses</u>
Use a comma before the words and, but, or, nor, for, yet when they join independent clauses.  To determine if two clauses are independent, remove the word that joins them.  If the two clauses are capable of being their own sentence by themselves, then they are independent and need a comma between them.

*Example:*
> He ran down the street, and then he ran over the bridge.

He ran down the street.  Then he ran over the bridge.  These are both clauses capable of being their own sentence.  Therefore a comma must be used along with the word "and" to join the two clauses together.

If one or more of the clauses would be a fragment if left alone, then it must be joined to another clause and does not need a comma between them.

*Example:*
> He ran down the street and over the bridge.

He ran down the street.  Over the bridge.  "Over the bridge" is a sentence fragment and is not capable of existing on its own.  No comma is necessary to join it with "He ran down the street".

Note that this does not cover the use of "and" when separating items in a series, such as "red, white, and blue".  In these cases a comma is not always necessary between the last two items in the series, but in general it is best to use one.

<u>Sentence beginnings</u>
Use a comma after words such as so, well, yes, no, and why when they begin a sentence.
> Example 1: So, you were there when they visited.
> Example 2: Well, I really haven't thought about it.
> Example 3: Yes, I heard your question.
> Example 4: No, I don't think I'll go to the movie.
> Example 5: Why, I can't imagine where I left my keys.

**Possessive Nouns and Pronouns**

For these questions the student should be able to recognize and correct inappropriate uses of possessive nouns and pronouns. They should also be able to differentiate between possessive and plural forms.

Possessive nouns
Possessive nouns show ownership. They often use apostrophes and the letter "s." For instance, a writer might say, "The house of the Owens is near a lake," but this is awkward so instead ownership is shown by using an apostrophe and the letter "s" to make the name "Owens" into a possessive. The writer would then say, "The Owens' house is near the lake." The apostrophe and "s" take the place of the "of" to show ownership or possession. The writer can check to see if a possessive is correct by inserting the word "of" instead of using the apostrophe and "s" and inverting the order of the words to see if the sentence makes sense.

Correct pronoun usage in combinations
To determine the correct pronoun form in a compound subject, try each subject separately with the verb, adapting the form as necessary. Your ear will tell you which form is correct.

*Example:*
    Bob and (I, me) will be going.

Restate the sentence twice, using each subject individually. Bob will be going. I will be going. "Me will be going" does not make sense.

When a pronoun is used with a noun immediately following (as in "we boys"), say the sentence without the added noun. Your ear will tell you the correct pronoun form.

*Example:*
    (We/Us) boys played football last year.

Restate the sentence twice, without the noun. We played football last year. Us played football last year. Clearly "We played football last year" makes more sense.

Apostrophes
If the noun is plural and ends in an "s", the possessive apostrophe would come after the word, without the addition of another "s".

*Example:*
    The students' hats were wet from the rain.

In the example above, there are plural or many students, all of whom have wet hats.

If the noun is plural and does not end in an "s", the possessive apostrophe would come after the word, with the addition of an "s".

*Example:*
    The mice's feet were wet from the rain.

If the noun is singular, the possessive apostrophe is followed by an "s".

*Example:*
    The student's hat was wet from the rain.

In the example above, there is only one student, whose hat is wet.

Errors involving nouns and pronouns
One error some people make when writing is spelling plural pronouns as if they were possessive, e.g., "Writer's need to punctuate correctly." There should be no apostrophe in this or ANY plural noun. Another punctuation error that is more understandable but still incorrect is using an apostrophe in the possessive pronoun "hers," i.e., "her's." This word NEVER has an apostrophe. A way to remember this is to compare it with "his," which also has no apostrophe. Contractions of a noun plus "is," e.g., "she's" contracting "she is" or "she has," require apostrophes; however, "hers" would never be a contraction because "her is" is not a grammatical construction, so it cannot be confused with a contraction needing an apostrophe. Still, the reason this error with a possessive pronoun is more understandable is that possessive nouns, both singular and plural, DO always use apostrophes; for example, "John's shoe," "Meryl's car," "the lady's house," "the company's name," and "the children's toys" indicate possession with apostrophes. Hence some writers confuse possessive pronouns with possessive nouns by equating them. Unlike "children's" above, plural nouns with –s endings take apostrophes after instead of before the –s, e.g., "The cats' fountain needs cleaning."

## Items in a Series

For these questions the student should be able to use the correct punctuation (commas and semicolons) to separate items in a series. They should also be able to recognize and correct the inappropriate use of this punctuation.

Semicolons
Semicolons are used to separate 3 or more items in a series that have a comma internally.

*Example:*

> The club president appointed the following to chair the various committees: John Smith, planning; Jessica Graham, membership; Paul Randolph, financial; and Jerry Short, legal.

Uses for commas and semicolons
Use commas for the following: Within-sentence breaks like appositives, e.g., "Bill Gates, head of Microsoft, developed Windows." List (short) items in a series. Separate adjectives modifying a noun, but NOT following the last adjective: "The sprawling, ramshackle house," NOT "sprawling, ramshackle, house." Separate geographical areas from those containing them, smallest to largest: "Their address is Building #7423, Dhahran Road, Al Mubarraz, Al Ahsa, Saudi Arabia." Also follow the last geographical area with a comma if it is not at the end of the sentence: "Washington, D.C., is the capital of the United States." Separate introductory (typically prepositional) phrases from the main clause: "After dinner, we went for a walk." "At our house, pets are necessities." Separate independent clauses joined by a conjunction ("and," "but," "or," "since," etc.): "He studied hard, but he failed the test." "Since people use air conditioning, electric bills typically increase during the summer." In dialogue, separate names in direct address: "Hugh, would you come here?" Separate direct, full quotations from words introducing them: "Sarah asked, 'Would you like a drink?'"

Separating items in a series by comma or semicolon
Short, easily understandable items listed in a series should be separated by commas. This is an example: "The United States Department of Agriculture divides the food groups into fruits, vegetables, grains, protein foods, dairy products, and oils." However, longer and/or more complex items that include additional explanation, description, or comments should be separated not with commas but with semicolons; for example: "I attended the event with Jennifer, my best friend; her friend, Joe; and his best friend, Rob." Semicolons should also be used to separate clauses in a sentence that contain commas within them to clarify and/or prevent confusion: "Some of these components of foods include saturated fats in meat, poultry, cheese, and butter; unsaturated fats in avocados, beans, nuts, and seeds; and starches in potatoes, corn, and bread." Do NOT use colons to introduce items in a series, as in "In the box were: cookies, candies, and other sweets." This is incorrect.

**Nonrestrictive and Parenthetical Elements**

These questions will require the student to use punctuation such as commas, parentheses, and dashes to set apart nonrestrictive and parenthetical sentence elements. They also need to be able to recognize and correct when restrictive or essential sentence elements are inappropriately set apart with punctuation.

Nonessential clauses and phrases
A comma should be used to set off nonessential clauses and nonessential participial phrases from the rest of the sentence. To determine if a clause is essential, remove it from the sentence. If the removal of the clause would alter the meaning of the sentence, then it is essential. Otherwise, it is nonessential.

*Example:*
      John Smith, who was a disciple of Andrew Collins, was a noted archeologist.

In the example above, the sentence describes John Smith's fame in archeology. The fact that he was a disciple of Andrew Collins is not necessary to that meaning. Therefore, separating it from the rest of the sentence with commas, is correct.

Do not use a comma if the clause or phrase is essential to the meaning of the sentence.

*Example:*
      Anyone who appreciates obscure French poetry will enjoy reading the book.

If the phrase "who appreciates obscure French poetry" is removed, the sentence would indicate that anyone would enjoy reading the book, not just those with an appreciation for obscure French poetry. However, the sentence implies that the book's enjoyment may not be for everyone, so the phrase is essential.

Another perhaps easier way to determine if the clause is essential is to see if it has a comma at its beginning or end. Consistent, parallel punctuation must be used, and so if you can determine a comma exists at one side of the clause, then you can be certain that a comma should exist on the opposite side.

Parenthetical expressions
Commas should separate parenthetical expressions such as the following: after all, by the way, for example, in fact, on the other hand.

*Example:*
      By the way, she is in my biology class.

If the parenthetical expression is in the middle of the sentence, a comma would be both before and after it.

*Example:*
      She is, after all, in my biology class.

However, these expressions are not always used parenthetically. In these cases, commas are not used. To determine if an expression is parenthetical, see if it would need a pause if you were reading the text. If it does, then it is parenthetical and needs commas.

*Example:*
> You can tell by the way she plays the violin that she enjoys its music.

No pause is necessary in reading that example sentence. Therefore the phrase "by the way" does not need commas around it.

## Years
Parentheses should be used around years.

*Example:*
> The presidency of Franklin Delano Roosevelt (1932-1945) was the longest one in American history.

## Nonessential information
Parentheses can be used around information that is added to a sentence but is not essential. Commas or dashes could also be used around these nonessential phrases.

*Example:*
> George Eliot (whose real name was Mary Ann Evans) wrote poems and several well-known novels.

## Identifying nonrestrictive elements
(1) "Woody Allen's original surname, Konigsberg, originated from two parts: *konig* and *berg,* German for 'king' and 'mountain'." When a teacher dictated this sentence for students to write with correct punctuation, some wrote it this way: (2) "...from two parts, '*konig*' and '*berg*'; German for...." Others wrote: (3) "...from two parts '*konig*' and '*berg*'; German for...." And still others wrote: (4) "...from two parts; '*konig*' and '*berg*' German for...." Version (1) uses the best punctuation. First, the colon following "parts" signals the introduction of what those parts were. Colons in sentences typically introduce or announce information that completes, defines, or explains the preceding thought. Second, the comma following "*'berg'*" correctly separates "'*konig*'" and "'*berg*'" and "German for 'king' and 'mountain'" as nonrestrictive appositives. Version (2) incorrectly connects the independent clause with a phrase by using a semicolon following "'*berg*'." Its comma following "parts" is too weak for the strong sentence break. Version (3) incorrectly connects an independent clause and phrase with a semicolon following "'*berg*'"; and omits punctuation following "parts" for nonrestrictive appositives. Version (4) incorrectly joins the independent clause with phrases using a semicolon following "parts"; and omits punctuation indicating nonrestrictive appositives following "'*berg*'."

## Unnecessary punctuation

For these questions the student will need to recognize and correct situations in which unnecessary punctuation was used.

## Correct punctuation vs incorrect punctuation
(1) "Students who undertake careers in the hospitality industry can come from a varied range of educational histories." Some students were assigned to identify correct punctuation in this sentence. Some found it needed no change as shown above. Some corrected it to read: (2) "Students, who undertake careers in the hospitality industry, can come from...." Some corrected it to read: (3) "Students who undertake careers, in the hospitality industry, can come from...." Others found it correct punctuated thusly: (4) "Students who undertake careers in the hospitality industry, can come from...." The first group was correct in leaving the sentence as is. The clause "who undertake careers in the hospitality industry" is a restrictive clause, i.e., essential to the

sentence meaning, by defining who the "students" are. Restrictive clauses are not punctuated. Version (2) sets this clause off with commas, which are only used with nonrestrictive clauses. Version (3) also incorrectly punctuates "in the hospitality industry" with commas like a nonrestrictive clause when it is essential to meaning, hence restrictive. Version (4) inserts an extraneous comma following "industry," separating the subject from the predicate.

Writing errors involving unnecessary punctuation
Some writers make the mistake of doubling, tripling, quadrupling, or even further multiplying exclamation marks and question marks, thinking they are adding the necessary emphasis they want to convey. While this may be acceptable in more casual formats such as e-mails, it should never be done in formal writing, e.g., "Why did he use so many question marks??? It's really annoying!!!" Another error is inserting a colon following a copula or linking verb (i.e., any form of "to be," "to become," "to seem," "to feel," etc. that connects the subject of a sentence to its complement, e.g., "You are a liar." No colon or other punctuation should be used between a linking verb and a subject complement. Colons should also not follow prepositions, e.g., "This book is by: Stephen King" is incorrect; "This book is by Stephen King" is correct. "This room will be painted yellow" is another construction needing no internal punctuation; some writers incorrectly insert a colon or comma between "painted" and "yellow."

Unnecessary use of commas
There is no need to place a comma between a sentence subject and verb. This includes long subjects, e.g., "The boy who wore a yellow hat and came to the party late spilled the punch" is correct as is. Some writers will incorrectly insert a comma between "late" and "spilled" thinking it clarifies the sentence because of the long subject, but subjects and verbs should not be separated by punctuation marks. When punctuation is needed, though, commas when correct are preferable over parentheses, brackets, dashes, or even semicolons. For example, in this sentence, "The elderly lady (who worked as a server) left at eight" uses unnecessary parentheses. It is more correctly punctuated, "The elderly lady, who worked as a server, left at eight." Commas between the sentence's verb and predicate adjectives or predicate nouns describing the subject are unnecessary. For example, "She was, nervous and anxious" is incorrect. "She was nervous and anxious" is correct. Commas are also unnecessary between two items and should only separate three or more items in a list. "She awoke, washed, dressed, and left" is correct; "She awoke, and left" is incorrect; "She awoke and left" is correct.

**Sentence errors**

Each question includes a sentence with parts underlined.  You must choose which, if any, of those underlined portions contains an error in mechanics, word choice, or structural and grammatical relationships.

Read the text four times, each time replacing the underlined portion with one of the choices. While reading the text, be sure to pause at each comma.  If the comma is necessary the pause will be logical.  If the comma is not needed, then the sentence will feel awkward.  Transitional words should create smooth, logical transitions and maintain a constant flow of text.

**Improving Sentences and Paragraphs**

Each question includes a sentence with part or all of it underlined.  Your answer choices will offer different ways to reword or rephrase the underlined portion of the sentence.  The first answer choice merely repeats the original underlined text, while the others offer different wording.

These questions will test your ability of correct and effective expression. Choose your answer carefully, utilizing the standards of written English, including grammar rules, the proper choice of words and of sentence construction.  The correct answer will flow smoothly and be both clear and concise.

## Parallelism

Often clues to the best answer are given within the text, if you know where to look for them. The correct answer will always be parallel in grammar type, punctuation, format, and tense as the rest of the sentence.

## Grammar type

If a series of nouns is given, then make sure your choice is a noun. If those nouns are plural, then ensure that your choice is plural.

*Example:*
>       Schools, politics, and governments

If a series of verbs is given, then make sure your choice is a verb.

*Example:*
>       eat, sleep, and drink

If a series of infinitives is given, then make sure your choice is an infinitive.

*Example:*
>       to trust, to honor, and to obey

If a series of phrases is given, then make sure your choice is a similar phrase.

*Example:*
>       of controlling, of policing, and of maintaining

## Added phrases

Any sentence or phrase added to a paragraph must maintain the same train of thought. This is particularly true when the word "and" is used. The word "and" joins two comments of like nature.
*Example:*
>       These men were tough. They were accustomed to a hard life, and could watch a man
>       die without blinking.

If an added phrase does not maintain a consistent train of thought, it will be set out with a word such as "but", "however", or "although". The new phrase would then be inconsistent to the train of thought and would offer a contrast.
*Example:*
>       These men were tough. They were accustomed to a hard life, but to watch a man die
>       would cause them to faint.

A tough man accustomed to a hard life is not expected to faint. Therefore the statements are contrasting and must have a contrasting transitional word, such as "but."

## Punctuation

If a section of text has an opening dash, parentheses, or comma at the beginning of a phrase, then you can be sure there should be a matching closing dash, parentheses, or comma at the end of the phrase. If items in a series all have commas between them, then any additional items in that series will also gain commas. Do not alternate punctuation. If a dash is at the beginning of a statement, then do not put a parenthesis at the ending of the statement.

**Final Tips**

Use your ear
Read each sentence carefully, inserting the answer choices in the blanks. Don't stop at the first answer choice if you think it is right, but read them all. What may seem like the best choice, at first, may not be after you have had time to read all of the choices. Allow your ear to determine what sounds right. Often one or two answer choices can be immediately ruled out because it doesn't make sound logical or make sense.

Contextual clues
It bears repeating that contextual clues offer a lot of help in determining the best answer. Key words in the sentence will allow you to determine exactly which answer choice is the best replacement text.

*Example:*

Archeology has shown that some of the ruins of the ancient city of Babylon are approximately 500 years <u>as old as any supposed</u> Mesopotamian predecessors.
    A.) as old as their supposed
    B.) older than their supposed

In this example, the key word "supposed" is used. Archaeology would either confirm that the predecessors to Babylon were more ancient or disprove that supposition. Since supposed was used, it would imply that archaeology had disproved the accepted belief, making Babylon actually older, not as old as, and answer choice "B" correct.

Furthermore, because "500 years" is used, answer choice A can be ruled out. Years are used to show either absolute or relative age. If two objects are as old as each other, no years are necessary to describe that relationship, and it would be sufficient to say, "The ancient city of Babylon is approximately as old as their supposed Mesopotamian predecessors," without using the term "500 years."

Simplicity is Bliss
Simplicity cannot be overstated. You should never choose a longer, more complicated, or wordier replacement if a simple one will do. When a point can be made with fewer words, choose that answer. However, never sacrifice the flow of text for simplicity. If an answer is simple, but does not make sense, then it is not correct.

Beware of added phrases that don't add anything of meaning, such as "to be" or "as to them". Often these added phrases will occur just before a colon, which may come before a list of items. However, the colon does not need a lengthy introduction. The phrases "of which [...] are" in the below examples are wordy and unnecessary. They should be removed and the colon placed directly after the words "sport" and "following".
    *Example 1: There are many advantages to running as a sport, of which the top advantages are:*
    *Example 2: The school supplies necessary were the following, of which a few are:*

# Mathematics Test

The math portion of the PSAT consists of a 45-minute section in which a calculator may be used and a 25-minute section in which no calculator may be used. The calculator portion contains 31 questions and the non calculator portion contains 17 questions.

*Concepts covered*
PSAT questions fall into four categories:
- Heart of Algebra
- Problem Solving and Data Analysis
- Passport to Advanced Math
- Additional Topics in Math

*The table below gives a complete breakdown of questions:*

| Calculator Portion | Number of Questions | % of Test |
|---|---|---|
| **Total Questions** | **31** | **100%** |
| Multiple Choice | 27 | 87% |
| Student-Produced Response | 4 | 13% |
| **Content Categories** | **31** | **100%** |
| Heart of Algebra | 8 | 26% |
| Problem Solving and Data Analysis | 16 | 52% |
| Passport to Advanced Math | 6 | 19% |
| Additional Math Topics | 1 | 3% |
| | | |
| **No-Calculator Portion** | | |
| **Total Questions** | **17** | **100%** |
| Multiple Choice | 13 | 76% |
| Student-Produced Response | 4 | 24% |
| **Content Categories** | **17** | **100%** |
| Heart of Algebra | 8 | 47% |
| Passport to Advanced Math | 8 | 47% |
| Additional Math Topics | 1 | 6% |

*Use the practice tests.*
The best thing you can do to prepare for the PSAT is to take several practice tests and review all your wrong answers very carefully. Work back through those problems until you understand how the answer was derived and you're confident you could answer a similar problem on your own.

This guide includes a practice test with answer key and explanations. Examples are also available on the College Board website. If you feel uncertain on a particular concept or problem type, use these tests to practice.

# How to Approach PSAT Math Questions

*Take an approved calculator you're familiar with. Check its batteries.*
If you normally use a scientific or graphic calculator, check the PSAT website to make sure it's one you'll be allowed to use. Use that calculator as you work through the practice tests.

*Remember that the test provides all the information you need.*
There's even a handy chart of "reference information" in the textbook with geometry formulas you might need, including the Pythagorean Theorem and special right triangles. The chart even tells you that the sum of angles in a triangle equals 180. Don't worry about cramming to memorize the formula for calculating the area of a circle. All you need to know is that A = area, C = circumference, and r = radius.

*Read carefully.*
Yes, it's a math test, but these questions require careful reading. Look for key words such as "is" (equals), "more than," "less than," "of" (percentage, ratio, or multiplication), and so forth. Ask yourself:
- "What do I know?"
- "What information does the problem provide?"
- "What is the question asking, exactly?"

*Remember that you don't always have to solve the whole problem to answer the question.*
Especially with algebra problems, answering the question may not actually require solving the entire equation or finding all the variables. This is another example of "read carefully" - be sure you understand what the question is asking for.

*Look at the answers before you begin calculating.*
What form do the possible answers take? If they're fractions, then work in fractions rather than decimals. Do they include negative numbers? (Negative numbers are an often-forgotten option for many problems involving exponents, roots, and absolute values.)

*Take it one step at a time.*
If a problem seems overwhelming at first, just look for the first step. Write down what information you know. Break it down. And remember that by just using logic and basic techniques, you can work through even the most complex multi-step problems.

*Draw a picture or write down expressions as you read.*
Many of the problems require more logic than raw mathematical knowledge. As you read a problem, make a sketch in the margin, draw on the figure in the test book, or write out the mathematical expression described. (For example, if you read "The area of Circle A is twice the area of Circle B," write down "A = 2B.")

*Substitute numbers for variables.*
Sometimes the easiest thing to do is pick a value for *x*, *n*, or another variable, and work through the problem using that number. It may be easier to work through that way, especially for geometry problems. (Just remember that the value isn't "true," merely convenient.)

*Use elimination.*
As with all PSAT questions, the first thing to do is eliminate obviously wrong answers. Are there choices that are clearly too big or too small? In an impossible form? Based on a common error, such as a sign or exponent error?

*Check your answers.*
When you solve a problem, plug the answer back in to confirm it makes sense. Make sure you haven't made careless mistakes such as skipping a step or making an arithmetic error.

*Fill in all the circles, then double-check.*
For the "student-produced" responses, where you have to supply the actual number instead of selecting from multiple choices, make sure to fill in all the circles. You get no credit for the number written at the top — those boxes are only there to help you mark the circles accurately. Make sure you've filled in the right spots.

*Give an educated guess.*
The PSAT no longer penalizes students for wrong answers. This means that you should always narrow down your answer choices by eliminating anything you know is wrong and then give an educated guess at the answer.

*Don't get mired down on any one question.*
The first, easiest problem on the test is worth the same points as the last, hardest question. If one problem is taking a long time, move on. You can come back to it later if you have time.

## Heart of Algebra

The questions in this section will cover a range of topics in algebra. Students will be tested on their ability to analyze and solve linear equations and systems of equations. They will also need to be able to create these equations to represent a relationship between two or more quantities and solve problems. Along with linear equations, students will need to be able to create and solve linear inequalities. Some questions will also require the student to interpret formulas and be able to rearrange them in order to solve the problem.

Solving a linear equation in one variable, where there are infinitely many solutions
When solving a linear equation in one variable, if the process results in a true equation of the form $a = a$ where $a$ is a real number, the equation has infinitely many solutions. This is because the equation is always true, independent of the value of the variable. For example, consider the solution of the equation below:

$$2x - 3(x + 1) = 2 - (x + 5)$$
$$2x - 3x - 3 = 2 - x - 5$$
$$-x - 3 = -x - 3$$
$$-3 = -3$$

For any value of $x$, each side of the equation evaluates to 3. So the solution is $x$ = any real number, and there are infinitely many solutions.

Solving a linear equation in one variable, where there are no solutions
When solving a linear equation in one variable, if the process results in a false equation of the form $a = b$ where $a$ and $b$ are different (not equal) numbers, the equation has no solution. This is because the equation is always false, independent of the value of the variable. For example, consider the solution of the equation below:

$$2x - 3(x + 1) = 2 - (x + 4)$$
$$2x - 3x - 3 = 2 - x - 4$$
$$-x - 3 = -x - 2$$
$$-3 = -2$$

For any value of $x$, each side of the equation evaluates to two different values. The equation therefore has no solution.

Types of questions – linear expressions
You should expect to create, solve, or interpret a linear equation in one variable. These equations will have rational coefficients and may require multiple steps to simplify or solve. Linear equations in one variable have just one unknown variable. That variable has an exponent of one. For example, $2m + 3 = 3m + 7$ and $1.2(2.5x + 3.2) = 6.7x$ are linear equations in one variable.

Typically, a question asks you to translate a verbal expression into an algebraic expression or a word problem into an equation. Then, you may need to solve the equation or answer another question related to that equation. The problems may include questions about any topic that lends itself to a linear expression or equation in one variable. For instance, you may see a question that says, "Jacob rents a car during his vacation. The rental agency's daily charge is $49.95, which is taxed at a rate of 7%. Jacob is also charged a one-time nonrefundable rental fee of $50. Which of the following represents Jacob's total car rental expenses, in dollars, for use of the car for $x$ days?" You would then need to create the expression that computes the total cost for $x$ days.

## Mathematical symbols

You must be able to translate verbal expressions or "math words" into math symbols. This chart contains several "math words" and their appropriate symbols:

| | |
|---|---|
| equal, is, was, will be, has, costs, gets to, is the same as, becomes | = |
| time, of, multiplied by, product of, twice, doubles, halves, triples | × |
| divided by, per, ratio of/to, out of | ÷ |
| plus, added to, sum, combined, and, more than, totals of | + |
| subtracted from, less than, decreased by, minus, difference between | - |
| what, how much, original value, how many, a number, a variable | $x$, $n$, etc |

For example, the phrase *four more than twice a number* can be written algebraically as $2x + 4$. The phrase *half a number decreased by six* can be written algebraically as $\frac{1}{2}x - 6$. The phrase *the sum of a number and the product of five and that number* can be written algebraically as $x + 5x$. You may see a test question that says, "Olivia is constructing a bookcase from seven boards. Two of them are for vertical supports and five are for shelves. The height of the bookcase is twice the width of the bookcase. If the seven boards total 36 feet in length, what will be the height of Olivia's bookcase?" You would need to make a sketch and then create the equation to determine the width of the shelves. The height can be represented as double the width. (If $x$ represents the width of the shelves in feet, then the height of the book shelf is $2x$. Since the seven boards total 36 feet, $2x + 2x + x + x + x + x + x = 36$; $9x = 36$; $x = 4$. The height is twice the width, or 8 feet.)

## Inequalities

Commonly in algebra and other upper-level fields of math you find yourself working with mathematical expressions that do not equal each other. The statement comparing such expressions with symbols such as < (less than) or > (greater than) is called an *Inequality*. An example of an inequality is $7x > 5$. To solve for $x$, simply divide both sides by 7 and the solution is shown to be $x > \frac{5}{7}$. Graphs of the solution set of inequalities are represented on a number line. Open circles are used to show that an expression approaches a number but is never quite equal to that number.

*Conditional Inequalities* are those with certain values for the variable that will make the condition true and other values for the variable where the condition will be false. *Absolute Inequalities* can have any real number as the value for the variable to make the condition true, while there is no real number value for the variable that will make the condition false. Solving inequalities is done by following the same rules as for solving equations with the exception that when multiplying or dividing by a negative number the direction of the inequality sign must be flipped or reversed. *Double Inequalities* are situations where two inequality statements apply to the same variable expression. An example of this is $-c < ax + b < c$.

A *Weighted Mean*, or weighted average, is a mean that uses "weighted" values. The formula is weighted mean $= \frac{w_1 x_1 + w_2 x_2 + w_3 x_3 \ldots + w_n x_n}{w_1 + w_2 + w_3 + \cdots + w_n}$. Weighted values, such as $w_1, w_2, w_3, \ldots w_n$ are assigned to each member of the set $x_1, x_2, x_3, \ldots x_n$. If calculating weighted mean, make sure a weight value for each member of the set is used.

## Solving linear inequalities

Solving linear inequalities is very similar to solving linear equations. You must isolate the variable on one side of the inequality by using the inverse, or opposite operations. To undo addition, you use subtraction and vice versa. To undo multiplication, you use division and vice versa. The only difference in solving linear inequalities occurs when you multiply or divide by a negative number. When this is the case, you must flip the inequality symbol. This means that less than becomes greater than, greater than becomes less than, etc. Another type of inequality is called a compound inequality. A compound inequality contains two inequalities separated by an "and" or an "or" statement. An "and" statement can also consist of a variable sandwiched in the middle of two inequality symbols. To solve this type of inequality, simply separate it into two inequalities applying the middle terms to each. Then, follow the steps to isolate the variable.

## Types of questions – linear inequalities

You should expect to create, solve, or interpret a linear inequality in one variable. Linear inequalities in one variable are inequalities with just one unknown variable. That variable has an exponent of one. For example, $4x + 2 > 10$ and $100 - 2x \geq 27$ are both linear equalities in one variable. Typically, the questions ask you to translate verbal expressions or word problems into algebraic inequalities. Then, you may be expected to solve the inequality or answer another question related to that inequality. Examples of key words and phrases indicating an inequality include *at least* ($\geq$), *no more than* ($\leq$), *more than* ($>$) and *less than* ($<$). You may see a test question that says, "Emily and Madison sold tickets to the school play. Emily sold 70 more tickets than Madison, but together they sold fewer than 200 tickets. Which of the following represents the number of tickets Madison sold?" You would then need to create an inequality from the given information and simplify that inequality using correct algebraic procedures; afterwards, when solving, remember to flip the inequality symbol if dividing or multiplying both sides by negative numbers.

## Types of questions – linear functions

You should expect to build or create a linear function or equation in two variables that models a context. Linear functions or equations in two variables are equations with two unknown variables. Both variables have an exponent of one. You might be required to express the relationship in functional notation. For example, $y = 3x + 12$ and $p = 0.5d + 14.7$ are both linear equations in two variables and can be expressed in functional notation as $f(x) = 3x + 12$ and $f(d) = 0.5d + 14.7$, respectively. You may be expected to simplify your equation or function. You may see a test question that says, "The pressure in a tank which contains an industrial chemical and which is open to the atmosphere increases linearly with the height of the chemical in the tank. The measured pressure is due to the combined hydrostatic pressure of the chemical and the atmospheric pressure. A pressure gauge at a depth of five feet beneath the surface reads 17.2 pounds per square inch (psi), and at a depth of ten feet reads 19.7 psi. Which of the following linear models best describes the pressure *p* in psi at a depth of *d* feet?" You must determine the relationship between pressure *p* and depth *d*. First, determine the rate at which the pressure changes with depth; then, consider the contribution of the atmospheric pressure to the total pressure.

## Modeling linear relationships in two variables

You should expect to build or create a linear function or equation in two variables that models a context. Linear functions or equations in two variables are equations with two unknown variables. Both variables have an exponent of one. You might be required to express the relationship in functional notation. For example, $y = 3x + 12$ and $p = 0.5d + 14.7$ are both linear equations in two variables and can be expressed in functional notation as $f(x) = 3x + 12$ and $f(d) = 0.5d + 14.7$, respectively. You may be expected to simplify your equation or function. You may see a test question that says, "The pressure in a tank which contains an industrial chemical and which is open to the atmosphere increases linearly with the height of the chemical in the tank. The measured pressure is due to the combined hydrostatic pressure of the chemical and the atmospheric pressure. A pressure gauge at a depth of five feet beneath the surface reads 17.2

pounds per square inch (psi), and at a depth of ten feet reads 19.7 psi. Which of the following linear models best describes the pressure p in psi at a depth of d feet?" You must determine the relationship between pressure p and depth d. First, determine the rate at which the pressure changes with depth; then, consider the contribution of the atmospheric pressure to the total pressure.

## Types of questions – linear inequalities in two variables

You should expect to create, solve, or interpret systems of linear inequalities in two variables. Linear inequalities in two variables resemble systems of equations except the equal signs are replaced with inequality symbols ($<, >, \leq, \geq$). You may be asked to solve a system of linear equalities. To solve a system of linear inequalities, each inequality must be graphed on the same coordinate plane. If both inequalities are written in slope intercept form, they can be graphed using the slope-intercept method. A dotted line is used when the inequality includes a $<$ or $>$ symbol. A solid line is used when the inequality includes a $\leq$ or $\geq$ symbol. Shade above the line if $y <$ or $\leq mx + b$ and above if $y >$ or $\geq mx + b$. The region where the two shaded areas overlap is the solution to the original system of inequalities; if there is no overlap, there is no solution. You may be asked to determine whether a given point is in the solution set of a system of linear inequalities. If a graph is provided, simply check to see if the given point is located in the region where the regions of the inequalities overlap. If you are not given a graph, see if the point satisfies each of the given inequalities. If the given point satisfies both inequalities, it is in the solution set for the system of inequalities.

## Systems of Equations

*Systems of Equations* are a set of simultaneous equations that all use the same variables. A solution to a system of equations must be true for each equation in the system. *Consistent Systems* are those with at least one solution. *Inconsistent Systems* are systems of equations that have no solution.

To solve a system of linear equations by *substitution*, start with the easier equation and solve for one of the variables. Express this variable in terms of the other variable. Substitute this expression in the other equation, and solve for the other variable. The solution should be expressed in the form (x, y). Substitute the values into both of the original equations to check your answer. Consider the following problem.

Solve the system using substitution:
$x + 6y = 15$
$3x - 12y = 18$

Solve the first equation for x:
$x = 15 - 6y$

Substitute this value in place of x in the second equation, and solve for y:
$3(15 - 6y) - 12y = 18$
$45 - 18y - 12y = 18$
$30y = 27$

$y = \dfrac{27}{30} = \dfrac{9}{10} = 0.9$

Plug this value for y back into the first equation to solve for x:
$x = 15 - 6(0.9) = 15 - 5.4 = 9.6$

Check both equations if you have time:
$9.6 + 6(0.9) = 9.6 + 5.4 = 15$
$3(9.6) - 12(0.9) = 28.8 - 10.8 = 18$
Therefore, the solution is (9.6, 0.9).

To solve a system of equations using *elimination*, begin by rewriting both equations in standard form $Ax + By = C$. Check to see if the coefficients of one pair of like variables add to zero. If not, multiply one or both of the equations by a non-zero number to make one set of like variables add to zero. Add the two equations to solve for one of the variables. Substitute this value into one of the original equations to solve for the other variable. Check your work by substituting into the other equation. Next we will solve the same problem as above, but using the addition method.

Solve the system using elimination:
$$x + 6y = 15$$
$$3x - 12y = 18$$

If we multiply the first equation by 2, we can eliminate the $y$ terms:
$$2x + 12y = 30$$
$$3x - 12y = 18$$

Add the equations together and solve for $x$:
$$5x = 48$$
$$x = \frac{48}{5} = 9.6$$

Plug the value for $x$ back into either of the original equations and solve for $y$:
$$9.6 + 6y = 15$$
$$y = \frac{15 - 9.6}{6} = 0.9$$

Check both equations if you have time:
$$9.6 + 6(0.9) = 9.6 + 5.4 = 15$$
$$3(9.6) - 12(0.9) = 28.8 - 10.8 = 18$$
Therefore, the solution is (9.6, 0.9).

## Solving systems of equations vs solving systems of inequalities

Solving systems of inequalities is very similar to solving systems of equations in that you are looking for a solution or a range of solutions that satisfy all of the equations in the system. Since solutions to inequalities are within a certain interval, it is best to solve this type of system by graphing. Follow the same steps to graph an inequality as you would an equation, but in addition, shade the portion of the graph that represents the solution. Recall that when graphing an inequality on the coordinate plane, you replace the inequality symbol with an equal sign and draw a solid line if the points are included (greater than or equal to or less than or equal to) or a dashed line if the points are not included (greater than or less than). Then replace the inequality symbol and shade the portion of the graph that is included in the solution. Choose a point that is not on the line and test it in the inequality to see if it is makes sense. In a system, you repeat this process for all of the equations and the solution is the region in which the graphs overlap. This is unlike solving a system of equations, in which the solution is a single point where the lines intersect.

## Possibilities of a system of 2 linear equations in 2 variables

There are 3 possibilities that can occur graphically for a given system of two linear equations in two variables:
1. The graphs intersect. The point at which they intersect is the solution of the system of equations.
2. The graphs are the same, or coincide with each other. This means that the two equations are actually the same equation. The solution of the system is all points on the line.
3. The graphs do not intersect, and the system has no solution. This occurs when the two equations have the same slope, or the two lines are distinct vertical lines. These lines are parallel.

## Types of questions – systems of equations

You should expect to be asked to write and solve a system of linear equations from a word problem. You may see a test question that says, "Alyssa's scout troop is selling tickets for the community fun fair. Adult tickets cost $8.50 each, and child tickets cost $5.50 each. The troop sells a total of 375 tickets and collects $2,512.50 in revenue. Solving which of these systems of equations yields the number of adult tickets, $x$, and the number of child tickets, $y$, sold by Alyssa's scout troop? How many of each ticket type are sold?" First, write an equation for the number of tickets sold ($x + y = 375$) and a second equation for revenue generated ($8.50x + 5.50y = 2512.50$). Then, solve the system of equations and answer the question that is asked. The methods used in solving systems of linear equations include elimination (addition), substitution, and graphing. To solve by elimination, write the equations in a way that the like variables line up when one equation is placed above the other. The goal is to add the two equations together to eliminate one of the variables. If necessary, multiply one or both of the equations by a constant to enable such elimination. To solve by substitution, select one of the equations and solve it for one of the variables; then, substitute this into the other equation and solve. To solve by graphing, find the point of intersection of the two lines graphed on the same coordinate plane.

## Solving linear equations in one variable

You should expect to be asked to solve linear equations in one variable without the use of a calculator. Linear equations in one variable are equations with just one unknown variable that has an exponent of one. The equation may be complicated with rational coefficients. For example, $\frac{10x-8}{6} = \frac{3x+12}{3}$ and $\frac{x-2}{x+3} = \frac{6}{8}$ are both linear equations in one variable that require several steps to solve. If any of the terms in the given equation has/have a denominator, first clear the equation of fractions by multiplying the entire equation by the least common denominator of all of the fractional terms. Then, simplify each side by collecting like terms. Finally, solve for the unknown variable by isolating the variable on one side.

## Solving linear equations in two variables

You should expect to be given a system of linear equations in two variables to solve without a calculator. For example, $\begin{cases} \frac{1}{2}x + \frac{1}{4}y = \frac{-1}{2} \\ 5x + 3y = -3 \end{cases}$ is a system of linear equations which you might be asked to solve. One of the coefficients may be replaced with a variable as shown here: $\begin{cases} \frac{1}{2}x + \frac{1}{4}y = \frac{-1}{2} \\ ax + 3y = -3 \end{cases}$; you may be asked to solve for $a$. You can solve systems of equations algebraically by elimination or substitution. Systems of equations may have no solution, one solution, or an infinite number of solutions. If when graphed the two lines are parallel, there is no solution. If the lines intersect at one point, there is one solution. If the lines graph as exactly the same line, there are an infinite number of solutions.

## Interpreting variables and constants

You should expect to be given a real-world scenario and the linear function associated with that scenario. You may be asked to identify variable terms or constant terms from the given function as well as interpret their meanings in the given real-world situation. You may see a test question like "The school van begins a field trip with 14 gallons of gasoline. After travelling 120 miles, the van has 8 gallons of gasoline. If this relationship is modeled by the linear function $f(x) = -20x + 280$, what does the $x$ represent?" Or you might be asked what -20 and 280 represent in the given function.

## Understanding the basic format

Understanding the basic format of a linear function is very helpful. A linear function has an input and an output. The value of the output is determined by substituting the value of the independent variable into the equation. If the function notation is $f(x)$, the $x$ is the input, and the $f(x)$ is the output. Linear functions are just linear equations written with functional notation. For example, the linear equation $y = 4x + 7$ can be written as the function $f(x) = 4x + 7$. You can compare this to the slope-intercept form of a line in which $y$ represents the output, $m$ represents the rate, $x$

represents the input, and *b* represents a constant. You may see a test question with a word problem that says, "A school play has $200 in production costs. If tickets are sold at $5.75, how many tickets must be sold before the play makes a profit?" In addition, you may be given a function $p(x) = 5.75x - 200$ and asked a questions such as, "What does the *x* represent?" or "Describe why the operator before the 200 is a minus sign."

<u>Helpful knowledge about interpreting variables and constants</u>
Understanding the term *slope* and the various forms of linear equations, such as slope-intercept form, is very useful. Slope indicates the slant of the line. Lines with positive slopes slant up and to the right. Lines with negative slopes slant down and to the right. A horizontal line has a slope of zero, and the slope of a vertical line is undefined. If a linear equation is written in the slope-intercept form $y = mx + b$, the slope of the line is given by *m*. Slope may be determined from a graph as $m = \frac{\Delta y}{\Delta x}$. This often referred to as "rise over run." Also, the *b* in the slope-intercept form $y = mx + b$ is the *y*-intercept of the line. The intercepts are the places where the graphed line crosses the axes. The *y*-intercept has coordinates (0, *b*), and the *x*-intercept has coordinates (*a*, 0). The two-intercept form of a line is given by $\frac{x}{a} + \frac{y}{b} = 1$, where *a* is the *x*-intercept and *b* is the *y*-intercept. The point-slope form of a line is given by $y - y_1 = m(x - x_1)$, where *m* is the slope and $(x_1, y_1)$ is a point on the line. A vertical line has the form $x = a$, and a horizontal line has the form $y = b$.

<u>Assessing understanding of the connection between algebraic and graphical representations</u>
You should expect five types of questions about the connections between algebraic and graphical representations. First, you may be given a linear equation and asked to select from several choices the graph which corresponds to that equation. Key features such as slope and *y*-intercept provide clues. Second, you may be given the graph of a linear equation and asked to select from several choices the equation which corresponds with that graph. Note the slant of the line, which indicates the slope, and the line's intercepts. Third, you may be given a verbal description of a linear graph and be asked to write the equation that matches the given description. Fourth, you may be given a graph of a linear equation and asked to determine key features such as slope (rate) and intercepts. Fifth, you may be given the graph of a linear equation and asked how a change in the equation impacts the graph. For example, you might be asked how a change in the slope or *y*-intercept affects the slant or position of the line graphed.

<u>Helpful knowledge about connections between algebraic and graphical representations</u>
Understanding the term *slope* and the various forms of linear equations, such as slope-intercept form, is very useful. Slope indicates the slant of the line. Lines with positive slopes slant up and to the right. Lines with negative slopes slant down and to the right. A horizontal line has a slope of zero, and the slope of a vertical line is undefined. If a linear equation is written in the slope-intercept form $y = mx + b$, the slope of the line is given by *m*. Slope may be determined from a graph as $m = \frac{\Delta y}{\Delta x}$. This often referred to as "rise over run." Also, the *b* in the slope-intercept form $y = mx + b$ is the *y*-intercept of the line. The intercepts are the places where the graphed line crosses the axes. The *y*-intercept has coordinates (0, *b*), and the *x*-intercept has coordinates (*a*, 0). The two-intercept form of a line is given by $\frac{x}{a} + \frac{y}{b} = 1$, where *a* is the *x*-intercept and *b* is the *y*-intercept. The point-slope form of a line is given by $y - y_1 = m(x - x_1)$, where *m* is the slope and $(x_1, y_1)$ is a point on the line. A vertical line has the form $x = a$, and a horizontal line has the form $y = b$.

**Problem Solving and Data Analysis**

The questions in this section will require students to create and analyze relationships. They will solve single- and multistep problems using ratios, rates, proportions, and percentages. Some questions will also require students to describe relationships that are presented graphically. In addition, students should be able to analyze and summarize both qualitative and quantitative data.

## Ratios
A ratio is a comparison of two quantities in a particular order. Example: If there are 14 computers in a lab, and the class has 20 students, there is a student to computer ratio of 20 to 14, commonly written as 20:14. Ratios are normally reduced to their smallest whole number representation, so 20:14 would be reduced to 10:7 by dividing both sides by 2.

## Proportions
A proportion is a relationship between two quantities that dictates how one changes when the other changes. A direct proportion describes a relationship in which a quantity increases by a set amount for every increase in the other quantity, or decreases by that same amount for every decrease in the other quantity.

Example: Assuming a constant driving speed, the time required for a car trip increases as the distance of the trip increases. The distance to be traveled and the time required to travel are directly proportional.

## Percentages
Percentages can be thought of as fractions that are based on a whole of 100; that is, one whole is equal to 100%. The word percent means "per hundred." Fractions can be expressed as percents by finding equivalent fractions with a denomination of 100. Example: $\frac{7}{10} = \frac{70}{100} = 70\%$; $\frac{1}{4} = \frac{25}{100} = 25\%$.

A percentage problem can be presented three main ways: (1) Find what percentage of some number another number is. Example: What percentage of 40 is 8? (2) Find what number is some percentage of a given number. Example: What number is 20% of 40? (3) Find what number another number is a given percentage of.

Example: What number is 8 20% of? The three components in all of these cases are the same: a whole ($W$), a part ($P$), and a percentage (%). These are related by the equation: $P = W \times \%$. This is the form of the equation you would use to solve problems of type (2). To solve types (1) and (3), you would use these two forms: $\% = \frac{P}{W}$ and $W = \frac{P}{\%}$.

The thing that frequently makes percentage problems difficult is that they are most often also word problems, so a large part of solving them is figuring out which quantities are what. Example: In a school cafeteria, 7 students choose pizza, 9 choose hamburgers, and 4 choose tacos. Find the percentage that chooses tacos. To find the whole, you must first add all of the parts: 7 + 9 + 4 = 20. The percentage can then be found by dividing the part by the whole ($\% = \frac{P}{W}$): $\frac{4}{20} = \frac{20}{100} = 20\%$.

## Unit rate
Unit rate expresses a quantity of one thing in terms of one unit of another. For example, if you travel 30 miles every two hours, a unit rate expresses this comparison in terms of one hour: in one hour you travel 15 miles, so your unit rate is 15 miles per hour. Other examples are how much one ounce of food costs (price per ounce), or figuring out how much one egg costs out of the dozen (price per 1 egg, instead of price per 12 eggs). The denominator of a unit rate is always 1.

Unit rates are used to compare different situations to solve problems. For example, to make sure you get the best deal when deciding which kind of soda to buy, you can find the unit rate of each. If Soda #1 costs $1.50 for a 1-liter bottle, and soda #2 costs $2.75 for a 2-liter bottle, it would be a better deal to buy Soda #2, because its unit rate is only $1.375 per 1-liter, which is cheaper than Soda #1. Unit rates can also help determine the length of time a given event will take. For example, if you can paint 2 rooms in 4.5 hours, you can determine how long it will take you to paint 5 rooms by solving for the unit rate per room and then multiplying that by 5.

## Types of questions – ratios, rates, proportional relationships

You should expect three types of questions in this category. First, you may be asked to use a proportional relationship between two quantities to solve a multistep problem or to find a ratio or rate. Proportional relationships can be direct relationships (as *x* increases, *y* increases) or inverse relationships (as *x* increases, *y* decreases). Remember, units can be cancelled just like factors. You may be expected to use some basic knowledge such as *distance = rate × time*. Second, you might be asked to calculate a ratio or rate and to use that rate or ratio to solve a multistep problem. Third, you might be given a ratio or rate and be expected to solve a multistep problem. You may see a test question that says, "The ratio of boys to girls in the children's choir is 2:3. If there are eight boys in the choir, how many total children are in the choir?" You may be given a mixture problem in the form of a ratio and be expected to determine how much of a component is needed. You may be asked to determine a ratio associated with a geometric relationship, such as the ratio of a circle's circumference to its radius. You may be given a scale drawing and be expected to find a ratio associated with that drawing.

## Types of questions – percentages

Questions involving percentages typically come in three basic forms. For example, "What is 10% of 50?" or "5 is what percent of 50?" or "5 is 10% of what number?" Questions involving percentages may also include percent increase or decrease. These questions may be worded using *percent change*. For example, "If gasoline prices rose from $2.76 to $3.61, what is the percent change?" More complicated questions may be asked, and you will need to have a solid understanding of percentages in order to approach such questions. You may be given a table of values or a pie chart and be expected to calculate percentages from the information given. You may be expected to use these calculations to answer a related question.

## Types of questions – units and unit conversion

You should expect to be asked to determine a unit rate and then use that rate to solve another problem. You may see a question that gives a conversion rate for an unfamiliar quantity to a familiar quantity, such as from a foreign currency to US dollars. You may be asked to solve a multistep unit problem using unfamiliar conversion rates along with other concepts, such as finding percentages. You may be asked to solve multistep problems to determine an item's density, or you may be asked to apply the concept of density. You may see a problem that says, "A bar of gold has dimensions of 5.0 cm by 5.0 cm by 10.0 cm. If gold has a density of 19,300 kg/m$^3$, what is the mass of the gold bar in grams?"

## Scatter plot

Scatter plots show the relationship between two sets of data. The first step in creating a scatter plot is to collect data. Suppose you are analyzing the relationship between age and hours of sleep. You would collect a representative sample of the population using a list or chart to organize your data. Next, you would arrange the data in a table with the independent variable on the left-hand side and the dependent variable on the right-hand side. To graph your data, look at the range in the values. In this situation, the independent variable, or x-values, and the dependent variable, or y-values, all are positive so you only need to draw and label Quadrant I on the coordinate grid. Look at the data and find the most appropriate intervals to label the axes. Plot the points using (*x*,*y*), moving over x units on the horizontal axis and up y units on the vertical axis to see the relationship between the two data sets.

## Types of questions – scatter plot

You should expect to be given a scatterplot in a real-world context. The scatterplot may already include a line of best fit, or you may be expected to select the equation of a line or curve of best fit. You may be expected to interpret the relationship between two variables based on the scatterplot. This relationship may be linear, quadratic, or exponential. You may be expected to use the line or curve of best fit to make a prediction about the situation. You may be given a scatter plot and asked, "Based on the line of best fit to the data shown, which of the following values is closest to the average yearly increase?." You must determine the slope of the line of best fit to answer the question. It is important to understand correlations shown by scatterplots. Make sure you do not try to apply a line of best fit to data that show no correlation. Make sure you do not try to apply a line to a curvilinear model. You probably will not have to actually find the equation of the line of best fit. You just need to be able to interpret the information that is given.

Correlations
A scatter plot is a way to represent the relationship between two data sets. The data can have one of three types of relationships, or correlations: a positive correlation, a negative correlation, or no correlation. A positive correlation is one in which the points increase from left to right. A negative correlation is one in which the points decrease from left to right. A scatter plot with no correlation is one in which the points show no relationship and neither rise nor fall. The correlation can help to determine the line of best fit. The line of best fit is a line drawn to best represent the data values. The line usually falls in the middle of the group of points and contains as many points as possible. When a graph has a positive or negative correlation, a line of regression can be drawn to determine an equation based on the relationship. When a graph has no correlation, a regression line cannot be drawn.

Summarize data in two-way frequency table
A two-way frequency table is a table that shows the number of data points falling into each combination of two categories in the form of a table, with one category on each axis. Creating a two-way frequency table is simply a matter of drawing a table with each axis labeled with the possibilities for the corresponding category, and then filling in the numbers in the appropriate cells. For instance, suppose you're told that at a given school, 30 male students take Spanish, 20 take French, and 25 German, while 26 female students take Spanish, 28 French, and 21 German. These data can be represented by the following two-way frequency table:

| # of students | SPANISH | FRENCH | GERMAN |
|---|---|---|---|
| MALE | 30 | 20 | 25 |
| FEMALE | 26 | 28 | 21 |

You should expect to see questions with categorical data summarized in two-way tables. You need to make comparisons among the data contained in the columns and rows of data. You may need to use proportions or calculate percentages. Two-way frequency tables typically include cells which total the data contained in the columns and rows, as well as an overall sum of data. These sums are used when calculating proportions and percentages. You may be asked to determine the relative frequencies of the data included in the rows or the columns. You may need to determine conditional probability, which is the probability of one event given the occurrence of another; additionally, you may be asked to compare conditional probabilities to determine the association between events. For example, consider a table with a row of data showing the number of students who study for a test more than and less than four hours a week and a row of data showing the number of students whose test grades are above and below 80%. The probability of a student making above 80% is calculated given a study time of more than four hours, and the probability of a student making below a 80% given a study time of more than four hours; if the probability of a student making above an 80% is much greater than the probability of making below an 80% given the same study time, there may be a correlation between study time and test score; alternatively, if the probabilities are approximately the same, there would appear to be no correlation.

Types of questions – inferences about population parameters
You may be asked to estimate a population parameter given the results from a random sample of a population. A question might say, "In the survey of a random sample of 1,200 cell phone users aged 18-25 from a particular region, 420 used their phones exclusively to do their banking. If the region had 160,000 residents aged 18-25, approximately how many of those residents could be

expected to use their cell phones exclusively to do their banking?" You are also expected to understand any confidence intervals and measurement errors included in the problem. You may see a question that says, "A researcher collected information from 1,000 randomly selected public high school science teachers in the United States and concluded that the median annual salary was between $52,400 and $63,800 with a 99% confidence level. Which of the following could represent the median annual salary for the same sample with a 95% confidence level?"

Estimating a conditional probability from a two-way frequency table

If we have a two-way frequency table, it is generally a straightforward matter to read off the probabilities of any two events A and B, as well as the joint probability of both events occurring, $P(A \cap B)$. We can then find the conditional probability P(A|B) by calculating $P(A|B) = \frac{P(A \cap B)}{P(B)}$.

For example, a certain store's recent T-shirt sales:

| | | Size | | | |
|---|---|---|---|---|---|
| | | Small | Medium | Large | Total |
| Color | Blue | 25 | 40 | 35 | 100 |
| | White | 27 | 25 | 22 | 74 |
| | Black | 8 | 23 | 15 | 26 |
| | Total | 60 | 88 | 72 | 220 |

Suppose we want to find the conditional probability that a customer buys a black shirt (event A), given that the shirt he buys is size small (event B). From the table, the probability P(A) that a customer buys a small shirt is $\frac{60}{220} = \frac{3}{11}$. The probability $P(A \cap B)$ that he buys a small, black shirt is $\frac{8}{220} = \frac{2}{55}$. The conditional probability P(A|B) that he buys a black shirt, given that he buys a small shirt, is therefore $P(A|B) = \frac{2/55}{3/11} = \frac{2}{15}$.

Probability

Probability is a branch of statistics that deals with the likelihood of something taking place. One classic example is a coin toss. There are only two possible results: heads or tails. The likelihood, or probability, that the coin will land as heads is 1 out of 2 (1/2, 0.5, 50%). Tails has the same probability. Another common example is a 6-sided die roll. There are six possible results from rolling a single die, each with an equal chance of happening, so the probability of any given number coming up is 1 out of 6.

Terms frequently used in probability:
- Event – a situation that produces results of some sort (a coin toss)
- Compound event – event that involves two or more independent events (rolling a pair of dice; taking the sum)
- Outcome – a possible result in an experiment or event (heads, tails)
- Desired outcome (or success) – an outcome that meets a particular set of criteria (a roll of 1 or 2 if we are looking for numbers less than 3)
- Independent events – two or more events whose outcomes do not affect one another (two coins tossed at the same time)
- Dependent events – two or more events whose outcomes affect one another (two cards drawn consecutively from the same deck)
- Certain outcome – probability of outcome is 100% or 1
- Impossible outcome – probability of outcome is 0% or 0
- Mutually exclusive outcomes – two or more outcomes whose criteria cannot all be satisfied in a single event (a coin coming up heads and tails on the same toss)

Probability is the likelihood of a certain outcome occurring for a given event.  The theoretical probability can usually be determined without actually performing the event.  The likelihood of a outcome occurring, or the probability of an outcome occurring, is given by the formula

$$P(A) = \frac{\text{Number of acceptable outcomes}}{\text{Number of possible outcomes}}$$

where $P(A)$ is the probability of an outcome $A$ occurring, and each outcome is just as likely to occur as any other outcome. If each outcome has the same probability of occurring as every other possible outcome, the outcomes are said to be equally likely to occur.  The total number of acceptable outcomes must be less than or equal to the total number of possible outcomes.  If the two are equal, then the outcome is certain to occur and the probability is 1.  If the number of acceptable outcomes is zero, then the outcome is impossible and the probability is 0.

*Example:*

There are 20 marbles in a bag and 5 are red.  The theoretical probability of randomly selecting a red marble is 5 out of 20, (5/20 = 1/4, 0.25, or 25%).

When trying to calculate the probability of an event using the $\frac{desired\ outcomes}{total\ outcomes}$ formula, you may frequently find that there are too many outcomes to individually count them.  Permutation and combination formulas offer a shortcut to counting outcomes.  A permutation is an arrangement of a specific number of a set of objects in a specific order.  The number of permutations of $r$ items given a set of $n$ items can be calculated as $_nP_r = \frac{n!}{(n-r)!}$.  Combinations are similar to permutations, except there are no restrictions regarding the order of the elements.  While ABC is considered a different permutation than BCA, ABC and BCA are considered the same combination.  The number of **combinations** of $r$ items given a set of $n$ items can be calculated as $_nC_r = \frac{n!}{r!(n-r)!}$ or $_nC_r = \frac{_nP_r}{r!}$.

Example: Suppose you want to calculate how many different 5-card hands can be drawn from a deck of 52 cards.  This is a combination since the order of the cards in a hand does not matter.  There are 52 cards available, and 5 to be selected.  Thus, the number of different hands is $_{52}C_5 = \frac{52!}{5! \times 47!} = 2,598,960$.

Sometimes it may be easier to calculate the possibility of something not happening, or the complement of an event.  Represented by the symbol $\bar{A}$, the complement of $A$ is the probability that event $A$ does not happen.  When you know the probability of event $A$ occurring, you can use the formula $P(\bar{A}) = 1 - P(A)$, where $P(\bar{A})$ is the probability of event $A$ not occurring, and $P(A)$ is the probability of event $A$ occurring.

The addition rule for probability is used for finding the probability of a compound event.  Use the formula $P(A \text{ or } B) = P(A) + P(B) - P(A \text{ and } B)$, where $P(A \text{ and } B)$ is the probability of both events occurring to find the probability of a compound event.  The probability of both events occurring at the same time must be subtracted to eliminate any overlap in the first two probabilities.

Conditional Probability

Conditional probability is the probability of an event occurring once another event has already occurred.  Given event $A$ and dependent event $B$, the probability of event $B$ occurring when event $A$ has already occurred is represented by the notation $P(A|B)$.  To find the probability of event $B$ occurring, take into account the fact that event $A$ has already occurred and adjust the total number of possible outcomes.  For example, suppose you have ten balls numbered 1–10 and you want ball number 7 to be pulled in two pulls.  On the first pull, the probability of getting the 7 is $\frac{1}{10}$ because there is one ball with a 7 on it and 10 balls to choose from. Assuming the first pull did not yield a 7, the probability of pulling a 7 on the second pull is now $\frac{1}{9}$ because there are only 9 balls remaining for the second pull.

The multiplication rule can be used to find the probability of two independent events occurring using the formula $P(A \text{ and } B) = P(A) \times P(B)$, where $P(A \text{ and } B)$ is the probability of two independent events occurring, $P(A)$ is the probability of the first event occurring, and $P(B)$ is the probability of the second event occurring.

The multiplication rule can also be used to find the probability of two dependent events occurring using the formula $P(A \text{ and } B) = P(A) \times P(B|A)$, where $P(A \text{ and } B)$ is the probability of two dependent events occurring and $P(B|A)$ is the probability of the second event occurring after the first event has already occurred.

Before using the multiplication rule, you MUST first determine whether the two events are dependent or independent.

Use a combination of the multiplication rule and the rule of complements to find the probability that at least one outcome of the element will occur. This given by the general formula $P(\text{at least one event occurring}) = 1 - P(\text{no outcomes occurring})$. For example, to find the probability that at least one even number will show when a pair of dice is rolled, find the probability that two odd numbers will be rolled (no even numbers) and subtract from one. You can always use a tree diagram or make a chart to list the possible outcomes when the sample space is small, such as in the dice-rolling example, but in most cases it will be much faster to use the multiplication and complement formulas.

Expected Value

Expected value is a method of determining expected outcome in a random situation. It is really a sum of the weighted probabilities of the possible outcomes. Multiply the probability of an event occurring by the weight assigned to that probability (such as the amount of money won or lost). A practical application of the expected value is to determine whether a game of chance is really fair. If the sum of the weighted probabilities is equal to zero, the game is generally considered fair because the player has a fair chance to at least to break even. If the expected value is less than zero, then players lose more than they win. For example, a lottery drawing might allow the player to choose any three-digit number, 000–999. The probability of choosing the winning number is 1:1000. If it costs \$1 to play, and a winning number receives \$500, the expected value is $\left(-\$1 \cdot \frac{999}{1,000}\right) + \left(\$500 \cdot \frac{1}{1,000}\right) = -0.499$ or $-\$0.50$. You can expect to lose on average 50 cents for every dollar you spend.

Empirical Probability

Most of the time, when we talk about probability, we mean theoretical probability. Empirical probability, or experimental probability or relative frequency, is the number of times an outcome occurs in a particular experiment or a certain number of observed events. While theoretical probability is based on what *should* happen, experimental probability is based on what *has* happened. Experimental probability is calculated in the same way as theoretical, except that actual outcomes are used instead of possible outcomes.

Theoretical and experimental probability do not always line up with one another. Theoretical probability says that out of 20 coin tosses, 10 should be heads. However, if we were actually to toss 20 coins, we might record just 5 heads. This doesn't mean that our theoretical probability is incorrect; it just means that this particular experiment had results that were different from what was predicted. A practical application of empirical probability is the insurance industry. There are no set functions that define life span, health, or safety. Insurance companies look at factors from hundreds of thousands of individuals to find patterns that they then use to set the formulas for insurance premiums.

## Measures of Central Tendency

The quantities of mean, median, and mode are all referred to as measures of central tendency. They can each give a picture of what the whole set of data looks like with just a single number. Knowing what each of these values represents is vital to making use of the information they provide.

The mean, also known as the arithmetic mean or average, of a data set is calculated by summing all of the values in the set and dividing that sum by the number of values. For example, if a data set has 6 numbers and the sum of those 6 numbers is 30, the mean is calculated as 30/6 = 5.

The median is the middle value of a data set. The median can be found by putting the data set in numerical order, and locating the middle value. In the data set (1, 2, 3, 4, 5), the median is 3. If there is an even number of values in the set, the median is calculated by taking the average of the two middle values. In the data set, (1, 2, 3, 4, 5, 6), the median would be (3 + 4)/2 = 3.5.

The mode is the value that appears most frequently in the data set. In the data set (1, 2, 3, 4, 5, 5, 5), the mode would be 5 since the value 5 appears three times. If multiple values appear the same number of times, there are multiple values for the mode. If the data set were (1, 2, 2, 3, 4, 4, 5, 5), the modes would be 2, 4, and 5. If no value appears more than any other value in the data set, then there is no mode.

## Confidence interval

A confidence interval gives a range of a values that is likely to include the parameter of interest. After a random sample, suppose a parameter, such as a median is estimated to be within a certain range with a 99% confidence level. This essentially means one time out of 100 times, the median value will not be in the specified interval. (You will not be asked to actually calculate the confidence levels; they will be given with the question.) For example, you may see a question that says, "A researcher collected information from 1,000 randomly selected public high school science teachers in the United States and concluded that the median annual salary was between $52,400 and $63,800 with a 99% confidence level. Which of the following could represent the median annual salary for the same sample with a 95% confidence level?" The key to answering this is to understand that a 95% confidence means that five out of 100 times the median value will not be in the specified interval. That means you are less confident that the median will be in that range. The range of salaries in the 95% confidence interval would be a subset of the range of salaries within the 99% confidence interval. The correct answer choice would show a narrower range of salaries, such as $55,000 to $60,000. This type of question can be answered without performing any calculations. You simply need to understand the meaning of confidence levels.

## Standard deviation

The standard deviation of a data set is a measurement of how much the data points vary from the mean. More precisely, it is equal to the square root of the average of the squares of the differences between each point and the mean: $s_x = \sqrt{\frac{\Sigma(X-\bar{X})^2}{N-1}}$.

The standard deviation is useful for determining the spread, or dispersion, of the data, or how far they vary from the mean. The smaller the standard deviation, the closer the values tend to be to the mean; the larger the standard deviation, the more they tend to be scattered far from the mean.

## Types of questions – center, shape, and spread of data

You may be given a data set and asked to calculate measures of center such as mean, median, and mode. You might be asked to determine spread, or range, for a given set of data. You may be asked to use given statistics to compare two separate sets of data. This comparison may involve mean, median, mode, range, and standard deviation, which are key topics in these types of questions. The mean is the numerical average of the data set. The median is the data point (or the average of two data points if there are an even number of data) when the data are ranked from least to greatest. The mode is the data point which occurs most often; there may be one mode, or there may be no mode or multiple modes. The range is the difference between the highest and lowest data points. The standard deviation is a measure of how much the data points differ from the mean. Basically, it describes how closely the data is clustered around the mean.

## Types of questions – evaluate reports to make inferences

You should expect to be given tables, graphs, and/or text summaries and to be asked to make inferences, justify conclusions, and determine the appropriateness of the data collection methods. Data is often collected from a subset of a large population in order to draw conclusions about the population as a whole; the subset must be sufficiently large and randomly selected in order for the statistics to be reliable. Sometimes, data is collected over a period of time in order to determine possible trends, such as "x increases over time." Two variables may be compared and conclusions such as "As one variable increases, the other decreases," or "When one variable increases, the other variable increases" may be drawn. While you can make a statistical association, you cannot determine causal relationships. That means you cannot say that one variable increased or decreased as a result of the other variable increasing or decreasing. Another way to say this is that correlation does not imply causation. Correlation tells how strongly two variables are associated. However, just because two variables are strongly correlated does not mean that one causes the other.

## Drawing conclusions from data trends

You will be asked to determine if there is a correlation between two variables, but you cannot conclude that a change in one variable causes a change in the other. Ask yourself questions like, "Do both variables increase or decrease?" or "Does one increase as the other decreases?" Then, find the answer choice that makes the best statement explaining that correlation. If there is no correlation, look for a statement that reflects that. Avoid answer choices that say, "The increase of _____ caused the increase of _____" or "The increase of _____ caused the decrease of _____." Again, correlation does not imply causation. You may simply have to choose between answer choices that say, "There is a correlation between _____," or "There is no correlation between _____."

## Types of questions – relating equations to graphs

You need to be able to match a given graph to the type of equation it represents, whether it be linear, quadratic, or exponential. Questions about bacteria cultures and radioactive isotopes are modeled with exponential equations. Questions about initial fees plus rates associated with a variable are modeled with linear equations. The projectiles of arrows, rocks, balls, missiles or anything that is shot or thrown are modeled with quadratic equations. You should know the general shapes for linear equations (line), quadratic equations (parabola), and exponential equations (steep curve). Also, you should have a firm grasp of the slope-intercept from of a line. When you are working with a linear equation, it is important to avoid making quick, erroneous conclusions about the line. Often, the equation of the line will be written in a form to "hide" the true nature of the line. For example, you may be given an equation like $y - x = k(x + y)$ and asked to determine which is necessarily true of its graph: the graph is a line passing through the origin; the graph is a parabola; the graph is a line with a positive slope; or the graph is a line with a slope of $k$. At first glance, you might think this is a factored quadratic equation, or you might think it is a linear equation in point-slope form with a slope of $k$. However, if you rearrange the equation into the slope-intercept form $y = \frac{1+k}{1-k}x$, you can see that the graph of the equation is a line with a $y$-intercept of zero, which means that the line passes through the origin. Depending on the value of $k$, the slope of the line can be positive, negative, zero, or undefined.

## Types of questions – relating two variables on a graph

You need to be able to match a given graph to the type of equation it represents, whether it be linear, quadratic, or exponential. Questions about bacteria cultures and radioactive isotopes are modeled with exponential equations. Questions about initial fees plus rates associated with a variable are modeled with linear equations. The projectiles of arrows, rocks, balls, missiles or anything that is shot or thrown are modeled with quadratic equations. You should know the general shapes for linear equations (line), quadratic equations (parabola), and exponential equations (steep curve). Also, you should have a firm grasp of the slope-intercept from of a line. When you are working with a linear equation, it is important to avoid making quick, erroneous conclusions about the line. Often, the equation of the line will be written in a form to "hide" the true nature of the line. For example, you may be given an equation like $y - x = k(x + y)$ and asked to determine which is necessarily true of its graph: the graph is a line passing through the origin; the graph is a parabola; the graph is a line with a positive slope; or the graph is a line with a slope of $k$. At first glance, you might think this is a factored quadratic equation, or you might think it is a linear equation in point-slope form with a slope of $k$. However, if you rearrange the equation into the slope-intercept form $y = \frac{1+k}{1-k}x$, you can see that the graph of the equation is a line with a $y$-intercept of zero, which means that the line passes through the origin. Depending on the value of $k$, the slope of the line can be positive, negative, zero, or undefined.

## Linear growth vs. exponential growth

Linear growth has a constant rate of growth. The growth over each interval is exactly the same. Linear growth is modeled by a line which has the growth rate as its slope. Exponential growth has a rate of growth that increases over time. The growth over each interval is not constant. This rate of growth is modeled by a steep curve. Linear growth can be modeled by an equation in the form slope-intercept form $y = mx + b$, in which $m$ is the slope and $b$ is the y-intercept. Exponential growth is modeled by an equation in the form $y = a(b^{kx}) + c$ in which $b$ is the base such that $b > 0$ and $b \neq 1$. Exponential functions are used to model growth and decay. The values of $b$ and $k$ determine if the function models growth or decay. If you are given a table of values, linear growth is shown as an arithmetic sequence. The value of $y$ increases (by addition) by a constant value over equal intervals of $x$. Exponential growth is shown as a geometric sequence. The value of $y$ is multiplied by a fixed value over a set interval. Comparing tables for the linear equation $y = 2x$ and the exponential function $y = 2^x$ shows that y-values for the exponential function quickly surpasses those of the linear function.

| $x$ | -3 | -2 | -1 | 0 | 1 | 2 | 3 | 4 |
|---|---|---|---|---|---|---|---|---|
| $y = 2x$ | -6 | -4 | -2 | 0 | 2 | 4 | 6 | 8 |

| $x$ | -3 | -2 | -1 | 0 | 1 | 2 | 3 | 4 |
|---|---|---|---|---|---|---|---|---|
| $y = 2^x$ | $\frac{1}{8}$ | $\frac{1}{4}$ | $\frac{1}{2}$ | 1 | 2 | 4 | 8 | 16 |

## Passport to Advanced Math

In this section the questions will deal with more advanced equations and expressions. Students need to be able to create quadratic and exponential equations that model a context. They also need to be able to solve these equations. Students should also be able to create equivalent expressions that involve radicals and rational exponents. Like the Heart of Algebra section this section will test systems of equations. These systems however will involve one linear and one quadratic equation in two variables. Finally, students should be able to perform operations such as addition, subtraction, and multiplication on polynomials.

## Solving Quadratic Equations

The *Quadratic Formula* is used to solve quadratic equations when other methods are more difficult. To use the quadratic formula to solve a quadratic equation, begin by rewriting the equation in standard form $ax^2 + bx + c = 0$, where $a$, $b$, and $c$ are coefficients. Once you have identified the values of the coefficients, substitute those values into the quadratic formula $= \frac{-b \pm \sqrt{b^2 - 4ac}}{2a}$. Evaluate the equation and simplify the expression. Again, check each root by substituting into the original equation. In the quadratic formula, the portion of the formula under the radical $(b^2 - 4ac)$ is called the *Discriminant*. If the discriminant is zero, there is only one root: zero. If the discriminant is positive, there are two different real roots. If the discriminant is negative, there are no real roots.

To solve a quadratic equation by *Factoring*, begin by rewriting the equation in standard form, if necessary. Factor the side with the variable then set each of the factors equal to zero and solve the resulting linear equations. Check your answers by substituting the roots you found into the original equation. If, when writing the equation in standard form, you have an equation in the form $x^2 + c = 0$ or $x^2 - c = 0$, set $x^2 = -c$ or $x^2 = c$ and take the square root of c. If c = 0, the only real root is zero. If c is positive, there are two real roots—the positive and negative square root values. If c is negative, there are no real roots because you cannot take the square root of a negative number.

To solve a quadratic equation by *Completing the Square*, rewrite the equation so that all terms containing the variable are on the left side of the equal sign, and all the constants are on the right side of the equal sign. Make sure the coefficient of the squared term is 1. If there is a coefficient with the squared term, divide each term on both sides of the equal side by that number. Next, work with the coefficient of the single-variable term. Square half of this coefficient, and add that value to both sides. Now you can factor the left side (the side containing the variable) as the square of a binomial. $x^2 + 2ax + a^2 = C \Rightarrow (x + a)^2 = C$, where x is the variable, and a and C are constants. Take the square root of both sides and solve for the variable. Substitute the value of the variable in the original problem to check your work.

Types of questions – quadratic function with rational coefficients
A quadratic function is a second degree equation that graphs as a parabola. The general form for a quadratic function is $f(x) = ax^2 + bx + c$, where $f(x) = y$. If $a > 0$, the parabola is concave up. If $a < 0$, the parabola is concave down. The axis of symmetry for the parabola is given by $x = \frac{-b}{2a}$. The turning point of the parabola (the minimum value for a concave down and maximum for a concave up parabola) is given by $\left( \frac{-b}{2a}, f\left( \frac{-b}{2a} \right) \right)$. Quadratic functions are often used to model projectile motion. A rocket or other projectile launched from the ground will follow a parabolic trajectory. You may be given a graph of a trajectory and asked to choose the function that best models that parabola. You must use the concavity, axis of symmetry, and turning point to work backwards to find the equation for the parabola.

Exponential function with rational coefficients
An exponential function has the general form of $f(x) = a(b^{kx}) + c$, in which b is the base and $b > 0$ and $b \neq 1$. Exponential functions are used to model growth and decay. The values of b and k determine if the function models exponential growth or exponential decay. When graphed, an exponential function has a horizontal asymptote at $y = c$. The y-intercept of an exponential function is located at $(0, a + c)$.

| Type | Values of b | Values of k | Example |
|------|-------------|-------------|---------|
| Exponential Growth | $b > 1$ | $k > 0$ | $f(x) = 2^x$ |
| Exponential Growth | $b < 1$ | $k < 0$ | $f(x) = \left(\frac{1}{2}\right)^{-x}$ |
| Exponential Decay | $b > 1$ | $k < 0$ | $f(x) = 2^{-x}$ |
| Exponential Decay | $b < 1$ | $k > 0$ | $f(x) = \left(\frac{1}{2}\right)^{x}$ |

You may be given the graph of an exponential function and asked to choose the correct equation. If $y$ increases rapidly as $x$ increases, the function models exponential growth. If $y$ decreases rapidly as $x$ increases, the function models exponential decay. You can determine $c$ from the horizontal asymptote. Then, you can determine $a$ from the $y$-intercept.

Types of questions – Writing expressions
You must be able to translate verbal expressions into mathematical language. These may be simple or complex algebraic expressions (linear, quadratic, or exponential); you must be able to simplify these expressions using order of operations. You may be asked to determine an algebraic model involving costs or interest and then use that model to perform a calculation. You may be given a geometric situation involving area or perimeter in which you have to write and simplify an expression. These problems may be complex and require sketches in order to choose or produce a correct answer.

Produce expressions or equations given a context
Often, complex geometry problems involve writing a system of equations. For example, if the problem gives the area and perimeter of a rectangular garden and asks for its length and width, you can use the formulas $A = lw$ and $p = 2l + 2w$ to write a system of equations. Sometimes, geometry problems involve two shapes, one of which is inside another. For example, you may be given the inner dimensions of a picture frame and asked to find the outer dimensions; in this case, if you designate the length and width of frame's inner rectangle as $l$ and $w$, respectively, then the length and width of the outer rectangle are respectively represented by $l + 2x$ and $w + 2x$, where $x$ is the width of the picture frame.

Consistent, inconsistent, or dependent systems
If a system of equations set up to represent a real-world problem turns out to be consistent (having exactly one solution), that solution is the solution to the problem.

If the system turns out to be dependent (having infinitely many solutions), that means that the original information given was redundant, and was therefore not enough information to solve the problem. Practically speaking, this may mean that any of that infinite set of solutions will do, or it may mean that more information is needed.

If the system turns out to be inconsistent (having no solutions), that means the real-world situation described cannot be true. If the situation described was a hypothetical desired outcome, we now know that it is not possible to achieve that outcome; if the situation described was supposed to have really occurred, we can only conclude that it must have been described inaccurately.

*Solve the rational equation:* $\frac{2}{x} - 2 = x - 1$

To solve the rational equation, multiply each side of the equation by the LCD, which is $x$. This will transform the rational equation into a quadratic equation that can be solved by factoring:

$$\frac{2}{x} - 2 = x - 1$$
$$x\left(\frac{2}{x} - 2\right) = x(x - 1)$$
$$2 - 2x = x^2 - x$$
$$x^2 + x - 2 = 0$$
$$(x + 2)(x - 1) = 0$$
$$x = -2, x = 1$$

Both $x = -2$ and $x = 1$ check out in the original equation. The solution is $x = \{-2, 1\}$.

*Solve the radical equation:* $\sqrt{x-1} + 3 = x$

To solve the radical equation, isolate the radical $\sqrt{x-1}$ on one side of the equation. Then square both sides and solve the resulting quadratic equation:

$$\sqrt{x-1} + 3 = x$$
$$\sqrt{x-1} = x - 3$$
$$\left(\sqrt{x-1}\right)^2 = (x-3)^2$$
$$x - 1 = x^2 - 6x + 9$$
$$x^2 - 7x + 10 = 0$$
$$(x-5)(x-2) = 0$$
$$x = 2, x = 5$$

Only $x = 5$ checks out in the original equation; $\sqrt{2-1} + 3 \overset{?}{\Leftrightarrow} 2 \xrightarrow{yields} \sqrt{1} + 3 = 4 \neq 2!$

The solution, then, is just $x = \{5\}$.

## Extraneous solution to rational and radical equation

An extraneous solution is the solution of an equation that arises during the process of solving an equation, which is not a solution of the original equation. When solving a rational equation, each side is often multiplied by x or an expression containing x. Since the value of x is unknown, this may mean multiplying by zero, which will make any equation the true statement 0 = 0. Similarly, when solving a radical expression, each side of the equation is often squared, or raised to some power. This can also change the sign of unknown expressions. For example, the equation 3 = –3 is false, but squaring each side gives 9 = 9, which is true.

## Rewriting radical expressions

Radical expressions can be rewritten as equivalent expressions with rational exponents. In general $\sqrt[b]{n^a}$ is equivalent to $n^{\frac{a}{b}}$ and $\sqrt[b]{m^c n^a}$ is equivalent to $m^{\frac{c}{b}} n^{\frac{a}{b}}$. For example, $\sqrt{x}$ is equivalent to $x^{\frac{1}{2}}$ and $\sqrt[3]{x^2}$ is equivalent to $x^{\frac{2}{3}}$. The radical $\sqrt[5]{x-1}$ is equivalent to $(x-1)^{\frac{1}{5}}$. Another point to remember is that, while $n^{\frac{a}{b}}$ can be rewritten as $\sqrt[b]{n^a}$, it can also be rewritten as $(\sqrt[b]{n})^a$. It is also important to understand the concept of negative exponents. A negative exponent basically flips a term from the numerator to the denominator or from the denominator to the numerator. You may see a question that says, "Rewrite the expression $2x^{-\frac{3}{4}}$ in radical form" or "Rewrite the expression $(\sqrt[3]{2xy})^2$ with rational exponents."

## Equivalent expressions with radical and rational exponents

You may see questions asking you to simplify a radical expression or perform operations with radicals. You may see a question that says, "Simplify $\sqrt[3]{-27x^6 y^{15}}$," or "Simplify the expression $\sqrt{2}(3\sqrt{5} + \sqrt{20})$." You many see a question that says, "Which of the following expressions is equivalent to $\sqrt{(20)(4) + (12)(16)}$?" You should expect to be asked to simplify rational expressions. You may need to factor the numerator and the denominator and then cancel like factors, as in this example: "Simplify $\frac{x^2-4}{x^2-x-2}$." You may also be asked to change a rational expression from one form into another. For example, you may see a question that says, "If the expression $\frac{6x^2-5}{x-1}$ is written in the equivalent form $\frac{1}{x-1} + B$, what is B in terms of x?" You could equate the two expressions and solve for B, or you could use long division to simplify the first expression and compare the result to the equivalent expression to determine B.

## Situations modeled by statements that use function notation

A statement using function notation can model any situation in which one quantity depends uniquely on one or more other quantities. For example, the area of a rectangle can be expressed as a function of its width and height. The maximum vertical distance a projectile travels can be expressed as a function of its initial vertical speed. An object's position, the amount of money in a bank account, or any other quantity that changes over time can be expressed as a function of time.

A relationship cannot be modeled with a function, however, if it involves two quantities neither of which is uniquely determined by the other—that is, if each quantity may have multiple values corresponding to the same value of the other. For example, we could not write a function to represent the relationship between peoples' height in inches and their weight in pounds. There are people of the same height with different weights, and people of the same weight but different heights.

## Using structure and mathematical operations

You might be given an algebraic expression and asked which, if any, of several other expressions is equivalent, or you might be given several pairs of algebraic expressions and be asked to determine which pairs are equivalent. For example, you may see a question that says, "Which of following pairs of algebraic expressions are equivalent" and an answer choice such as "$(2x + 3)(3x-4)$ and $6x^2 + x + 12$." You would determine that is an incorrect choice since these are not equivalent expressions. You might see a question that says, "Which of the following rational expressions is equivalent to $\frac{x+3}{x-5}$?" You may be given choices in which the numerators and denominators can factored and some of the factors canceled.

## Determining if two equations are equivalent

One way to check for equivalence is to evaluate each expression at a chosen value, say $x = 0$ or $x = 1$, and see if the results agree. If the expressions do not yield the same result, then they are not equivalent, but it is important to note that yielding the same result does not necessarily mean the expressions are equivalent. This is only a method to eliminate incorrect answers; as the choices are narrowed, you may continue to try other values until all but the correct choice have been eliminated. Another way to determine whether two algebraic expressions are equivalent is to choose the most complex expression and simplify it algebraically to see if you can produce the second expression. This may involve factoring and canceling like factors or distributing and combining like terms.

## Methods to solve quadratic equations

Quadratic equations may be solved by graphing, factoring, completing the square, or using the quadratic formula. Since these types of questions are in the no calculator section of the test, graphing is not your best choice due to time constraints. Set the equation equal to zero; if the quadratic expression is easily factored, factor it, and then solve the equation by setting each factor equal to zero. If the expression is not factorable and $a = 1$ when the equation is written in the general form $ax^2 + bx + c = 0$, you may choose to complete the square. Remember, if $a \neq 1$, you must divide the entire equation by $a$ and work with resulting fractions. In these situations, it is easier to solve the equation using the quadratic formula $x = \frac{-b \pm \sqrt{b^2-4ac}}{2a}$. You may simply be asked to find the roots of a quadratic equation, or you may be asked to perform some operation with one of the roots once you have found the roots. Be careful to answer the question that is asked. For example, you may see a question that says, "If $3x^2 + 4x = 4$ and $x > 0$, what is the value of $x + \frac{1}{3}$?" First, you would write the equation in the form $3x^2 + 4x - 4 = 0$ and solve by factoring or by using the quadratic formula; then, you would use the positive root to find $x + \frac{1}{3}$.

## Performing arithmetic operations on polynomials

You should expect to add, subtract, and multiply polynomial expressions and simplify the results. These expressions will have rational coefficients. You may see a question that says, "Add $(2x^2 + 4y + 5xy)$, $(3x^2 - 3xy - x)$, and $(xy + 1)$" or "Subtract $(6x^2 + 6y - xy + 1)$ from $(2x^2 + 3xy - 2)$." You may see a question that says, "If $p = 3x^3 - 2x^2 + 5x - 7$ and $q = 2x^3 - 7x^2 - x + 3$, what is $p - 2q$?" You may see a question that says, "Multiply $(x + 2y)(4x - 3y + 1)$" or "What is the product of $(2x + 1)$, $(2x - 1)$, and $(2x^2 + 1)$?" In each of these types of questions, you should perform the operation, collecting like terms to simplify the result.

## Adding and subtracting polynomials

When adding or subtracting two polynomials, you should first identify the like terms. Like terms have the same base and the same exponent but not necessarily the same coefficient. When adding or subtracting polynomials, only like terms can be combined. For example, $2xy$ and $3xy$ are like terms, but $2x^2$ and $2x^3$ are not like terms. When finding a difference, make sure you have the polynomials written in the correct order. When removing parentheses from an expression which follows a minus sign, remember to change the sign of every term inside the parentheses. For example, when subtracting $(2x - y)$ from $(5x + 3y)$, the problem is written as $(5x + 3y) - (2x - y)$. Removing the parentheses yields $5x + 3y - 2x + y$, which is further simplified to $3x + 4y$. When multiplying two polynomials, you should multiply each term of one polynomial by each term of the other and then simplify the result when necessary. Remember, when multiplying monomial terms, you should multiply coefficients but add the exponents of like bases.

## Single- variable equation with radicals

To solve an equation with radicals, first, isolate the radical on one side of the equation. If there is more than one radical, isolate the most complex radical. Then, raise the equation to the appropriate power. For example, if the radical is a square root, you should square both sides. If there is still a radical in the equation, isolate the radical and repeat. Once the radicals are removed, solve for the unknown variable. Be sure to check every solution to determine if any are extraneous ones. You may see a question such as "What is one possible solution to the equation $\sqrt{x - 1} = x - 7$?" You would need to solve for $x$ and substitute each solution back into the original equation to see if the resulting statement is true. If the resulting statement is false, the solution is extraneous. (Note: if=f you are given choices for this type of question, you may simply plug each possible solution into the equation until you find one that works.) To solve an equation with a variable in the denominator of a fraction, multiply the equation by the least common denominator of every fraction included in the equation. This will clear the equation of fractions. Then, solve normally. Remember to check all solutions by substituting them back to the original equations. If any substituted value does not result in a true statement, it is an extraneous solution.

## Types of questions – solving systems of equations

You may see a question with a graph of a line intersecting a circle or parabola. The question may ask about the number of solutions (which would be the number of times the line and circle or parabola intersect) or about the actual solutions (which would be the points of those intersections).

You may see a question with the equation of a line and the equation of a circle or parabola. In this case, you need to solve the linear equation for one variable and then substitute for that variable in the quadratic equation. If the question simply asks for the number of solutions, you may choose to make a quick sketch of the line and circle or parabola to see if you can see if they intersect and, if so, how many times.

One method to solve a system of equations is by graphing. A line with slope $m$ and $y$-intercept $b$ has the general form $y = mx + b$. A circle with radius $r$ and center $(h, k)$ has the general form $(x - h)^2 + (y - k)^2 = r^2$. A parabola has the general form $y = ax^2 + bx + c$. A line may intersect a circle or parabola at no point, one point, or two points. For example, if you are asked for the solutions to the system $\begin{cases} y = -x + 5 \\ x^2 + y^2 = 25 \end{cases}$, you would graph a line with a slope of -1 and a $y$-intercept of 5 and a circle centered at the origin with a radius of 5 units. You should be able to see even from a simple sketch that line intersects the circle at (0, 5) and (5, 0). More complicated systems of equations can be solved by substitution. For example, if you are asked for the solutions to the system $\begin{cases} 2x + 3y = 7 \\ (x - 4)^2 + y^2 = 10 \end{cases}$, it would be difficult to find the coordinates of the intersection points with a quick sketch. The quickest option is to solve the linear equation for one of the variables and then substitute the result for the corresponding variable in the quadratic equation.

## Adding or subtracting rational exponents

You should expect questions asking you to add or subtract rational expressions. You may see a question that says, "Add $\frac{2a+3}{3ab} + \frac{3a-2}{2bc}$," or "Subtract $\frac{m-2}{m-3} - \frac{m-1}{m-2}$." The questions may have more than two terms and may combine addition and subtraction, such as "Simplify $\frac{1}{x} + \frac{2}{y} - \frac{3}{z}$." In order to be able to add or subtract rational expressions, the expressions must have the same denominator. Find the least common denominator (LCD) of the terms in the expression. Then, multiply each term of the expression by the ratio $\frac{LCD}{LCD}$. Simplify where possible and present your answer as one term over the LCD. Since these are rational expressions, not equations, you cannot clear the fractions as you do in an equation.

## Multiplying and dividing rational expressions

You should expect questions asking you to multiply or divide rational expressions. You may see a question that says, "Multiply $\frac{n^2+n-6}{4} \cdot \frac{8}{2n+6}$" or "Divide $\frac{m^2+6m+5}{m^2-2m-3} \div \frac{m^2+8m+15}{3m^2-9m}$." In order to multiply rational expressions, the numerators and the denominators of each expression must be factored. Always check for a common monomial factor first. Then, check for differences of squares or a perfect square trinomials. A difference of squares $a^2 - b^2$ factors to $(a + b)(a - b)$. A perfect square trinomial factors to a binomial squared: $a^2 + 2ab + b^2$ factors to $(a + b)^2$, and $a^2 - 2ab + b^2$ factors to $(a - b)^2$. Also, check for other factorable trinomials. After factoring the numerators and denominators, cancel like factors and then multiply. To divide a rational expression, change the problem to a multiplication problem by multiplying the dividend by the reciprocal of the divisor, just like you would do if you were asked to divide two fractions containing no variables.

## Types of questions – Interpreting nonlinear expressions

You should to be given a nonlinear expression that represents a real-life context. These nonlinear expressions may be rational expressions with a variable in the denominator. They may be exponential expressions or quadratic expressions or any other type of expression that is not linear. You should also expect to interpret non-linear functions. For example, if the nonlinear function is a quadratic function that models a projectile's trajectory, you may be given the equation and asked, "What are the values of $x$ for which $y$ is minimum?" You may be given a nonlinear function that models a scientific concept. For example, Newton's Universal Law of Gravitation states that the gravitational force ($F$) in Newtons is inversely proportional to the square of the distance ($r$) in meters between the centers of those two objects; this is represented by the relationship $F \propto \frac{1}{r^2}$. You may be asked a question like, "If the distance between two objects is doubled, what happens to the strength of the force between them?"

## Modeling a projectile's trajectory

Since quadratic equations graph as parabolas, they are often used to model trajectories. To find the values of $x$ for which a quadratic equation is equal to zero, you should set the equation equal to zero and then solve by factoring or by using the quadratic equation. For a trajectory problem, usually one zero is at $x = 0$, representing the launch of the projectile, and the other zero represents the landing. Inverse square relationships model scientific concepts, such as the relationship between gravitational force and the distance between two objects, the electric force between two charges, and the magnetic force between two poles. In each of these laws, the force increases as the distance between the objects decreases, and the force decreases as the distance between the objects increase. More specifically, if the distance is doubled, the force is reduced to one fourth of the original value; if the distance is halved, the force quadruples. When working with exponential relationships, a common mistake is to handle the exponent incorrectly. If you are given an equation and values to plug into that equation, be sure to apply the exponent to every factor inside the parenthesis under the exponent. Remember, when raising a power to a power, you should multiply exponents.

## Zeros and factors of polynomials

Zeros are roots or solutions of polynomials when the polynomials are set equal to zero. These zeros are the locations where the graph of the polynomial intersects the x-axis. If the polynomials are set equal to zero and then factored, each individual factor is set equal to zero and solved; this gives the root or zero associated with that factor. If a polynomial equation has a zero of $-2$, the polynomial has a factor of $(x + 2)$. The Factor Theorem can be used to determine whether a given value is a zero. The polynomial is divided (using synthetic division) by the value, and if there is no remainder, the given value is a zero of the polynomial; if remainder is not zero, the value is not a root. If you are given one or more factors or roots of a polynomial function, you can use these factors or roots to determine the remaining factors and roots of the polynomial by dividing the polynomial by the given factor.

## Types of questions – zeros and factors of polynomials

You may be expected to factor a polynomial, or you may be given the factored form of a polynomial and asked to select the appropriate graph from a set of given graphs. You may see a question that says, "Which of the following graphs represents the polynomial $f(x) = (x-1)(x+2)(x+5)$?" or "Which of the following graphs represents the quadratic equation $y = x^2 + 4x - 5$?" You may be given a polynomial function with the ordered pairs of its zeros and be asked to solve for a missing coefficient or a missing coordinate. You may be given a function such as $f(x) = 2x^4 + 3x^2 - 5x + 7$ and be expected to use the Factor Theorem to find zeros or verify zeros. You may be given the zeros of a quadratic or cubic function and asked to write the function. You might see a question that says, "If the zeros of a cubic function are -2, 3, and 5 and the graph of that function passes through (1, 8), what is the equation of the function?"

## Types of questions – nonlinear relationships between two variables

You may be asked to select a graph for a given nonlinear equation. You may be asked to select an equation given a nonlinear graph. You may be given a system of equations with both algebraic and graphical representations. You may be given a verbal description of the curve of a nonlinear relationship and asked to determine the equation of the function. You may be asked to determine key features of the graph of a nonlinear function from its equation. For example, you may see a question in which you are given a graph containing an intersecting circle, parabola, and line as well as the equations associated with them which says. "A system of equations and their graphs are shown above. How many solutions does the system have?" You may be given the equations of two exponential functions and asked if the graphs (which are not given) show that they are increasing or decreasing. You may see a question that says, "The functions $y_1 = 2\left(\frac{1}{2}\right)^x$ and $y_2 = 2\left(\frac{3}{2}\right)^x$ are graphed in the $xy$ plane. Which of the following statements correctly describes whether each function is increasing or decreasing?"

## Finding a solution to a system of three equations

This test typically has one problem with a system of three equations. Usually the graphs as well as the equations are given. The key point is that the only solutions to this graph are the points at which all three graphs coincide or intersect. For example, the graph might include a circle, a parabola, and a line. There are no solutions to the given system if all three graphs do not intersect at one or more points. If the three graphs intersect at one point, then there is one solution to the given system, and that solution is the point of intersection. If the line intersects the circle at two points, and the line also intersects the parabola at the same exact two points, there are two solutions to the given system, and those solutions are the points of intersection. This system has at most two solutions.

## Types of questions – using function notation

You may be asked to evaluate a given function. For example, you may see a question that says, "If $f(x) = x^3 - 4x^2 + 3x - 1$, find $f(2)$." You should expect to be given two functions such as $f(x)$ and $g(x)$ and be asked to find $f(g(x))$ or $g(f(x))$. For example, you may see a question that says, "Let $f(x) = x^2 - 1$ and $g(x) = x + 1$. Which of the following describes $f(g(x))$?" Or you may be asked to work a similar problem given $f(x)$ and $g(f(x))$ and be asked to find $g(x)$. For example, you may see a question that says, "Let $f(x) = x^2 - 3$. If $g(f(x)) = \sqrt{x^2 + 1}$, which of the following describes $g(x)$?" You may be asked to evaluate composite functions, as in this example: "Two functions are defined as $f(t) = 4t^2 - t$ and $g(x) = -3x^2 - 2x - 1$. Find the value of $g(f(2))$."

## Types of questions – isolate or identify

You will be given a literal equation and be asked to be solve for one of the unknowns. Literal equations are equations often referred to as formulas. For example, in geometry, the formula for the area of a trapezoid is $A = \frac{h(b_1 + b_2)}{2}$, and in physics, the mirror equation is $\frac{1}{f} = \frac{1}{d_o} + \frac{1}{d_i}$. You may see a question that says, "The area of a trapezoid with bases $b_1$ and $b_2$ and height $h$ can be found by $A = \frac{h(b_1 + b_2)}{2}$. Which of the following is the correct expression to find the height of a trapezoid given the area and lengths of the bases?" You may see a question that says, "The focal length $f$ of a mirror can be determined from the object distance $d_o$ and image distance $d_i$ by the equation $\frac{1}{f} = \frac{1}{d_o} + \frac{1}{d_i}$. Which of the following is the correct expression to find the image distance of an image formed by a lens with a given object distance and focal length?"

*Solving $A = \frac{h(b_1 + b_2)}{2}$*

Literal equations can be solved for one of the unknown variables using basic algebraic operations. To solve $A = \frac{h(b_1 + b_2)}{2}$ for $b_2$, first multiply both sides of the equation by 2: $2A = h(b_1 + b_2)$. Then, divide by $h$: $\frac{2A}{h} = b_1 + b_2$. Then, subtract $b_1$: $\frac{2A}{h} - b_1 = b_2$. To solve $\frac{1}{f} = \frac{1}{d_o} + \frac{1}{d_i}$ for $d_i$, first subtract $\frac{1}{d_o}$ from both sides of the equation: $\frac{1}{f} - \frac{1}{d_o} = \frac{1}{d_i}$. Then, find a common denominator to combine the terms on the left-hand side of the equation: $\frac{d_o - f}{f d_o} = \frac{1}{d_i}$. Then, solve by taking the reciprocal of both sides: $\frac{f d_o}{d_o - f} = d_i$.

## Additional Topics in Math

Questions in this section will test geometric and trigonometric concepts and the Pythagorean Theorem. The student should be familiar with geometric concepts such as volume, radius, diameter, chord length, angle, arc, and sector area. The questions will give certain information about a figure and require the student to solve for some missing information. Any required volume formulas will be provided on the test. The trigonometry questions will require students to use trigonometric ratios and the Pythagorean Theorem to solve problems dealing with right triangles. The student should be able to use these ratios and the Pythagorean Theorem to solve for missing lengths and angle measures in right triangles.

## Volume formulas

The formula for a prism or a cylinder is $V = Bh$, where $B$ is the area of the base and $h$ is the height of the solid. For a cylinder, the area of the circular base is determined by the formula $B = \pi r^2$. For a prism, the area of the base depends on the shape of the base; for example, a triangular base would have area $\frac{1}{2}bh$, while a rectangular base would have area $bh$.

For a pyramid or cone, the volume is $V = \frac{1}{3}Bh$, where $B$ once again is the area of the base and $h$ is the height. In other words, the volume of a pyramid or cone is one-third the volume of a prism or cylinder with the same base and the same height.

## Pythagorean Theorem

The side of a triangle opposite the right angle is called the hypotenuse. The other two sides are called the legs. The Pythagorean Theorem states a relationship among the legs and hypotenuse of a right triangle: $a^2 + b^2 = c^2$, where $a$ and $b$ are the lengths of the legs of a right triangle, and $c$ is the length of the hypotenuse. Note that this formula will only work with right triangles.

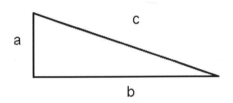

## Types of questions – volume formulas

You should expect to be asked questions concerning volumes of figures such as rectangular prisms and cylinders. You may be asked to use information such as length of a side, area of a face, or volume of a solid to calculate missing information. Area formulas for circles, rectangles, and triangles and volume formulas for rectangular prisms and cylinders are provided with the test. It is important to understand that the volume calculations may be more complicated than simply applying basic formulas. For example, you may be asked to find the volume of a hexagonal nut and given that the volume of a prism is $V = Bh$, where $B$ is the area of the base and $h$ is the height of the prism. Since you are not given the area formula for a regular hexagon, however, you must find the area by adding the areas of the six equilateral triangles which comprise the hexagon. Once you calculate the area of the base, you can find the volume of a hexagonal prism by multiplying the area of the base and the height; afterward, you must subtract the volume of the cylindrical hole from the volume of the hexagonal prism in order to find the volume of the hexagonal nut.

## Types of questions – applied problems with right triangles

You should expect questions requiring you to use the Pythagorean Theorem and trigonometric ratios to find missing side lengths and angles of right triangles. The Pythagorean Theorem as well as the 30°-60°-90° and 45°-45°-90° special right triangles are provided on the test. You should be able to recognize situations in which the Pythagorean Theorem, trigonometry, and special right triangles can be applied. For example, a square can be divided by a diagonal into two 45°-45°-90° triangles. An equilateral triangle can be divided by an altitude into two 30°-60°-90° right triangles. Hexagons can be divided into six equilateral triangles, each of which can be further divided into two 30°-60°-90° triangles. You need to be able to apply the special right triangles to given triangles. For example, if you are given a 45°-45°-90° triangle with a side length of 5 cm, you should be able to determine that the hypotenuse has a length of $5\sqrt{2}$ cm. If you are given a 30°-60°-90° triangle with a short leg of length 3 inches, you should be able to determine that the hypotenuse has a length of 6 inches.

## Trigonometric ratio sine for an acute angle using ratios of sides in similar right triangles

Similar triangles have three pairs of congruent angles and three pairs of proportional sides. The proportion has the same value for all pairs of sides, so $\frac{a}{d} = \frac{c}{f}$ or (using cross multiplication and division to reorganize) $\frac{a}{c} = \frac{d}{f}$. The trigonometric ratio sine is opposite over hypotenuse. In $\triangle ABC$, $\sin A = \frac{a}{c}$ and in $\triangle DEF$, $\sin D = \frac{d}{f}$. So since $\frac{a}{c} = \frac{d}{f}$, $\sin A = \sin D$. This shows that the trigonometric ratio sine is a property of the angle because the ratio is the same in both triangles even though the triangles are different sizes.

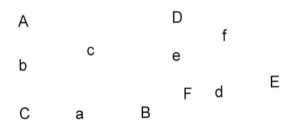

## Trigonometric ratio cosine for an acute angle using ratios of sides in similar right triangles

Similar triangles have three pairs of congruent angles and three pairs of proportional sides. The proportion has the same value for all pairs of sides, so $\frac{b}{e} = \frac{c}{f}$ or (using cross multiplication and division to reorganize) $\frac{b}{c} = \frac{e}{f}$. The trigonometric ratio cosine is adjacent over hypotenuse. In $\triangle ABC$, $\cos A = \frac{b}{c}$ and in $\triangle DEF$, $\cos D = \frac{e}{f}$. So since $\frac{b}{c} = \frac{e}{f}$, $\cos A = \cos D$. This shows that the trigonometric ratio cosine is a property of the angle because the ratio is the same in both triangles even though the triangles are different sizes.

## Trigonometric ratio tangent for an acute angle using ratios of sides in similar right triangles

Similar triangles have three pairs of congruent angles and three pairs of proportional sides. The proportion has the same value for all pairs of sides, so $\frac{a}{d} = \frac{b}{e}$ or (using cross multiplication and division to reorganize) $\frac{a}{b} = \frac{d}{e}$. The trigonometric ratio tangent is opposite over adjacent. In $\triangle ABC$, $\tan A = \frac{a}{b}$ and in $\triangle DEF$, $\tan D = \frac{d}{e}$. So since $\frac{a}{b} = \frac{d}{e}$, $\tan A = \tan D$. This shows that the trigonometric ratio tangent is a property of the angle because the ratio is the same in both triangles even though the triangles are different sizes.

## Complex numbers

Complex numbers consist of a real component and an imaginary component. Complex numbers are expressed in the form $a + bi$ with real component $a$ and imaginary component $bi$. The imaginary unit $i$ is equal to $\sqrt{-1}$. That means $i^2 = -1$. The imaginary unit provides a way to find the square root of a negative number. For example, $\sqrt{-25}$ is $5i$. You should expect questions asking you to add, subtract, multiply, divide, and simplify complex numbers. You may see a question that says, "Add $3 + 2i$ and $5 - 7i$" or "Subtract $4 + i\sqrt{5}$ from $2 + i\sqrt{5}$." Or you may see a question that says, "Multiply $6 + 2i$ by $8 - 4i$" or "Divide $1 - 3i$ by $9 - 7i$."

## Perform operations on complex numbers

Operations with complex numbers resemble operations with variables in algebra. Complex numbers are expressed in the form $a + bi$ with real component $a$ and imaginary component $bi$. When adding or subtracting complex numbers, you can only combine like terms − real terms with real terms and imaginary terms with imaginary terms. For example, if you are asked to simplify $-2 + 4i - (-3 + 7i) - 5i$, you should first remove the parentheses to yield $-2 + 4i + 3 - 7i - 5i$. Combining likes terms yields $1 - 8i$. One interesting aspect with imaginary number is that if $i$ has an exponent greater than 1, it can be simplified. For example, $i^2 = -1$, $i^3 = -i$, and $i^4 = 1$. When multiplying complex numbers, remember to simplify each $i$ with an exponent greater than 1. For example, you might see a question that says, "Simplify $(2-i)(3+2i)$." You need to distribute and multiply to get $6 + 4i - 3i - 2i^2$. This is further simplified to $6 + i - 2(-1)$, or $8 + i$.

## Simplifying with $i$ in the denominator

If an expression contains an $i$ in the denominator, it must be simplified. Remember, roots cannot be left in the denominator of a fraction. Since $i$ is equivalent to $\sqrt{-1}$, $i$ cannot be left in the denominator of a fraction. You must rationalize the denominator of a fraction that contains a complex denominator by multiplying the numerator and denominator by the conjugate of the denominator. The conjugate of the complex number $a + bi$ is $a - bi$. You can simplify $\frac{2}{5i}$ by simply multiplying $\frac{2}{5i} \cdot \frac{i}{i}$, which yields $-\frac{2}{5}i$. And you can simplify $\frac{5+3i}{2-4i}$ by multiplying $\frac{5+3i}{2-4i} \cdot \frac{2+4i}{2+4i}$. This yields $\frac{10+20i+6i-12}{4-8i+8i+16}$ which simplifies to $\frac{-2+26i}{20}$ or $\frac{-1+13i}{10}$, which can also be written as $-\frac{1}{10} + \frac{13}{10}i$.

## Converting between degrees and radians

To convert from degrees to radians, multiply by $\frac{\pi \text{ rad}}{180°}$. For example $60° \cdot \frac{\pi \text{ rad}}{180°}$ is $\frac{\pi}{3}$ radians. To convert from radians to degrees, multiply by $\frac{180°}{\pi \text{ rad}}$. For example, $\frac{\pi}{4}$ radians $\frac{180°}{\pi \text{ rad}}$ is 45°. The equation to determine are length is $s = r\theta$, in which $s$ is the arc length, $r$ is the radius of the circle, and $\theta$ is the angular displacement or the angle subtended in radians. For example, if you are asked to find the length of the arc that subtends a 60° central angle in a circle with a radius of 10 cm, you would solve $s = (10 \text{ cm})(60°)\left(\frac{\pi \, rad}{180°}\right)$ to obtain an arc length in centimeters. You also need to be able to evaluate trigonometric functions of angles in radian measure without your calculator. You may see a question that involves finding the $\sin x$ in which $\frac{\pi}{2} < x < \pi$. It is important to be able recognize given intervals which indicate angle-containing quadrants, which are bound by $0$, $\frac{\pi}{2}$, $\pi$, $\frac{3\pi}{2}$, and $2\pi$. The statement "all students take calculus" or ASTC can help you to remember the signs of $\sin x$, $\cos x$, and $\tan x$ for an angle measuring $x°$ or $x$ radians. In Quadrant I, the values of $\sin x$, $\cos x$, and $\tan x$ are all positive. In Quadrant II, only $\underline{\sin x}$ is positive. In Quadrant III, only $\underline{\tan x}$ is positive. In Quadrant IV, only $\underline{\cos x}$ is positive.

## Area of a sector of a circle and arc length of a sector of a circle

The area of a sector of a circle is found by the formula, $A = \frac{\theta r^2}{2}$, where A is the area, $\theta$ is the measure of the central angle in radians, and r is the radius. To find the area when the central angle is in degrees, use the formula, $A = \theta \pi r^2$, where $\theta$ is the measure of the central angle in degrees and r is the radius. The arc length of a sector of a circle is found by the formula: arc length=$r\theta$, where r is the radius and $\theta$ is the measure of the central angle in radians. To find the arc length when the central angle is given in degrees, use the formula: arc length=$\theta 2\pi r$, where $\theta$ is the measure of the central angle in degrees and r is the radius.

## Circles

The center is the single point inside the circle that is equidistant from every point on the circle. (Point O in the diagram below.)

The radius is a line segment that joins the center of the circle and any one point on the circle. All radii of a circle are equal. (Segments OX, OY, and OZ in the diagram below.)

The diameter is a line segment that passes through the center of the circle and has both endpoints on the circle. The length of the diameter is exactly twice the length of the radius. (Segment *XZ* in the diagram below.)

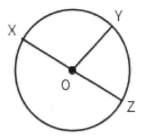

The area of a circle is found by the formula $A = \pi r^2$, where *r* is the length of the radius. If the diameter of the circle is given, remember to divide it in half to get the length of the radius before proceeding.

The circumference of a circle is found by the formula $C = 2\pi r$, where *r* is the radius. Again, remember to convert the diameter if you are given that measure rather than the radius.

Concentric circles are circles that have the same center, but not the same length of radii. A bulls-eye target is an example of concentric circles.

An arc is a portion of a circle. Specifically, an arc is the set of points between and including two points on a circle. An arc does not contain any points inside the circle. When a segment is drawn from the endpoints of an arc to the center of the circle, a sector is formed.

A central angle is an angle whose vertex is the center of a circle and whose legs intercept an arc of the circle. Angle *XOY* in the diagram above is a central angle. A minor arc is an arc that has a measure less than 180°. The measure of a central angle is equal to the measure of the minor arc it intercepts. A major arc is an arc having a measure of at least 180°. The measure of the major arc can be found by subtracting the measure of the central angle from 360°.

A semicircle is an arc whose endpoints are the endpoints of the diameter of a circle. A semicircle is exactly half of a circle.

An inscribed angle is an angle whose vertex lies on a circle and whose legs contain chords of that circle. The portion of the circle intercepted by the legs of the angle is called the intercepted arc. The measure of the intercepted arc is exactly twice the measure of the inscribed angle. In the following diagram, angle *ABC* is an inscribed angle. $\overarc{AC} = 2(m\angle ABC)$

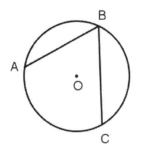

Any angle inscribed in a semicircle is a right angle. The intercepted arc is 180°, making the inscribed angle half that, or 90°. In the diagram below, angle *ABC* is inscribed in semicircle *ABC*, making angle *ABC* equal to 90°.

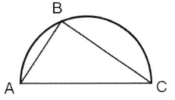

A chord is a line segment that has both endpoints on a circle. In the diagram below, $\overline{EB}$ is a chord.

Secant: A line that passes through a circle and contains a chord of that circle. In the diagram below, $\overleftrightarrow{EB}$ is a secant and contains chord $\overline{EB}$.

A tangent is a line in the same plane as a circle that touches the circle in exactly one point. While a line segment can be tangent to a circle as part of a line that is tangent, it is improper to say a tangent can be simply a line segment that touches the circle in exactly one point. In the diagram below, $\overleftrightarrow{CD}$ is tangent to circle *A*. Notice that $\overrightarrow{FB}$ is not tangent to the circle. $\overline{FB}$ is a line segment that touches the circle in exactly one point, but if the segment were extended, it would touch the circle in a second point. The point at which a tangent touches a circle is called the point of tangency. In the diagram below, point *B* is the point of tangency.

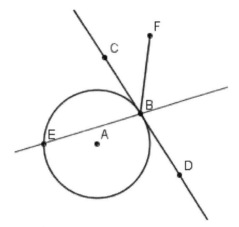

A secant is a line that intersects a circle in two points. Two secants may intersect inside the circle, on the circle, or outside the circle. When the two secants intersect on the circle, an inscribed angle is formed.

When two secants intersect inside a circle, the measure of each of two vertical angles is equal to half the sum of the two intercepted arcs. In the diagram below, $m\angle AEB = \frac{1}{2}(\widehat{AB} + \widehat{CD})$ and $m\angle BEC = \frac{1}{2}(\widehat{BC} + \widehat{AD})$.

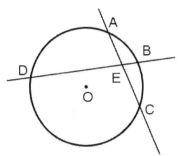

When two secants intersect outside a circle, the measure of the angle formed is equal to half the difference of the two arcs that lie between the two secants. In the diagram below, $m\angle E = \frac{1}{2}(\widehat{AB} - \widehat{CD})$.

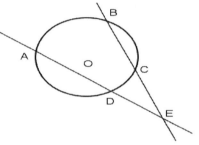

The arc length is the length of that portion of the circumference between two points on the circle. The formula for arc length is $s = \frac{\pi r \theta}{180°}$ where $s$ is the arc length, $r$ is the length of the radius, and $\theta$ is the angular measure of the arc in degrees, or $s = r\theta$, where $\theta$ is the angular measure of the arc in radians ($2\pi$ radians $= 360$ degrees).

A sector is the portion of a circle formed by two radii and their intercepted arc. While the arc length is exclusively the points that are also on the circumference of the circle, the sector is the entire area bounded by the arc and the two radii.

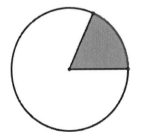

The area of a sector of a circle is found by the formula, $A = \frac{\theta r^2}{2}$, where $A$ is the area, $\theta$ is the measure of the central angle in radians, and $r$ is the radius. To find the area when the central angle is in degrees, use the formula, $A = \frac{\theta \pi r^2}{360}$, where $\theta$ is the measure of the central angle in degrees and $r$ is the radius.

Formulas for circles
One formula for arc length is $s = r\theta$, in which $s$ is the arc length, $r$ is the radius of the circle, and $\theta$ is the angular displacement or the angle subtended in radians. Another formula for arc length involving the circumference is given by $C$ is $\frac{s}{C} = \frac{\theta}{360°}$ when central angle $\theta$ is measured in degrees or $\frac{s}{C} = \frac{\theta}{2\pi}$ when $\theta$ is measured in radians. These formulas can be rearranged to solve for $s$, $C$, or $\theta$; of course, if you know a circle's circumference, you can also determine its diameter $d$ or radius $r$ using the formula $C = \pi d$ or $C = 2\pi r$. The area of a sector is given by $\frac{A_{Sector}}{A_{Circle}} = \frac{\theta}{360°}$ when $\theta$ is measured in degrees or $\frac{A_{Sector}}{A_{Circle}} = \frac{\theta}{2\pi}$ when $\theta$ is measured in radians. Chord lengths are often found by drawing the perpendicular bisector of the chord through the center of the circle and then drawing line segments from the center of the circle to each of the chord's endpoints. This forms two congruent right triangles. The length of the chord can be found using a trigonometric function or the Pythagorean Theorem. On some questions, you may be expected to combine your knowledge of circles with your knowledge of other geometric concepts, such as properties of parallel lines. The formulas for the area and circumference of a circle and the Pythagorean Theorem are provided with the test.

Similarity and Congruence Rules
Similar triangles are triangles whose corresponding angles are equal and whose corresponding sides are proportional. Represented by AA. Similar triangles whose corresponding sides are congruent are also congruent triangles.

Three sides of one triangle are congruent to the three corresponding sides of the second triangle. Represented as SSS.

Two sides and the included angle (the angle formed by those two sides) of one triangle are congruent to the corresponding two sides and included angle of the second triangle. Represented by SAS.

Two angles and the included side (the side that joins the two angles) of one triangle are congruent to the corresponding two angles and included side of the second triangle. Represented by ASA.

Two angles and a non-included side of one triangle are congruent to the corresponding two angles and non-included side of the second triangle. Represented by AAS.

Note that AAA is not a form for congruent triangles. This would say that the three angles are congruent, but says nothing about the sides. This meets the requirements for similar triangles, but not congruent triangles.

Solving problems with similarity and congruence
Congruent figures have the same size and same shape. Similar figures have the same shape but not the same size; their corresponding angles are congruent and their sides are proportional. All circles are similar. All squares are similar; likewise, all regular n-gons are similar to other regular n-gons. These concepts may appear in different types of test questions. For example, if a line is drawn through that triangle such that it is parallel to one side, a triangle similar to the original triangle is formed. The corresponding angles are congruent, and proportional relationships can be used to determine missing side lengths from the given information. Also, if parallel lines are cut by

two transversals which intersect between or outside of parallel lines, two similar triangles are formed. If an altitude is drawn from the vertex of an isosceles triangle, two congruent triangles are formed. If an altitude is drawn from the vertex of the right angle to the hypotenuse of a right triangle, the two triangles that are formed are similar to each other and to the original right triangle.

<u>Relationship between similarity, right triangles, and trigonometric ratios</u>
An interesting relationship exists between similarity, right triangles, and the trigonometric ratios. If a line that is parallel to one of the legs of a right triangle is drawn through the right triangle, a right triangle is formed which is similar to the original triangle since the triangles share one acute angle and both contain a right angle. Therefore, the trigonometric ratios of similar right triangles are equal.

Complementary angles have a sum of 90°. The acute angles in a right triangle are complementary. In a right triangle, the sine of one of the acute angles equals the cosine of the other acute angle.

If an altitude is drawn from the vertex of the right angle to the hypotenuse of a right triangle as shown, the two triangles that are formed are similar to each other and to the original right triangle: $\Delta ACH \sim \Delta CBH$, $\Delta ACH \sim \Delta ABC$, and $\Delta CBH \sim \Delta ABC$.

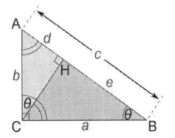

<u>Equation of a circle</u>
A circle with radius $r$ centered at the origin on the coordinate plane can be represented by the equation $x^2 + y^2 = r^2$. A circle with radius $r$ and center $(h, k)$ is represented by the equation $(x-h)^2 + (y-k)^2 = r^2$. For example, a circle at the origin with a radius of 5 units is represented by the equation $x^2 + y^2 = 25$. If this circle is shifted three units right and two units down, the translated circle is represented by the equation $(x-3)^2 + (y+2)^2 = 25$.

<u>Integrating information from a circle into more complex questions</u>
A single question on this test may require knowledge of multiple geometric concepts. You may see a question about concentric circles or two intersecting circles; you might need to use information given about one circle to find information about the other. A question may provide the points of intersection of a line and a circle, and you may be asked to write and solve the system of equations, which would include both an equation for the line and an equation for the circle. You may be asked to convert between polar coordinates $(r, \theta)$ and rectangular (or Cartesian) coordinates $(x, y)$. The relationship between polar and rectangular coordinates is shown below.

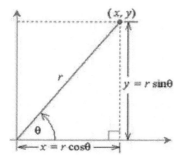

<u>Angles</u>
An angle is formed when two lines or line segments meet at a common point. It may be a common starting point for a pair of segments or rays, or it may be the intersection of lines. Angles are represented by the symbol $\angle$.

The vertex is the point at which two segments or rays meet to form an angle. If the angle is formed by intersecting rays, lines, and/or line segments, the vertex is the point at which four angles are formed. The pairs of angles opposite one another are called vertical angles, and their measures are equal.

An acute angle is an angle with a degree measure less than 90°.
A right angle is an angle with a degree measure of exactly 90°.
An obtuse angle is an angle with a degree measure greater than 90° but less than 180°.
A straight angle is an angle with a degree measure of exactly 180°. This is also a semicircle.
A reflex angle is an angle with a degree measure greater than 180° but less than 360°.
A full angle is an angle with a degree measure of exactly 360°.

Two angles whose sum is exactly 90° are said to be complementary. The two angles may or may not be adjacent. In a right triangle, the two acute angles are complementary.

Two angles whose sum is exactly 180° are said to be supplementary. The two angles may or may not be adjacent. Two intersecting lines always form two pairs of supplementary angles. Adjacent supplementary angles will always form a straight line.

Two angles that have the same vertex and share a side are said to be adjacent. Vertical angles are not adjacent because they share a vertex but no common side.

**Adjacent**
**Share vertex and side**

**Not adjacent**
**Share part of side, but not vertex**

When two parallel lines are cut by a transversal, the angles that are between the two parallel lines are interior angles. In the diagram below, angles 3, 4, 5, and 6 are interior angles.

When two parallel lines are cut by a transversal, the angles that are outside the parallel lines are exterior angles. In the diagram below, angles 1, 2, 7, and 8 are exterior angles.

When two parallel lines are cut by a transversal, the angles that are in the same position relative to the transversal and a parallel line are corresponding angles. The diagram below has four pairs of corresponding angles: angles 1 and 5; angles 2 and 6; angles 3 and 7; and angles 4 and 8. Corresponding angles formed by parallel lines are congruent.

When two parallel lines are cut by a transversal, the two interior angles that are on opposite sides of the transversal are called alternate interior angles. In the diagram below, there are two pairs of alternate interior angles: angles 3 and 6, and angles 4 and 5. Alternate interior angles formed by parallel lines are congruent.

When two parallel lines are cut by a transversal, the two exterior angles that are on opposite sides of the transversal are called alternate exterior angles.

In the diagram below, there are two pairs of alternate exterior angles: angles 1 and 8, and angles 2 and 7. Alternate exterior angles formed by parallel lines are congruent.

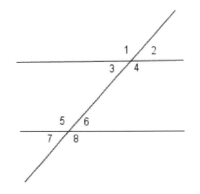

When two lines intersect, four angles are formed. The non-adjacent angles at this vertex are called vertical angles. Vertical angles are congruent. In the diagram, $\angle ABD \cong \angle CBE$ and $\angle ABC \cong \angle DBE$.

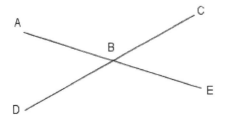

98

## Triangles

An equilateral triangle is a triangle with three congruent sides. An equilateral triangle will also have three congruent angles, each 60°. All equilateral triangles are also acute triangles.

An isosceles triangle is a triangle with two congruent sides. An isosceles triangle will also have two congruent angles opposite the two congruent sides.

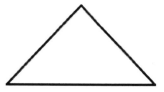

A scalene triangle is a triangle with no congruent sides. A scalene triangle will also have three angles of different measures. The angle with the largest measure is opposite the longest side, and the angle with the smallest measure is opposite the shortest side.

An acute triangle is a triangle whose three angles are all less than 90°. If two of the angles are equal, the acute triangle is also an isosceles triangle. If the three angles are all equal, the acute triangle is also an equilateral triangle.

A right triangle is a triangle with exactly one angle equal to 90°. All right triangles follow the Pythagorean Theorem. A right triangle can never be acute or obtuse.

An obtuse triangle is a triangle with exactly one angle greater than 90°. The other two angles may or may not be equal. If the two remaining angles are equal, the obtuse triangle is also an isosceles triangle.

<u>Terminology</u>
Altitude of a Triangle: A line segment drawn from one vertex perpendicular to the opposite side. In the diagram below, $\overline{BE}$, $\overline{AD}$, and $\overline{CF}$ are altitudes. The three altitudes in a triangle are always concurrent.

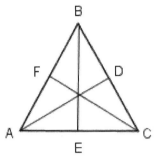

Height of a Triangle: The length of the altitude, although the two terms are often used interchangeably.

Orthocenter of a Triangle: The point of concurrency of the altitudes of a triangle. Note that in an obtuse triangle, the orthocenter will be outside the circle, and in a right triangle, the orthocenter is the vertex of the right angle.

Median of a Triangle: A line segment drawn from one vertex to the midpoint of the opposite side. This is not the same as the altitude, except the altitude to the base of an isosceles triangle and all three altitudes of an equilateral triangle.

Centroid of a Triangle: The point of concurrency of the medians of a triangle. This is the same point as the orthocenter only in an equilateral triangle. Unlike the orthocenter, the centroid is always inside the triangle. The centroid can also be considered the exact center of the triangle. Any shape triangle can be perfectly balanced on a tip placed at the centroid. The centroid is also the point that is two-thirds the distance from the vertex to the opposite side.

# Other Useful Math Concepts

## Numbers and Operations

Numbers are the basic building blocks of mathematics. Specific features of numbers are identified by the following terms:
- Integers – The set of whole positive and negative numbers, including zero. Integers do not include fractions ($\frac{1}{3}$), decimals (0.56), or mixed numbers ($7\frac{3}{4}$).
- Prime number – A whole number greater than 1 that has only two factors, itself and 1; that is, a number that can be divided evenly only by 1 and itself.
- Composite number – A whole number greater than 1 that has more than two different factors; in other words, any whole number that is not a prime number. For example: The composite number 8 has the factors of 1, 2, 4, and 8.
- Even number – Any integer that can be divided by 2 without leaving a remainder. For example: 2, 4, 6, 8, and so on.
- Odd number – Any integer that cannot be divided evenly by 2. For example: 3, 5, 7, 9, and so on.
- Decimal number – a number that uses a decimal point to show the part of the number that is less than one. Example: 1.234.
- Decimal point – a symbol used to separate the ones place from the tenths place in decimals or dollars from cents in currency.

- Decimal place – the position of a number to the right of the decimal point. In the decimal 0.123, the 1 is in the first place to the right of the decimal point, indicating tenths; the 2 is in the second place, indicating hundredths; and the 3 is in the third place, indicating thousandths.

The decimal, or base 10, system is a number system that uses ten different digits $(0, 1, 2, 3, 4, 5, 6, 7, 8, 9)$. An example of a number system that uses something other than ten digits is the binary, or base 2, number system, used by computers, which uses only the numbers 0 and 1. It is thought that the decimal system originated because people had only their 10 fingers for counting.

Rational, irrational, and real numbers can be described as follows:
- Rational numbers include all integers, decimals, and fractions. Any terminating or repeating decimal number is a rational number.
- Irrational numbers cannot be written as fractions or decimals because the number of decimal places is infinite and there is no recurring pattern of digits within the number. For example, pi ($\pi$) begins with 3.141592 and continues without terminating or repeating, so pi is an irrational number.
- Real numbers are the set of all rational and irrational numbers.

**Operations**

There are four basic mathematical operations:
- Addition increases the value of one quantity by the value of another quantity. Example: $2 + 4 = 6; 8 + 9 = 17$. The result is called the sum. With addition, the order does not matter. $4 + 2 = 2 + 4$.
- Subtraction is the opposite operation to addition; it decreases the value of one quantity by the value of another quantity. Example: $6 - 4 = 2; 17 - 8 = 9$. The result is called the difference. Note that with subtraction, the order does matter. $6 - 4 \neq 4 - 6$.
- Multiplication can be thought of as repeated addition. One number tells how many times to add the other number to itself. Example: $3 \times 2$ (three times two) $= 2 + 2 + 2 = 6$. With multiplication, the order does not matter. $2 \times 3 = 3 \times 2$ or $3 + 3 = 2 + 2 + 2$.
- Division is the opposite operation to multiplication; one number tells us how many parts to divide the other number into. Example: $20 \div 4 = 5$; if 20 is split into 4 equal parts, each part is 5. With division, the order of the numbers does matter. $20 \div 4 \neq 4 \div 20$.

An exponent is a superscript number placed next to another number at the top right. It indicates how many times the base number is to be multiplied by itself. Exponents provide a shorthand way to write what would be a longer mathematical expression. Example: $a^2 = a \times a$; $2^4 = 2 \times 2 \times 2 \times 2$. A number with an exponent of 2 is said to be "squared," while a number with an exponent of 3 is said to be "cubed." The value of a number raised to an exponent is called its power. So, $8^4$ is read as "8 to the 4th power," or "8 raised to the power of 4." A negative exponent is the same as the reciprocal of a positive exponent. Example: $a^{-2} = \frac{1}{a^2}$.

Parentheses are used to designate which operations should be done first when there are multiple operations. Example: 4 – (2 + 1) = 1; the parentheses tell us that we must add 2 and 1, and then subtract the sum from 4, rather than subtracting 2 from 4 and then adding 1 (this would give us an answer of 3).

Order of Operations is a set of rules that dictates the order in which we must perform each operation in an expression so that we will evaluate at accurately. If we have an expression that includes multiple different operations, Order of Operations tells us which operations to do first. The most common mnemonic for Order of Operations is PEMDAS, or "Please Excuse My Dear Aunt Sally." PEMDAS stands for Parentheses, Exponents, Multiplication, Division, Addition, Subtraction. It is important to understand that multiplication and division have equal precedence, as do addition and subtraction, so those pairs of operations are simply worked from left to right in order.

Example: Evaluate the expression $5 + 20 \div 4 \times (2 + 3)^2 - 6$ using the correct order of operations.
P: Perform the operations inside the parentheses, $(2 + 3) = 5$.
E: Simplify the exponents, $(5)^2 = 25$.
The equation now looks like this: $5 + 20 \div 4 \times 25 - 6$.
MD: Perform multiplication and division from left to right, $20 \div 4 = 5$; then $5 \times 25 = 125$.
The equation now looks like this: $5 + 125 - 6$.
AS: Perform addition and subtraction from left to right, $5 + 125 = 130$; then $130 - 6 = 124$.

The laws of exponents are as follows:
1) Any number to the power of 1 is equal to itself: $a^1 = a$.
2) The number 1 raised to any power is equal to 1: $1^n = 1$.
3) Any number raised to the power of 0 is equal to 1: $a^0 = 1$.
4) Add exponents to multiply powers of the same base number: $a^n \times a^m = a^{n+m}$.
5) Subtract exponents to divide powers of the same number; that is $a^n \div a^m = a^{n-m}$.
6) Multiply exponents to raise a power to a power: $(a^n)^m = a^{n \times m}$.
7) If multiplied or divided numbers inside parentheses are collectively raised to a power, this is the same as each individual term being raised to that power:
$(a \times b)^n = a^n \times b^n$; $(a \div b)^n = a^n \div b^n$.

Note: Exponents do not have to be integers. Fractional or decimal exponents follow all the rules above as well. Example: $5^{\frac{1}{4}} \times 5^{\frac{3}{4}} = 5^{\frac{1}{4}+\frac{3}{4}} = 5^1 = 5$.

A root, such as a square root, is another way of writing a fractional exponent. Instead of using a superscript, roots use the radical symbol ($\sqrt{\phantom{a}}$) to indicate the operation. A radical will have a number underneath the bar, and may sometimes have a number in the upper left: $\sqrt[n]{a}$, read as "the $n^{\text{th}}$ root of $a$." The relationship between radical notation and exponent notation can be described by this equation: $\sqrt[n]{a} = a^{\frac{1}{n}}$. The two special cases of $n$ = 2 and $n$ = 3 are called square roots and cube roots. If there is no number to the upper left, it is understood to be a square root ($n$ = 2). Nearly all of the roots you encounter will be square roots. A square root is the same as a number raised to the one-half power. When we say that $a$ is the square root of $b$ ($a = \sqrt{b}$), we mean that $a$ multiplied by itself equals $b$: ($a \times a = b$).

A perfect square is a number that has an integer for its square root. There are 10 perfect squares from 1 to 100: 1, 4, 9, 16, 25, 36, 49, 64, 81, 100 (the squares of integers 1 through 10).

Scientific notation is a way of writing large numbers in a shorter form. The form $a \times 10^n$ is used in scientific notation, where $a$ is greater than or equal to 1, but less than 10, and $n$ is the number of places the decimal must move to get from the original number to $a$.

Example: The number 230,400,000 is cumbersome to write. To write the value in scientific notation, place a decimal point between the first and second numbers, and include all digits through the last non-zero digit ($a$ = 2.304). To find the appropriate power of 10, count the number of places the decimal point had to move ($n$ = 8). The number is positive if the decimal moved to the left, and negative if it moved to the right. We can then write 230,400,000 as $2.304 \times 10^8$. If we look instead at the number 0.00002304, we have the same value for $a$, but this time the decimal moved 5 places to the right ($n = -5$). Thus, 0.00002304 can be written as $2.304 \times 10^{-5}$. Using this notation makes it simple to compare very large or very small numbers. By comparing exponents, it is easy to see that $3.28 \times 10^4$ is smaller than $1.51 \times 10^5$, because 4 is less than 5.

## Positive and Negative Numbers

A precursor to working with negative numbers is understanding what absolute values are. A number's *Absolute Value* is simply the distance away from zero a number is on the number line. The absolute value of a number is always positive and is written $|x|$.

When adding signed numbers, if the signs are the same simply add the absolute values of the addends and apply the original sign to the sum. For example, $(+4) + (+8) = +12$ and $(-4) + (-8) = -12$. When the original signs are different, take the absolute values of the addends and subtract the smaller value from the larger value, then apply the original sign of the larger value to the difference. For instance, $(+4) + (-8) = -4$ and $(-4) + (+8) = +4$.

For subtracting signed numbers, change the sign of the number after the minus symbol and then follow the same rules used for addition. For example, $(+4) - (+8) = (+4) + (-8) = -4$.

If the signs are the same the product is positive when multiplying signed numbers. For example, $(+4) \times (+8) = +32$ and $(-4) \times (-8) = +32$. If the signs are opposite, the product is negative. For example, $(+4) \times (-8) = -32$ and $(-4) \times (+8) = -32$. When more than two factors are multiplied together, the sign of the product is determined by how many negative factors are present. If there are an odd number of negative factors then the product is negative, whereas an even number of negative factors indicates a positive product. For instance, $(+4) \times (-8) \times (-2) = +64$ and $(-4) \times (-8) \times (-2) = -64$.

The rules for dividing signed numbers are similar to multiplying signed numbers. If the dividend and divisor have the same sign, the quotient is positive. If the dividend and divisor have opposite signs, the quotient is negative. For example, $(-4) \div (+8) = -0.5$.

## Factors and Multiples

Factors are numbers that are multiplied together to obtain a product. For example, in the equation $2 \times 3 = 6$, the numbers 2 and 3 are factors. A prime number has only two factors (1 and itself), but other numbers can have many factors.

A common factor is a number that divides exactly into two or more other numbers. For example, the factors of 12 are 1, 2, 3, 4, 6, and 12, while the factors of 15 are 1, 3, 5, and 15. The common factors of 12 and 15 are 1 and 3.

A prime factor is also a prime number. Therefore, the prime factors of 12 are 2 and 3. For 15, the prime factors are 3 and 5.

The greatest common factor (GCF) is the largest number that is a factor of two or more numbers. For example, the factors of 15 are 1, 3, 5, and 15; the factors of 35 are 1, 5, 7, and 35. Therefore, the greatest common factor of 15 and 35 is 5.

The least common multiple (LCM) is the smallest number that is a multiple of two or more numbers. For example, the multiples of 3 include 3, 6, 9, 12, 15, etc.; the multiples of 5 include 5, 10, 15, 20, etc. Therefore, the least common multiple of 3 and 5 is 15.

## Fractions, Percentages, and Related Concepts

A fraction is a number that is expressed as one integer written above another integer, with a dividing line between them ($\frac{x}{y}$). It represents the quotient of the two numbers "x divided by y." It can also be thought of as x out of y equal parts.

The top number of a fraction is called the numerator, and it represents the number of parts under consideration. The 1 in $\frac{1}{4}$ means that 1 part out of the whole is being considered in the calculation. The bottom number of a fraction is called the denominator, and it represents the total number of equal parts. The 4 in $\frac{1}{4}$ means that the whole consists of 4 equal parts. A fraction cannot have a denominator of zero; this is referred to as "undefined."

Fractions can be manipulated, without changing the value of the fraction, by multiplying or dividing (but not adding or subtracting) both the numerator and denominator by the same number. If you divide both numbers by a common factor, you are reducing or simplifying the fraction. Two fractions that have the same value, but are expressed differently are known as equivalent fractions. For example, $\frac{2}{10}, \frac{3}{15}, \frac{4}{20}$, and $\frac{5}{25}$ are all equivalent fractions. They can also all be reduced or simplified to $\frac{1}{5}$.

When two fractions are manipulated so that they have the same denominator, this is known as finding a common denominator. The number chosen to be that common denominator should be the least common multiple of the two original denominators. Example: $\frac{3}{4}$ and $\frac{5}{6}$; the least common multiple of 4 and 6 is 12. Manipulating to achieve the common denominator: $\frac{3}{4} = \frac{9}{12}; \frac{5}{6} = \frac{10}{12}$.

If two fractions have a common denominator, they can be added or subtracted simply by adding or subtracting the two numerators and retaining the same denominator. Example: $\frac{1}{2} + \frac{1}{4} = \frac{2}{4} + \frac{1}{4} = \frac{3}{4}$. If the two fractions do not already have the same denominator, one or both of them must be manipulated to achieve a common denominator before they can be added or subtracted.

Two fractions can be multiplied by multiplying the two numerators to find the new numerator and the two denominators to find the new denominator. Example: $\frac{1}{3} \times \frac{2}{3} = \frac{1 \times 2}{3 \times 3} = \frac{2}{9}$.

Two fractions can be divided flipping the numerator and denominator of the second fraction and then proceeding as though it were a multiplication. Example: $\frac{2}{3} \div \frac{3}{4} = \frac{2}{3} \times \frac{4}{3} = \frac{8}{9}$.

A fraction whose denominator is greater than its numerator is known as a proper fraction, while a fraction whose numerator is greater than its denominator is known as an improper fraction. Proper fractions have values less than one and improper fractions have values greater than one.

A mixed number is a number that contains both an integer and a fraction. Any improper fraction can be rewritten as a mixed number. Example: $\frac{8}{3} = \frac{6}{3} + \frac{2}{3} = 2 + \frac{2}{3} = 2\frac{2}{3}$. Similarly, any mixed number can be rewritten as an improper fraction. Example: $1\frac{3}{5} = 1 + \frac{3}{5} = \frac{5}{5} + \frac{3}{5} = \frac{8}{5}$.

Percentages can be thought of as fractions that are based on a whole of 100; that is, one whole is equal to 100%. The word percent means "per hundred." Fractions can be expressed as percents by finding equivalent fractions with a denomination of 100. Example: $\frac{7}{10} = \frac{70}{100} = 70\%; \frac{1}{4} = \frac{25}{100} = 25\%$. To express a percentage as a fraction, divide the percentage number by 100 and reduce the fraction to its simplest possible terms. Example: $60\% = \frac{60}{100} = \frac{3}{5}; 96\% = \frac{96}{100} = \frac{24}{25}$.

Converting decimals to percentages and percentages to decimals is as simple as moving the decimal point. To convert from a decimal to a percent, move the decimal point two places to the right. To convert from a percent to a decimal, move it two places to the left. Example: 0.23 = 23%; 5.34 = 534%; 0.007 = 0.7%; 700% = 7.00; 86% = 0.86; 0.15% = 0.0015. It may be helpful to remember that the percentage number will always be larger than the equivalent decimal number.

A percentage problem can be presented three main ways: (1) Find what percentage of some number another number is. Example: What percentage of 40 is 8? (2) Find what number is some percentage of a given number. Example: What number is 20% of 40? (3) Find what number another number is a given percentage of. Example: What number is 8 20% of? The three components in all of these cases are the same: a whole (W), a part (P), and a percentage (%). These are related by the equation: $P = W \times \%$. This is the form of the equation you would use to solve problems of type (2). To solve types (1) and (3), you would use these two forms: $\% = \frac{P}{W}$ and $W = \frac{P}{\%}$.

The thing that frequently makes percentage problems difficult is that they are most often also word problems, so a large part of solving them is figuring out which quantities are what. Example: In a school cafeteria, 7 students choose pizza, 9 choose hamburgers, and 4 choose tacos. Find the percentage that chooses tacos. To find the whole, you must first add all of the parts: 7 + 9 + 4 = 20. The percentage can then be found by dividing the part by the whole ($\% = \frac{P}{W}$): $\frac{4}{20} = \frac{20}{100} = 20\%$.

A ratio is a comparison of two quantities in a particular order. Example: If there are 14 computers in a lab, and the class has 20 students, there is a student to computer ratio of 20 to 14, commonly written as 20:14. Ratios are normally reduced to their smallest whole number representation, so 20:14 would be reduced to 10:7 by dividing both sides by 2.

A proportion is a relationship between two quantities that dictates how one changes when the other changes. A direct proportion describes a relationship in which a quantity increases by a set amount for every increase in the other quantity, or decreases by that same amount for every decrease in the other quantity. Example: Assuming a constant driving speed, the time required for a car trip increases as the distance of the trip increases. The distance to be traveled and the time required to travel are directly proportional.

Inverse proportion is a relationship in which an increase in one quantity is accompanied by a decrease in the other, or vice versa. Example: the time required for a car trip decreases as the speed increases, and increases as the speed decreases, so the time required is inversely proportional to the speed of the car.

## Algebra, Functions, and Graphs

### Polynomial Algebra

To multiply two binomials, follow the *FOIL* method. FOIL stands for:
- First: Multiply the first term of each binomial
- Outer: Multiply the outer terms of each binomial
- Inner: Multiply the inner terms of each binomial
- Last: Multiply the last term of each binomial

Using FOIL $(Ax + By)(Cx + Dy) = ACx^2 + ADxy + BCxy + BDy^2$.

### Equations and Graphing

When algebraic functions and equations are shown graphically, they are usually shown on a *Cartesian Coordinate Plane*. The Cartesian coordinate plane consists of two number lines placed perpendicular to each other, and intersecting at the zero point, also known as the origin. The horizontal number line is known as the *x*-axis, with positive values to the right of the origin, and negative values to the left of the origin. The vertical number line is known as the *y*-axis, with positive values above the origin, and negative values below the origin. Any point on the plane can be identified by an ordered pair in the form $(x, y)$, called coordinates. The x-value of the coordinate is called the abscissa, and the y-value of the coordinate is called the ordinate. The two number lines divide the plane into four quadrants: I, II, III, and IV.

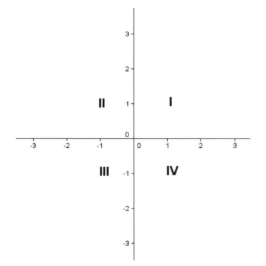

Before learning the different forms equations can be written in, it is important to understand some terminology. A ratio of the change in the vertical distance to the change in horizontal distance is called the *Slope*. On a graph with two points, $(x_1, y_1)$ and $(x_2, y_2)$, the slope is represented by the formula $= \frac{y_2 - y_1}{x_2 - x_1}$; $x_1 \neq x_2$. If the value of the slope is posfitive, the line slopes upward from left to right. If the value of the slope is negative, the line slopes downward from left to right. If the y-coordinates are the same for both points, the slope is 0 and the line is a *Horizontal Line*. If the x-coordinates are the same for both points, there is no slope and the line is a *Vertical Line*. Two or more lines that have equal slopes are *Parallel Lines*. *Perpendicular Lines* have slopes that are negative reciprocals of each other, such as $\frac{a}{b}$ and $\frac{-b}{a}$.

Equations are made up of monomials and polynomials. A *Monomial* is a single variable or product of constants and variables, such as $x$, $2x$, or $\frac{2}{x}$. There will never be addition or subtraction symbols in a monomial. Like monomials have like variables, but they may have different coefficients. *Polynomials* are algebraic expressions which use addition and subtraction to combine two or more monomials. Two terms make a binomial; three terms make a trinomial; etc.. The *Degree of a Monomial* is the sum of the exponents of the variables. The *Degree of a Polynomial* is the highest degree of any individual term.

As mentioned previously, equations can be written many ways. Below is a list of the many forms equations can take.
- *Standard Form*: $Ax + By = C$; the slope is $\frac{-A}{B}$ and the y-intercept is $\frac{C}{B}$
- *Slope Intercept Form*: $y = mx + b$, where $m$ is the slope and $b$ is the y-intercept
- *Point-Slope Form*: $y - y_1 = m(x - x_1)$, where $m$ is the slope and $(x_1, y_1)$ is a point on the line
- *Two-Point Form*: $\frac{y - y_1}{x - x_1} = \frac{y_2 - y_1}{x_2 - x_1}$, where $(x_1, y_1)$ and $(x_2, y_2)$ are two points on the given line
- *Intercept Form*: $\frac{x}{x_1} + \frac{y}{y_1} = 1$, where $(x_1, 0)$ is the point at which a line intersects the x-axis, and $(0, y_1)$ is the point at which the same line intersects the y-axis

Equations can also be written as $ax + b = 0$, where $a \neq 0$. These are referred to as *One Variable Linear Equations*. A solution to such an equation is called a *Root*. In the case where we have the equation $5x + 10 = 0$, if we solve for $x$ we get a solution of $x = -2$. In other words, the root of the equation is -2. This is found by first subtracting 10 from both sides, which gives $5x = -10$. Next, simply divide both sides by the coefficient of the variable, in this case 5, to get $x = -2$. This can be checked by plugging -2 back into the original equation $(5)(-2) + 10 = -10 + 10 = 0$.

The *Solution Set* is the set of all solutions of an equation. In our example, the solution set would simply be -2. If there were more solutions (there usually are in multivariable equations) then they would also be included in the solution set. When an equation has no true solutions, this is referred to as an *Empty Set*. Equations with identical solution sets are *Equivalent Equations*. An *Identity* is a term whose value or determinant is equal to 1.

## Calculations Using Points

Sometimes you need to perform calculations using only points on a graph as input data. Using points, you can determine what the midpoint and distance are. If you know the equation for a line you can calculate the distance between the line and the point.

To find the *Midpoint* of two points $(x_1, y_1)$ and $(x_2, y_2)$, average the x-coordinates to get the x-coordinate of the midpoint, and average the y-coordinates to get the y-coordinate of the midpoint. The formula is Midpoint $= \left(\frac{x_1+x_2}{2}, \frac{y_1+y_2}{2}\right)$.

The *Distance* between two points is the same as the length of the hypotenuse of a right triangle with the two given points as endpoints, and the two sides of the right triangle parallel to the x-axis and y-axis, respectively. The length of the segment parallel to the x-axis is the difference between the x-coordinates of the two points. The length of the segment parallel to the y-axis is the difference between the y-coordinates of the two points. Use the Pythagorean Theorem $a^2 + b^2 = c^2$ or $c = \sqrt{a^2 + b^2}$ to find the distance. The formula is Distance $= \sqrt{(x_2 - x_1)^2 + (y_2 - y_1)^2}$.

When a line is in the format $Ax + By + C = 0$, where A, B, and C are coefficients, you can use a point $(x_1, y_1)$ not on the line and apply the formula $d = \frac{|Ax_1 + By_1 + C|}{\sqrt{A^2+B^2}}$ to find the distance between the line and the point $(x_1, y_1)$.

# Geometry

## Lines and Planes

A point is a fixed location in space; has no size or dimensions; commonly represented by a dot.

A line is a set of points that extends infinitely in two opposite directions. It has length, but no width or depth. A line can be defined by any two distinct points that it contains. A line segment is a portion of a line that has definite endpoints. A ray is a portion of a line that extends from a single point on that line in one direction along the line. It has a definite beginning, but no ending.

A plane is a two-dimensional flat surface defined by three non-collinear points. A plane extends an infinite distance in all directions in those two dimensions. It contains an infinite number of points, parallel lines and segments, intersecting lines and segments, as well as parallel or intersecting rays. A plane will never contain a three-dimensional figure or skew lines. Two given planes will either be parallel or they will intersect to form a line. A plane may intersect a circular conic surface, such as a cone, to form conic sections, such as the parabola, hyperbola, circle or ellipse.

Perpendicular lines are lines that intersect at right angles. They are represented by the symbol ⊥. The shortest distance from a line to a point not on the line is a perpendicular segment from the point to the line.

Parallel lines are lines in the same plane that have no points in common and never meet. It is possible for lines to be in different planes, have no points in common, and never meet, but they are not parallel because they are in different planes.

A bisector is a line or line segment that divides another line segment into two equal lengths. A perpendicular bisector of a line segment is composed of points that are equidistant from the endpoints of the segment it is dividing.

Intersecting lines are lines that have exactly one point in common. Concurrent lines are multiple lines that intersect at a single point.

A transversal is a line that intersects at least two other lines, which may or may not be parallel to one another. A transversal that intersects parallel lines is a common occurrence in geometry.

## General Rules

The Triangle Inequality Theorem states that the sum of the measures of any two sides of a triangle is always greater than the measure of the third side. If the sum of the measures of two sides were equal to the third side, a triangle would be impossible because the two sides would lie flat across the third side and there would be no vertex. If the sum of the measures of two of the sides was less than the third side, a closed figure would be impossible because the two shortest sides would never meet.

The sum of the measures of the interior angles of a triangle is always 180°. Therefore, a triangle can never have more than one angle greater than or equal to 90°.

In any triangle, the angles opposite congruent sides are congruent, and the sides opposite congruent angles are congruent. The largest angle is always opposite the longest side, and the smallest angle is always opposite the shortest side.

The line segment that joins the midpoints of any two sides of a triangle is always parallel to the third side and exactly half the length of the third side.

## Area and Perimeter Formulas

The perimeter of any triangle is found by summing the three side lengths; $P = a + b + c$. For an equilateral triangle, this is the same as $P = 3s$, where $s$ is any side length, since all three sides are the same length.

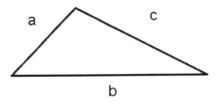

The area of any triangle can be found by taking half the product of one side length (base or $b$) and the perpendicular distance from that side to the opposite vertex (height or $h$). In equation form, $A = \frac{1}{2}bh$. For many triangles, it may be difficult to calculate $h$, so using one of the other formulas given here may be easier.

Another formula that works for any triangle is $A = \sqrt{s(s-a)(s-b)(s-c)}$, where $A$ is the area, $s$ is the semiperimeter $s = \frac{a+b+c}{2}$, and $a$, $b$, and $c$ are the lengths of the three sides.

The area of an equilateral triangle can found by the formula $A = \frac{\sqrt{3}}{4}s^2$, where $A$ is the area and $s$ is the length of a side. You could use the $30° - 60° - 90°$ ratios to find the height of the triangle and then use the standard triangle area formula, but this is faster.

The area of an isosceles triangle can found by the formula, $A = \frac{1}{2}b\sqrt{a^2 - \frac{b^2}{4}}$, where $A$ is the area, $b$ is the base (the unique side), and $a$ is the length of one of the two congruent sides. If you do not remember this formula, you can use the Pythagorean Theorem to find the height so you can use the standard formula for the area of a triangle.

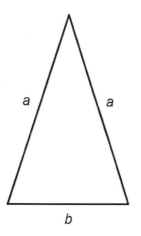

Congruent figures are geometric figures that have the same size and shape. All corresponding angles are equal, and all corresponding sides are equal. It is indicated by the symbol $\cong$.

Congruent polygons

Similar figures are geometric figures that have the same shape, but do not necessarily have the same size. All corresponding angles are equal, and all corresponding sides are proportional, but they do not have to be equal. It is indicated by the symbol $\sim$.

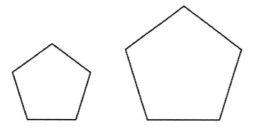

Similar polygons

Note that all congruent figures are also similar, but not all similar figures are congruent.

Line of Symmetry: The line that divides a figure or object into two symmetric parts. Each symmetric half is congruent to the other. An object may have no lines of symmetry, one line of symmetry, or more than one line of symmetry.

  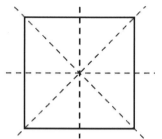

No lines of symmetry            One line of symmetry            Multiple lines of symmetry

Quadrilateral: A closed two-dimensional geometric figure composed of exactly four straight sides. The sum of the interior angles of any quadrilateral is 360°.

Parallelogram: A quadrilateral that has exactly two pairs of opposite parallel sides. The sides that are parallel are also congruent. The opposite interior angles are always congruent, and the consecutive interior angles are supplementary. The diagonals of a parallelogram bisect each other. Each diagonal divides the parallelogram into two congruent triangles.

Trapezoid: Traditionally, a quadrilateral that has exactly one pair of parallel sides. Some math texts define trapezoid as a quadrilateral that has at least one pair of parallel sides. Because there are no rules governing the second pair of sides, there are no rules that apply to the properties of the diagonals of a trapezoid.

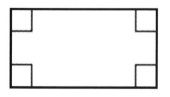

Rectangles, rhombuses, and squares are all special forms of parallelograms.

Rectangle: A parallelogram with four right angles. All rectangles are parallelograms, but not all parallelograms are rectangles. The diagonals of a rectangle are congruent.

Rhombus: A parallelogram with four congruent sides. All rhombuses are parallelograms, but not all parallelograms are rhombuses. The diagonals of a rhombus are perpendicular to each other.

110

Square: A parallelogram with four right angles and four congruent sides. All squares are also parallelograms, rhombuses, and rectangles. The diagonals of a square are congruent and perpendicular to each other.

A quadrilateral whose diagonals bisect each other is a parallelogram. A quadrilateral whose opposite sides are parallel (2 pairs of parallel sides) is a parallelogram.

A quadrilateral whose diagonals are perpendicular bisectors of each other is a rhombus. A quadrilateral whose opposite sides (both pairs) are parallel and congruent is a rhombus.

A parallelogram that has a right angle is a rectangle. (Consecutive angles of a parallelogram are supplementary. Therefore if there is one right angle in a parallelogram, there are four right angles in that parallelogram.)

A rhombus with one right angle is a square. Because the rhombus is a special form of a parallelogram, the rules about the angles of a parallelogram also apply to the rhombus.

**Area and Perimeter Formulas**

The area of a square is found by using the formula $A = s^2$, where and $s$ is the length of one side.

The perimeter of a square is found by using the formula $P = 4s$, where $s$ is the length of one side. Because all four sides are equal in a square, it is faster to multiply the length of one side by 4 than to add the same number four times. You could use the formulas for rectangles and get the same answer.

The area of a rectangle is found by the formula $A = lw$, where $A$ is the area of the rectangle, $l$ is the length (usually considered to be the longer side) and $w$ is the width (usually considered to be the shorter side). The numbers for $l$ and $w$ are interchangeable.

The perimeter of a rectangle is found by the formula $P = 2l + 2w$ or $P = 2(l + w)$, where $l$ is the length, and $w$ is the width. It may be easier to add the length and width first and then double the result, as in the second formula.

The area of a parallelogram is found by the formula $A = bh$, where $b$ is the length of the base, and $h$ is the height. Note that the base and height correspond to the length and width in a rectangle, so this formula would apply to rectangles as well. Do not confuse the height of a parallelogram with the length of the second side. The two are only the same measure in the case of a rectangle.

The perimeter of a parallelogram is found by the formula $P = 2a + 2b$ or $P = 2(a + b)$, where $a$ and $b$ are the lengths of the two sides.

The area of a trapezoid is found by the formula $A = \frac{1}{2}h(b_1 + b_2)$, where $h$ is the height (segment joining and perpendicular to the parallel bases), and $b_1$ and $b_2$ are the two parallel sides (bases). Do not use one of the other two sides as the height unless that side is also perpendicular to the parallel bases.

The perimeter of a trapezoid is found by the formula $P = a + b_1 + c + b_2$, where $a$, $b_1$, $c$, and $b_2$ are the four sides of the trapezoid.

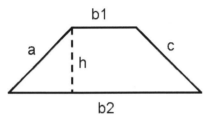

## Data Analysis, Statistics, and Probability

**Statistics**

Statistics is the branch of mathematics that deals with collecting, recording, interpreting, illustrating, and analyzing large amounts of data. The following terms are often used in the discussion of data and statistics:
- Data – the collective name for pieces of information (singular is datum).
- Quantitative data – measurements (such as length, mass, and speed) that provide information about quantities in numbers
- Qualitative data – information (such as colors, scents, tastes, and shapes) that cannot be measured using numbers
- Discrete data – information that can be expressed only by a specific value, such as whole or half numbers; For example, since people can be counted only in whole numbers, a population count would be discrete data.
- Continuous data – information (such as time and temperature) that can be expressed by any value within a given range
- Primary data – information that has been collected directly from a survey, investigation, or experiment, such as a questionnaire or the recording of daily temperatures; Primary data that has not yet been organized or analyzed is called raw data.
- Secondary data – information that has been collected, sorted, and processed by the researcher
- Ordinal data – information that can be placed in numerical order, such as age or weight
- Nominal data – information that cannot be placed in numerical order, such as names or places

## Displaying data

A bar graph is a graph that uses bars to compare data, as if each bar were a ruler being used to measure the data. The graph includes a scale that identifies the units being measured.

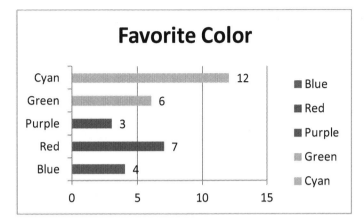

A line graph is a graph that connects points to show how data increases or decreases over time. The time line is the horizontal axis. The connecting lines between data points on the graph are a way to more clearly show how the data changes.

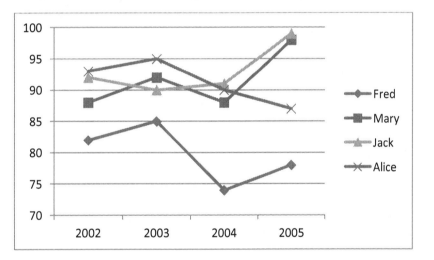

A pictograph is a graph that uses pictures or symbols to show data. The pictograph will have a key to identify what each symbol represents. Generally, each symbol stands for one or more objects.

A pie chart or circle graph is a diagram used to compare parts of a whole. The full pie represents the whole, and it is divided into sectors that each represent something that is a part of the whole. Each sector or slice of the pie is either labeled to indicate what it represents, or explained on a key associated with the chart. The size of each slice is determined by the percentage of the whole that the associated quantity represents. Numerically, the angle measurement of each sector can be computed by solving the proportion: x/360 = part/whole.

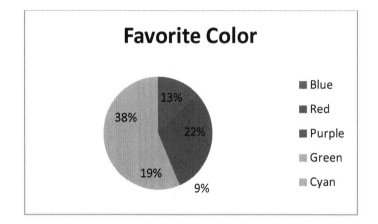

A histogram is a special type of bar graph where the data are grouped in intervals (for example 20-29, 30-39, 40-49, etc.). The frequency, or number of times a value occurs in each interval, is indicated by the height of the bar. The intervals do not have to be the same amount but usually are (all data in ranges of 10 or all in ranges of 5, for example). The smaller the intervals, the more detailed the information.

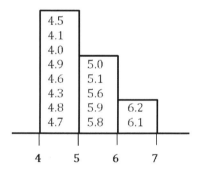

A stem-and-leaf plot is a way to organize data visually so that the information is easy to understand. A stem-and-leaf plot is simple to construct because a simple line separates the stem (the part of the plot listing the tens digit, if displaying two-digit data) from the leaf (the part that shows the ones digit). Thus, the number 45 would appear as 4│ 5. The stem-and-leaf plot for test scores of a group of 11 students might look like the following:

9│ 5
8│ 1, 3, 8
7│ 0, 2, 4, 6, 7
6│ 2, 8

A stem-and-leaf plot is similar to a histogram or other frequency plot, but with a stem-and-leaf plot, all the original data is preserved. In this example, it can be seen at a glance that nearly half the students scored in the 70's, yet all the data has been maintained. These plots can be used for larger numbers as well, but they tend to work better for small sets of data as they can become unwieldy with larger sets.

**Student-Produced Response**

The PSAT test includes 8 questions that are not multiple choice. Instead, they require you to solve the problem, then fill the exact number into a grid very similar to the one you used to enter your name and address on the form. The grid has a row of four boxes on top, with a column of numbers 0–9, a slash, and a decimal beneath each box.

To fill in the grid, write your answer in the boxes on top, then fill in the corresponding circle underneath. Use the slash to indicate fractions. It's a machine-scored test, so you don't get any credit for the number you write on top — that's strictly to help you fill in the circles correctly. If your answer doesn't fill up all four columns, that's okay. And it doesn't matter whether you left-justify or right-justify your answers. What *does* matter is that the circles be filled in correctly.

*If you can't write it using the characters provided, it's not right.*
No student-produced response will be a negative number or a percent. If you get a negative number, you've made a mistake. Percentages should be expressed as a ratio or decimal; for example, 50% can be written as .50.

*Start on the left.*
There are a few reasons to start with the first box every time. For one thing, it's faster. It will also help you be as precise as possible. If your answer is <1, though, don't use a leading 0 before the decimal. The PSAT omits the 0 from column one to help you be as precise as possible. For decimals, use as many columns as you can. Don't round or truncate answers. If you calculate an answer to be .125, enter the full number, not .13.

*Repeat a repeating decimal.*
Repeating decimals such as .666666 *are* only counted correct if you fill all the available columns. Either .666 or .667 will get credit. However, .66 will be counted as wrong.

*Don't use mixed numbers.*
If you try to write 2 ½, the computer will think you've written 21/2 and count it wrong. Instead, use the improper fraction form of such numbers; for example, 2 ½ = 5/2.

*Use your calculator.*
You brought a calculator; use it. Work the problem twice to make sure you entered all the numbers correctly.

*Check your work.*
More than any other questions in the math section, student-produced responses need to be double-checked. Try working the problem backward, plugging answers back into the original equation.

*It's okay to get multiple answers.*
Some questions may have more than one answer. In that case, any correct answer will do.

*In general:*
Approach the problem systematically. Take time to understand what is being asked for. In many cases there is a drawing or graph that you can write on. Draw lines, jot notes, do whatever is necessary to create a visual picture and to allow you to understand what is being asked.

# *Practice Test*

## Reading

**U.S. Literature**

Focus: Students must read and understand a passage from U.S. Literature.

*Questions 1-9 refer to the following selection from Little Women by Louisa May Alcott:*

"Christmas won't be Christmas without any presents," grumbled Jo, lying on the rug.

"It's so dreadful to be poor!" sighed Meg, looking down at her old dress.

"I don't think it's fair for some girls to have plenty of pretty things, and other girls nothing at all," added little Amy, with an injured sniff.

"We've got Father and Mother, and each other," said Beth contentedly from her corner.

The four young faces on which the firelight shone brightened at the cheerful words, but darkened again as Jo said sadly, "We haven't got Father, and shall not have him for a long time." She didn't say "perhaps never," but each silently added it, thinking of Father far away, where the fighting was.

Nobody spoke for a minute; then Meg said in an altered tone, "You know the reason Mother proposed not having any presents this Christmas was because it is going to be a hard winter for everyone; and she thinks we ought not to spend money for pleasure, when our men are suffering so in the army. We can't do much, but we can make our little sacrifices, and ought to do it gladly. But I am afraid I don't," and Meg shook her head, as she thought regretfully of all the pretty things she wanted.

"But I don't think the little we should spend would do any good. We've each got a dollar, and the army wouldn't be much helped by our giving that. I agree not to expect anything from Mother or you, but I do want to buy Undine and Sintran for myself. I've wanted it so long," said Jo, who was a bookworm.

"I planned to spend mine in new music," said Beth, with a little sigh, which no one heard but the hearth brush and kettle-holder.

"I shall get a nice box of Faber's drawing pencils; I really need them," said Amy decidedly.

"Mother didn't say anything about our money, and she won't wish us to give up everything. Let's each buy what we want, and have a little fun; I'm sure we work hard enough to earn it," cried Jo, examining the heels of her shoes in a gentlemanly manner.

"I know I do—teaching those tiresome children nearly all day, when I'm longing to enjoy myself at home," began Meg, in the complaining tone again.

"You don't have half such a hard time as I do," said Jo. "How would you like to be shut up for hours with a nervous, fussy old lady, who keeps you trotting, is never satisfied, and worries you till you're ready to fly out the window or cry?"

"It's naughty to fret, but I do think washing dishes and keeping things tidy is the worst work in the world. It makes me cross, and my hands get so stiff, I can't practice well at all." And Beth looked at her rough hands with a sigh that anyone could hear that time.

"I don't believe any of you suffer as I do," cried Amy, "for you don't have to go to school with impertinent girls, who plague you if you don't know your lessons, and laugh at your dresses, and label your father if he isn't rich, and insult you when your nose isn't nice."

"If you mean libel, I'd say so, and not talk about labels, as if Papa was a pickle bottle," advised Jo, laughing.

1. Which of the following sentences best describes the theme of this passage?
    a. You should always use the biggest words you know.
    b. The youngest member of a family should do the most work.
    c. Everyone has problems, and it is important to think of others.
    d. You should spend your money on yourself because you deserve it.

2. Which choice gives the best summary of the problems presented in this passage?
    a. Father is away at war, money is scarce, and the sisters are unhappy with their responsibilities.
    b. Mother forbade any presents this Christmas, and the sisters are unhappy with their responsibilities.
    c. The sisters do not have as much money to spend as they would like, and Amy is made fun of at school.
    d. Beth is tired of cleaning and washing dishes, and Father is away at war.

3. What do you know to be true about Father?
    a. He wants the sisters to spend their money on themselves.
    b. He misses his wife and children.
    c. He wants the sisters to give their money to the army.
    d. He is with the army.

4. What do you know to be true about Mother?
    a. She misses her husband.
    b. She is sorry that the family is poor.
    c. She proposed not having presents.
    d. She wants the sisters to spend their money on themselves.

5. Who is the only sister who does NOT specify what she wants to buy with her money?
    a. Amy
    b. Beth
    c. Jo
    d. Meg

6. What does the phrase "no one heard but the hearth brush and kettle holder" tell the reader about where Beth is located in the room?
"I planned to spend mine in new music," said Beth, with a little sigh, which no one heard but the hearth brush and kettle-holder.
    a. Near the stove
    b. By the window
    c. In the kitchen
    d. Closest to the fireplace

7. "'I don't think it's fair for some girls to have plenty of pretty things, and other girls nothing at all,' added little Amy, with an injured sniff." In this sentence, what is the best meaning of "injured"?
    a. Amy sniffs in pain at having injured herself.
    b. Amy sniffs to show her sense of unfairness.
    c. Amy sniffs with hurt feelings at Meg's words.
    d. Amy sniffs because she caught a winter cold.

8. Beth says, "'It makes me cross, and my hands get so stiff, I can't practice well at all.'" In the context of this entire passage, Beth refers to what when she says "'practice'"?
    a. Practicing music
    b. Practicing drawing
    c. Practicing teaching
    d. Practicing schoolwork

9. Which evidence shows that this passage takes place during a war?
   a. "...thinking of Father far away, where the fighting was."
   b. "...when our men are suffering so in the army."
   c. "We haven't got Father, and shall not...for a long time."
   d. (a) primarily and also (b) secondarily, but not (c)

## History/Social Studies

## Passage Set 1
Focus: Students must read and understand a passage on a history topic.

*Questions 10-19 refer to the Second Inaugural Address and the Gettysburg Address, both by Abraham Lincoln:*

### Second Inaugural Address

Fellow-Countrymen:

AT this second appearing to take the oath of the Presidential office there is less occasion for an extended address than there was at the first. Then a statement somewhat in detail of a course to be pursued seemed fitting and proper. Now, at the expiration of four years, during which public declarations have been constantly called forth on every point and phase of the great contest which still absorbs the attention and engrosses the energies of the nation, little that is new could be presented. The progress of our arms, upon which all else chiefly depends, is as well known to the public as to myself, and it is, I trust, reasonably satisfactory and encouraging to all. With high hope for the future, no prediction in regard to it is ventured.

On the occasion corresponding to this four years ago all thoughts were anxiously directed to an impending civil war. All dreaded it, all sought to avert it. While the inaugural address was being delivered from this place, devoted altogether to saving the Union without war, insurgent agents were in the city seeking to destroy it without war—seeking to dissolve the Union and divide effects by negotiation. Both parties deprecated war, but one of them would make war rather than let the nation survive, and the other would accept war rather than let it perish, and the war came.

One-eighth of the whole population were colored slaves, not distributed generally over the Union, but localized in the southern part of it. These slaves constituted a peculiar and powerful interest. All knew that this interest was somehow the cause of the war. To strengthen, perpetuate, and extend this interest was the object for which the insurgents would rend the Union even by war, while the Government claimed no right to do more than to restrict the territorial enlargement of it. Neither party expected for the war the magnitude or the duration which it has already attained. Neither anticipated that the cause of the conflict might cease with or even before the conflict itself should cease. Each looked for an easier triumph, and a result less fundamental and astounding. Both read the same Bible and pray to the same God, and each invokes His aid against the other. It may seem strange that any men should dare to ask a just God's assistance in wringing their bread from the sweat of other men's faces, but let us judge not, that we be not judged. The prayers of both could not be answered. That of neither has been answered fully. The Almighty has His own purposes. "Woe unto the world because of offenses; for it must needs be that offenses come, but woe to that man by whom the offense cometh." If we shall suppose that American slavery is one of those offenses which, in the providence of God, must needs come, but which, having continued through His appointed time, He now wills to remove, and that He gives to both North and South this terrible war as the woe

118

due to those by whom the offense came, shall we discern therein any departure from those divine attributes which the believers in a living God always ascribe to Him? Fondly do we hope, fervently do we pray, that this mighty scourge of war may speedily pass away. Yet, if God wills that it continue until all the wealth piled by the bondsman's two hundred and fifty years of unrequited toil shall be sunk, and until every drop of blood drawn with the lash shall be paid by another drawn with the sword, as was said three thousand years ago, so still it must be said "the judgments of the Lord are true and righteous altogether."

With malice toward none, with charity for all, with firmness in the right as God gives us to see the right, let us strive on to finish the work we are in, to bind up the nation's wounds, to care for him who shall have borne the battle and for his widow and his orphan, to do all which may achieve and cherish a just and lasting peace among ourselves and with all nations.

### Gettysburg Address

Four score and seven years ago our fathers brought forth on this continent, a new nation, conceived in Liberty, and dedicated to the proposition that all men are created equal.

Now we are engaged in a great civil war, testing whether that nation, or any nation so conceived and so dedicated, can long endure. We are met on a great battle-field of that war. We have come to dedicate a portion of that field, as a final resting place for those who here gave their lives that that nation might live. It is altogether fitting and proper that we should do this.

But, in a larger sense, we can not dedicate -- we can not consecrate -- we can not hallow -- this ground. The brave men, living and dead, who struggled here, have consecrated it, far above our poor power to add or detract. The world will little note, nor long remember what we say here, but it can never forget what they did here. It is for us the living, rather, to be dedicated here to the unfinished work which they who fought here have thus far so nobly advanced. It is rather for us to be here dedicated to the great task remaining before us -- that from these honored dead we take increased devotion to that cause for which they gave the last full measure of devotion -- that we here highly resolve that these dead shall not have died in vain -- that this nation, under God, shall have a new birth of freedom -- and that government of the people, by the people, for the people, shall not perish from the earth.

10. In his Second Inaugural Address, Lincoln said, "These slaves constituted a peculiar and powerful interest." In this context, what does "peculiar" most nearly mean?
    a. Odd
    b. Bizarre
    c. Specific
    d. Appropriate

11. In the last sentence of the Gettysburg Address, what did Lincoln most closely mean by "...that this nation, under God, shall have a new birth of freedom"?
    a. Freedom from war
    b. Freedom for all citizens
    c. Freedom for the soldiers
    d. Freedom to own slaves or not

12. In his Second Inaugural Address, Lincoln said, <u>"If we shall suppose that... [God] gives to both North and South this terrible war as the woe due to those by whom the offense came..."</u> Which of the following did he provide as evidence of this supposition?

   a. "Neither party expected for the war the magnitude or the duration which it has already attained."
   b. "Both read the same Bible and pray to the same God, and each invokes His aid against the other."
   c. "Yet, if God wills that it continue...so still it must be said 'the judgments of the Lord are true and righteous altogether.'"
   d. "'Woe unto the world because of offenses; for it must needs be that offenses come, but woe to that man by whom the offense cometh.'"

13. Which of the following comes closest to summarizing the main idea of the Gettysburg Address?

   a. In dedicating this ground, we must moreover save our democracy so soldiers did not die in vain.
   b. In dedicating this ground, we must consecrate and hallow it to honor the soldiers living and dead.
   c. In dedicating this ground, we must ensure the world remembers what we said and they did here.
   d. In dedicating this ground, we must complete soldiers' unfinished work by declaring a cease-fire.

14. In the sentence, <u>"The world will little note, nor long remember what we say here, but it can never forget what they did here"</u>, which rhetorical device did Lincoln use?

   a. Epiphora
   b. Anaphora
   c. Repetition
   d. Parallelism

15. Which idea did Lincoln overtly include in both his Second Inaugural Address and Gettysburg Address?

   a. Achieving an enduring peace
   b. The Civil War being God's will
   c. Completing some ongoing tasks
   d. Wishing the war would end soon

16. Why does Lincoln discuss his first inaugural address in this passage?

   a. To prove that the country could have gone in a different direction.
   b. To illustrate how the country had changed since his first inauguration.
   c. To show how much he improved the country during his first term.
   d. To explain that the country was once a place of peace.

17. Which sentence from the address supports the idea that Lincoln believed the North and the South did not have equally justifiable reasons for taking part in the war?

   a. All knew that this interest was somehow the cause of the war.
   b. Neither anticipated that the cause of the conflict might cease with or even before the conflict, itself, should cease.
   c. Both parties deprecated war, but one of them would make war rather than let the nation survive, and the other would accept war rather than let it perish, and the war came.
   d. Each looked for an easier triumph, and a result less fundamental and astounding.

18. How does Lincoln unite the themes of war and religion in his second inaugural address?
    a. He suggests that the war and its end are parts of God's plan.
    b. He says that no man would ask God to help him win a war.
    c. He insists that it is God's responsibility, not his own, to resolve the war.
    d. He quotes from the Bible liberally in order to extend an address he knew was too short.

19. How might reading Lincoln's second inaugural address online differ from hearing it in person?
    a. Lincoln likely was angry while reading his address, and this anger is lost in its translation to online text.
    b. Lincoln's original address was much longer than the version that later appeared online.
    c. Lincoln was an impressive-looking man, and this characteristic could be conveyed online only if the web page includes a photograph of him.
    d. Lincoln would have been able to use his voice to heighten the emotion in his address.

**Passage2**
Focus: Students must read and understand a passage from History/Social Studies.

*Read the selection from Roosevelt's 1941 State of the Union Address to answer questions 20-29:*

Many subjects connected with our social economy call for immediate improvement.

As examples:

We should bring more citizens under the coverage of old-age pensions and unemployment insurance.

We should widen the opportunities for adequate medical care.

We should plan a better system by which persons deserving or needing gainful employment may obtain it.

I have called for personal sacrifice. And I am assured of the willingness of almost all Americans to respond to that call.

A part of the sacrifice means the payment of more money in taxes. In my Budget Message I will recommend that a greater portion of this great defense program be paid for from taxation than we are paying for today. No person should try, or be allowed, to get rich out of the program; and the principle of tax payments in accordance with ability to pay should be constantly before our eyes to guide our legislation.

If the Congress maintains these principles, the voters, putting patriotism ahead of pocketbooks, will give you their applause.

In the future days, which we seek to make secure, we look forward to a world founded upon four essential human freedoms.

The first is freedom of speech and expression—everywhere in the world.

The second is freedom of every person to worship God in his own way—everywhere in the world.

The third is freedom from want—which, translated into world terms, means economic understandings which will secure to every nation a healthy peacetime life for its inhabitants—everywhere in the world.

The fourth is freedom from fear—which, translated into world terms, means a world-wide reduction of armaments to such a point and in such a thorough fashion that no nation will be in a position to commit an act of physical aggression against any neighbor—anywhere in the world.

That is no vision of a distant millennium. It is a definite basis for a kind of world attainable in our own time and generation. That kind of world is the very antithesis of the so-called new order of tyranny which the dictators seek to create with the crash of a bomb.

To that new order we oppose the greater conception—the moral order. A good society is able to face schemes of world domination and foreign revolutions alike without fear.

Since the beginning of our American history, we have been engaged in change—in a perpetual peaceful revolution—a revolution which goes on steadily, quietly adjusting itself to changing conditions—without the concentration camp or the quick-lime in the ditch. The world order which we seek is the cooperation of free countries, working together in a friendly, civilized society.

This nation has placed its destiny in the hands and heads and hearts of its millions of free men and women; and its faith in freedom under the guidance of God. Freedom means the supremacy of human rights everywhere. Our support goes to those who struggle to gain those rights and keep them. Our strength is our unity of purpose.

To that high concept there can be no end save victory.

20. Which statement best supports the idea that FDR believed that America is constantly evolving toward a better situation?

a. Since the beginning of our American history, we have been engaged in change—in a perpetual peaceful revolution—a revolution which goes on steadily, quietly adjusting itself to changing conditions—without the concentration camp or the quick-lime in the ditch.

b. This nation has placed its destiny in the hands and heads and hearts of its millions of free men and women; and its faith in freedom under the guidance of God.

c. To that new order we oppose the greater conception—the moral order. A good society is able to face schemes of world domination and foreign revolutions alike without fear.

d. The fourth is freedom from fear—which, translated into world terms, means a world-wide reduction of armaments to such a point and in such a thorough fashion that no nation will be in a position to commit an act of physical aggression against any neighbor—anywhere in the world.

21. Read the following selection from a blog entry on FDR's speech. What aspect of the speech is emphasized?

…There is, of course, a lot to love in the speech. It highlights the important social issues of the day, the very same issues our nation is struggling with at the moment. What can we do about our elderly? Do class distinctions matter? The fact of the matter is, no one wants to take care of a sickly aging relative, regardless of class. Then again, most of our elderly don't want to live with their offspring, either—rich or poor. It begs the question…

a. It emphasizes the need for a social safety net for the aging populace.

b. It emphasizes the need for a lack of social class distinctions.

c. It highlights the fact that many of the elderly do not want long-term care.

d. It highlights the idea that people want to live independently.

22. In this text, FDR claims that raising taxes will result in a patriotic populace that will happily support the government. What might be one argument against this idea?

a. Americans are uninterested in pursuing freedom of any kind, and the four freedoms listed here are not considered important.

b. The average citizen already feels overburdened by taxes and feels the money is not being well-spent by the government.

c. Individuals will easily assent to the idea of a greater tax burden since it will naturally lead to a more prosperous state.

d. Patriots of all kinds are part of the natural makeup of America, and some will feel that the support of government is something that should be contemplated and debated.

23. What is a major theme that Roosevelt articulates in his speech?

a. It is important for all people to have access to the benefits of an old-age system that supports citizens when they can no longer work.

b. Patriotic people will feel the need to pay more taxes to the government in order to obtain certain benefits they would not be able to afford.

c. People who want to work should be able to find work without bias and without undue hardship.

d. There are four basic freedoms that are vital to the health of people: speech, worship, freedom from want, and freedom from fear.

24. The last sentence in this passage is, "To that high concept there can be no end save victory." In the context of the preceding text, which of the following is the most precise meaning of the word "**end**"?

    a. Death

    b. Purpose

    c. Outcome

    d. Conclusion

25. FDR spoke of "the so-called new order of tyranny which the dictators seek to create with the crash of a bomb." In the context of this passage, which is the most accurate meaning of the word "**order**"?

    a. A command given by a military leader

    b. An authoritative decision or direction

    c. An arrangement of items in sequence

    d. A system of societal and world politics

26. When FDR spoke of "personal sacrifice", which of these did he explicitly give as an example of it?

    a. Higher taxation

    b. Military service

    c. Arms reduction

    d. Four freedoms

27. FDR described America's constant engagement in change as "a perpetual peaceful revolution...without the concentration camp or the quick-lime in the ditch." In this description, we can infer his implicit reference to which war(s)?

    a. Revolutionary

    b. World War I

    c. World War II

    d. To all of them

28. FDR identified aspects of the social economy needing to be improved immediately. As evidence of this need, which example did he NOT cite in this passage?

    a. Expanding retirement benefits

    b. Expanding healthcare benefits

    c. Expanding draft by the military

    d. Expanding labor opportunities

29. In identifying the four freedoms in this passage, FDR ended his definition of the first three freedoms with "—everywhere in the world" and the fourth with "—anywhere in the world." This is an example of which rhetorical device?

    a. Anastrophe

    b. Antistrophe

    c. Apostrophe

    d. Aposiopesis

**Science**

Focus: Students must read and understand a passage from a science topic.

*Questions 30-38 pertain to the following passage:*

<u>Annelids</u>

The phylum Annelida, named for the Latin word *anellus*, meaning "ring", includes earthworms, leeches, and other similar organisms. In their typical form, these animals exhibit bilateral symmetry, a cylindrical cross section, and an elongate body divided externally into segments (*metameres*) by a series of rings (*annuli*). They are segmented internally as well, with most of the internal organs repeated in series in each segment. This organization is termed *metamerism*. Metameric segmentation is the distinguishing feature of this phylum, and provides it with a degree of evolutionary plasticity in that certain segments can be modified and specialized to perform specific functions. For example, in some species certain of the locomotor *parapodia*, or feet, may be modified for grasping, and some portions of the gut may evolve digestive specializations.

The gut is a straight, muscular tube that functions independently of the muscular activity in the body wall. The Annelida resemble the nematodes, another worm phylum, in possessing a fluid-filled internal cavity separating the gut from the body wall. In both phyla, this cavity is involved in locomotion. However, in the annelids this space is formed at a much later time during the development of the embryo, and presumably evolved much later as well. This fluid-filled internal space is called a true *coelom*.

The annelid excretory and circulatory systems are well developed, and some members of the phylum have evolved respiratory organs. The nervous system offers a particular example of metameric specialization. It is concentrated anteriorly into enlarged cerebral ganglia connected to a ventral nerve cord that extends posteriorly and is organized into repeating segmental ganglia.

This phylum includes members bearing adaptations required for aquatic (marine or freshwater) or terrestrial habitats. They may be free-living entities or exist as parasites. Among the best known are the earthworm *Lumbricus*, the water leech *Hirudo*, and the marine worm *Nereis*.

30. What is the purpose of this passage?
    a. To describe the annelid nervous system.
    b. To describe the annelid digestive system.
    c. To introduce distinctive features of annelid anatomy.
    d. To define metamerism.

31. What is meant by the term *metamerism*?
    a. Segmentation of the anatomy
    b. A series of rings
    c. Bilateral symmetry
    d. Evolutionary plasticity

32. What is meant by the term *parapodia*?
    a. Specialization
    b. Grasping appendages
    c. Locomotion
    d. Feet

33. One evolutionary advantage of segmentation is that
    a. Segmented animals have many feet.
    b. Segmented animals have a fluid-filled coelom.
    c. Parts of some segments can become specialized to perform certain functions.
    d. Segments can evolve.

34. Some annelid feet may be specialized in order to
    a. be used for locomotion.
    b. be segmented.
    c. be fluid-filled.
    d. grasp things.

35. The main difference between the Annelida and all other animal phyla is that
    a. the Annelida are worms.
    b. the Annelida include the leeches.
    c. the Annelida are metameric.
    d. the Annelida are aquatic.

36. The purpose of the last paragraph in the passage is to
    a. give familiar examples of members of the annelid phylum.
    b. show that annelids may be parasites.
    c. tell the reader that annelids may be adapted to aquatic environments.
    d. show that there are many annelids in nature and that they are adapted to a wide
    variety of habitats.

37. Which of the following provide(s) evidence to support the statement that metamerism confers
some evolutionary flexibility?
    a. "in some species certain of the...feet may be modified for grasping..."
    b. "...and some portions of the gut may evolve digestive specializations."
    c. "Metameric segmentation is the distinguishing feature of this phylum."
    d. (a) and (b) are both examples of evolutionary flexibility, but (c) is not.

38. The second paragraph discusses annelids and nematodes. Which relationship(s) between
these two phyla does the author establish by describing their respective characteristics?
    a. Comparison
    b. Contrast
    c. Neither
    d. Both

**Passage 2**
Focus: Students must read and understand a passage from a science topic.

*Questions 39-47 are based on the following selection from Albert Einstein's paper on Relativity:
The Special and General Theory (1916, revised 1924).*
                THE PRINCIPLE OF RELATIVITY (IN THE RESTRICTED SENSE)

        In order to attain the greatest possible clearness, let us return to our example of
        the railway carriage supposed to be travelling uniformly. We call its motion a
        uniform translation ("uniform" because it is of constant velocity and direction,
        "translation" because although the carriage changes its position relative to the
        embankment yet it does not rotate in so doing). Let us imagine a raven flying
        through the air in such a manner that its motion, as observed from the
        embankment, is uniform and in a straight line. If we were to observe the flying
        raven from the moving railway carriage, we should find that the motion of the
        raven would be one of different velocity and direction, but that it would still be
        uniform and in a straight line. Expressed in an abstract manner we may say : If a

mass m is moving uniformly in a straight line with respect to a co-ordinate system K, then it will also be moving uniformly and in a straight line relative to a second co-ordinate system K1 provided that the latter is executing a uniform translatory motion with respect to K. In accordance with the discussion contained in the preceding section, it follows that:

If K is a Galilean co-ordinate system, then every other co-ordinate system K' is a Galilean one, when, in relation to K, it is in a condition of uniform motion of translation. Relative to K1 the mechanical laws of Galilei-Newton hold good exactly as they do with respect to K.

We advance a step farther in our generalization when we express the tenet thus: If, relative to K, K1 is a uniformly moving co-ordinate system devoid of rotation, then natural phenomena run their course with respect to K1 according to exactly the same general laws as with respect to K. This statement is called the principle of relativity (in the restricted sense).

As long as one was convinced that all natural phenomena were capable of representation with the help of classical mechanics, there was no need to doubt the validity of this principle of relativity…

Nevertheless, there are two general facts which at the outset speak very much in favor of the validity of the principle of relativity. Even though classical mechanics does not supply us with a sufficiently broad basis for the theoretical presentation of all physical phenomena, still we must grant it a considerable measure of **"truth,"** since it supplies us with the actual motions of the heavenly bodies with a delicacy of detail little short of wonderful. The principle of relativity must therefore apply with great accuracy in the domain of mechanics. But that a principle of such broad generality should hold with such exactness in one domain of phenomena, and yet should be invalid for another, is a priori not very probable.

We now proceed to the second argument, to which, moreover, we shall return later. If the principle of relativity (in the restricted sense) does not hold, then the Galilean co-ordinate systems K, K1, K2, etc., which are moving uniformly relative to each other, will not be equivalent for the description of natural phenomena. In this case we should be constrained to believe that natural laws are capable of being formulated in a particularly simple manner, and of course only on condition that, from amongst all possible Galilean co-ordinate systems, we should have chosen one (K[0]) of a particular state of motion as our body of reference. We should then be justified (because of its merits for the description of natural phenomena) in calling this system "absolutely at rest," and all other Galilean systems K "in motion." If, for instance, our embankment were the system K[0] then our railway carriage would be a system K, relative to which less simple laws would hold than with respect to K[0]. This diminished simplicity would be due to the fact that the carriage K would be in motion (i.e. "really") with respect to K[0]. In the general laws of nature which have been formulated with reference to K, the magnitude and direction of the velocity of the carriage would necessarily play a part. We should expect, for instance, that the note emitted by an organ pipe placed with its axis parallel to the direction of travel would be different from that emitted if the axis of the pipe were placed perpendicular to this direction.

Now in virtue of its motion in an orbit round the sun, our earth is comparable with a railway carriage travelling with a velocity of about 30 kilometers per second. If the principle of relativity were not valid we should therefore expect that the direction of motion of the earth at any moment would enter into the laws of nature, and also that physical systems in their behavior would be dependent on the orientation in space with respect to the earth. For owing to the alteration in direction of the velocity of revolution of the earth in the course of a year, the earth cannot be at rest relative to the hypothetical system K[0] throughout the whole year. However, the most careful observations have never revealed such anisotropic properties in terrestrial physical space, i.e. a physical non-equivalence of different directions. This is very powerful argument in favor of the principle of relativity.

39. Which of the following choices best supports the claim of Einstein's theory of special relativity as accurate?
    a. the movement of the Earth around the sun
    b. Galilean co-ordinate systems and their application in classical mechanics
    c. the idea of chance in quantum mechanics
    d. the two different parts of relativity

40. What might be one question to ask to begin an argument against Einstein's theory of relativity?
    a. If relativity holds true, what does that say about the classical rules of motion?
    b. If relativity is valid, then why can it not explain all parts of the natural world, including the rules of quantum mechanics?
    c. If the natural laws concerning quantum mechanics are true, then shouldn't the classical rules of motion be suspect?
    d. If the natural laws formulated with reference to K are measurable, then wouldn't the magnitude and direction of the velocity of the carriage be important?

41. Which of the following choices provides the best meaning for the underlined "truth"?
    a. correctness regarding the abstract meaning of classical mechanics
    b. honesty regarding the movement of objects according to the rules of relativity
    c. validity regarding an understanding of the classical rules of motion
    d. exactness regarding the movement of small bodies on a coordinate plane

42. Einstein writes that classical mechanics describes astronomical movements with "a delicacy of detail little short of wonderful." In this context, what is the best synonym for the meaning of "delicacy"?
    a. A fragility
    b. A sensitivity
    c. A rare delight
    d. A soft texture

43. If a reader did not know the meaning of the phrase a priori, s/he could ascertain it from the sentence: "But that a principle of such broad generality should hold with such exactness in one domain of phenomena, and yet should be invalid for another, is a priori not very probable." Based on this context, to which of these is its meaning closest?
    a. Existing in the first place
    b. Having the highest priority
    c. Something happening after the fact
    d. General to specific/independently true

44. In the last paragraph, Einstein used the word "anisotropic". What is true about its meaning?
    a. Einstein used and explicitly defined it in the same sentence.
    b. Einstein's meaning is implicit; only physicists would know it.
    c. Einstein coined this term, defining it in an earlier paragraph.
    d. Einstein never defined it, but anyone can tell from context.

45. Within this passage, which of the following conclusions proposed by Einstein is predicated upon the condition that the principle of relativity is valid?

a. "...then the Galilean co-ordinate systems K, K1, K2, etc., which are moving uniformly relative to each other, will not be equivalent for the description of natural phenomena."

b. "...natural laws are capable of being formulated in a particularly simple manner, and...only on condition that...we...have chosen one...of a particular state of motion as our body of reference."

c. "If, relative to K, K1 is a uniformly moving co-ordinate system devoid of rotation...then natural phenomena run their course with respect to K1 according to exactly the same general laws as with respect to K."

d. "...we should therefore expect that the direction of motion of the earth at any moment would enter into the laws of nature, and also that physical systems in their behavior would be dependent on the orientation in space with respect to the earth."

46. Einstein describes the detail with which classical mechanics describes celestial motions as "little short of wonderful." Rhetorically, this is most an example of which of these?

a. Understatement
b. Overstatement
c. Amplification
d. Metabasis

47. Which of the following most accurately represents Einstein's use of claims and counterclaims in this passage?

a. From one paragraph to the next, statements of claims and statements of counterclaims are presented alternately; the last two sentences summarize how these contrast.

b. The first three paragraphs present a series of counterclaims; the following four present arguments that logically refute those counterclaims and then support his claims.

c. The first five paragraphs mainly explain his claims; the last two state counterclaims, explaining results to expect if they were true; the last two sentences reassert his claims.

d. Every paragraph begins by presenting a claim, then a counterclaim, then refutation of the counterclaim; and ends with repeating the original claim for emphasis.

# Writing and Language

## Careers

Focus: Students must make revising and editing decisions in the context of a passage on a careers-related topic.

### Software Developer

Software developers are in charge of the entire development process for a software program. They begin by asking how the customer plans to use the software. They design the program and then give instructions to programmers, who write computer code and test it. If the program does not work as expected or people find it too difficult to use, software developers go back to the design process to fix the problems or improve the program. After the program is released to the customer, a developer may perform upgrades and maintenance.

Developers usually work closely with <u>computer programmers</u>. However, in some companies, developers write code themselves instead of giving instructions to computer programmers.

Developers who supervise a software project from the planning stages through implementation sometimes are called information technology (IT) project managers. These workers monitor the project's progress to ensure that it meets deadlines, standards, and cost targets. IT project managers who plan and direct an organization's IT department or IT policies are included in the profile on <u>computer and information systems managers</u>.

The following are types of software developers:
*Applications software developers* design computer applications, such as word processors and games, for consumers. They may create custom software for a specific customer or commercial software to be sold to the general public. Some applications software developers create complex databases for organizations. They also create programs that people use over the Internet and within a company's intranet.

*Systems software developers* create the systems that keep computers functioning properly. These could be operating systems that are part of computers the general public buys or systems built specifically for an organization. Often, systems software developers also build the system's interface, which is what allows users to interact with the computer. Systems software developers create the operating systems that control most of the consumer electronics in use today, including those in phones or cars.

1. Which of the following best represents how information is connected in this passage?
   a. Transitions from paragraphs 1-2 and 2-3 begin paragraphs 2 and 3; the transition to both paragraphs 4 and 5 ends paragraph 3.
   b. Transitions from paragraphs 1-2, 2-3, and 3-4 end paragraphs 1, 2, and 3; there is no transition between paragraph 4 and paragraph 5.
   c. Transitions between paragraphs are not present in this passage; each paragraph introduces a new topic with no reference to the last.
   d. Transitions between paragraphs are only evident in the transition from paragraph 3 to paragraph 4, but not in any other place.

2. According to the information in this passage, readers can conclude that Apple's iOS and Google's Android were designed by which of these?
   a. Steve Jobs and Bill Gates respectively
   b. Both (c) and (d) software designers
   c. Applications software designers
   d. Systems software designers

3. Which of the following best describes the organizational structure of this passage from the first paragraph to the others?
   a. Problem to solution
   b. General to specific
   c. Compare-contrast
   d. Cause-and-effect

4. If someone wanted to claim that software developers have nothing more to do with their designs after their programs become available to the public, how would evidence from this passage relate to such a claim?
   a. There is no evidence that relates to such a claim.
   b. There is evidence there that supports this claim.
   c. There is evidence here that will refute this claim.
   d. There is evidence both for and against this claim.

5. Which of the following accurately describes the use of introductions and conclusions in this passage?
   a. An introduction but no conclusion
   b. No introduction but a conclusion
   c. An introduction and a conclusion
   d. No introduction and no conclusion

6. "Software developers are in charge of the entire development process for a software program." Which version has the best noun agreement?
   a. No change
   b. for software programs.
   c. for one software program.
   d. for many software programs.

7. The second paragraph of the passage says that "...in some companies, developers write code themselves" instead of having programmers do it. Which of these is the correct convention in current Standard English?
   a. No change
   b. developers write codes
   c. developers write a code
   d. developers write coding

8. In this passage, the third paragraph states, "Developers who supervise a software project from the planning stages through implementation sometimes are called information technology (IT) project managers." Which version is both least awkward and most correct?
   a. No change
   b. are sometimes called information technology (IT) managers.
   c. are called information technology (IT) managers sometimes.
   d. are called sometimes information technology (IT) managers.

9. A reader unfamiliar with the term "intranet" could determine from the context of the passage that it most precisely means which of these?
   a. A network inside the Internet to which anyone has access
   b. A network the same size as but separate from the Internet
   c. A network smaller than the Internet, specific to a company
   d. A network that is the Internet but as used by one company

10. Based on the context of this passage, which of the following is correct concerning "databases"?
   a. Databases are software operating systems.
   b. Databases are sold to the general public.
   c. Databases are software applications.
   d. Databases are system interfaces.

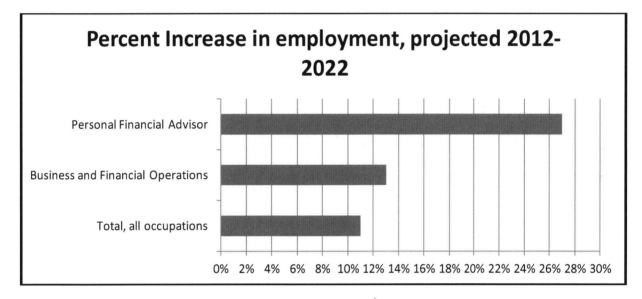

Adapted from United States Bureau of Labor Statistics, Employment Projections Program. "All occupations" includes all occupations in the United States economy.

11. Based on the information provided in the graph, which of the following is true?
   a. Software developers will be hired more than employees in business and financial or other jobs.
   b. Software developers will be hired at the same rate as business and financial, but not other jobs.
   c. Software developers will be hired more than in all jobs but less than business and financial jobs.
   d. Software developers will not be hired as much as those in business, financial, and all other jobs.

**History/Social Studies**

Focus: Students must make revising and editing decisions in the context of a passage on a history/social studies-related topic.

### Ernst Lubitsch

The comedy of manners was a style of film popular in the 1930s. These movies expressed the frustrations of the depression-era poor by mocking the swells of the upper classes, and contrasting their gilded lives to the daily grind of the downtrodden masses. One of the greatest directors of this type of film was Ernst Lubitsch, a German filmmaker who eventually came to Hollywood to make some of his greatest films.

Lubitsch's film career began in the silent era. Born in Berlin, in 1892, he worked at first as an actor, subsequently debuting as a director with the film Passion in 1912. He made more than 40 films in Germany, but the advent of sound brought him to Hollywood, where the new technology was most readily available. After the producer Albert Zukor invited him to come to the U.S. in 1923, he pursued his career in the capital of film until the late 1940s. His signature style – a focus on seemingly insignificant details that **(12)** <u>imbued</u> them with symbolism in the context of the film – was just as effective in the "talkies" as it had been in silent films. One of his greatest comedies, Trouble in Paradise, starred Herbert Marshall and Miriam Hopkins and was shot in 1932. A stinging social comedy that skewers the illusions of the upper classes, it would not have been well received in his native Germany of the time.

Trouble in Paradise tells the story of a charming, elegant thief. Marshall plays Gaston Monescu, a man whose charm and elegant manners allow him to work his way into the bosom of high society. In the hotels and clubs of the rich, he manages to gain the trust of wealthy individuals until he swindles them. Monescu courts the rich perfume heiress, Mariette, **(13)** <u>and we can never know of certain of how sincere his affection for her may be.</u> But he is also in love with his accomplice, Lily, a clever thief in her own right. His eventual decision to leave Mariette for her can be seen as an affirmation of the unity of the working class in this very class-conscious film.

The opening scenes of the film provide a classic example of Lubitsch's wry symbolism. The opening shot is of a garbage can, which is duly picked up by a garbage man and dumped onto what seems to be a truck. But, as the camera pans back, we realize that the truck is, in fact, a gondola, and that the scene takes place in Venice. As the gondolier-garbage man breaks into a romantic song, the camera contrasts the elegant city, its palaces and beautiful canals, with the mundane reality of garbage and necessary, low-wage work.

The film continues to contrast the elegant surfaces of society with the corruption that lies beneath. A classic scene is the first meeting between Monescu and Lily, two thieves with polished manners. In an elegant hotel room, the two engage in a genteel banter filled with seductive double-entendres and urbane banalities. But they are not the baron and countess they profess to be, as their behavior soon makes clear. As the supper progresses, they manage to steal one another's wallets, jewelry, and watches. Finally, they reveal the thefts to one another and sort out their belongings, but Monescu has been won over by Lily's cleverness, for he admires her resourcefulness far more than the undeserved wealth of the upper classes.

Lubitsch went on to make many more films during the 1930s, comedies of manners and musical comedies as well. Among his greatest Hollywood films are Design for Living (1933), The Merry Widow (1934), Ninotchka (1939), and Heaven Can Wait (1943). One of the wittiest directors of all time, he made films in English, German and French, always exhibiting the sharpest eye for detail. His films challenged the intellect of his viewers, and they never disappointed. The juxtaposition of seemingly contradictory elements was always central to his style, as he exposed the falsehoods he found in his world.

12.
    a. No Change
    b. engulfed
    c. enchanted
    d. emboldened

13.
    a. No Change
    b. and we are not to certain of how sincere his affection for her may be.
    c. and we will never know certain of how sincere his affection for her may be.
    d. and we are never certain of how sincere his affection for her may be.

14. Which of the following terms would *not* be a good description of Lubitsch's film style, as it is described in the text?
    a. Sophisticated
    b. Erudite
    c. Chic
    d. Boisterous

15. One of the tools that Lubitsch used to mock the upper classes, as shown in the text, was
    a. Lighting.
    b. Talking pictures.
    c. Juxtaposition of contradictory elements.
    d. Urbane banalities.

16. Lubitsch's signature style can be described as
    a. Double-entendres and urbane banalities.
    b. Using apparently insignificant details as symbols.
    c. Charm and elegant manners.
    d. Corruption underlying high society.

17. Lubitsch first came to the U.S in 1923 because
    a. His films were not well received in Germany.
    b. He was fleeing the Nazi regime.
    c. He was invited by a producer.
    d. He could not make films with sound in Germany.

18. The text tells us that Lubitsch's first film, *Passion* was
    a. An early "talkie."
    b. A comedy of manners.
    c. A film starring Miriam Hopkins.
    d. None of the above.

19. Without considering gender, which two characters have the most in common?
    a. Monescu and Lily
    b. Monescu and Mariette
    c. Lily and Mariette
    d. Monescu and Lubitsch

20. The scene with the garbage gondola at the opening of the film shows that
    a. The rich need supporting services.
    b. Venice is kept clean by gondoliers.
    c. Elegance may be only a veneer.
    d. Gondoliers sing romantic ballads.

21. Monescu most admires
    a. Lily's wealth.
    b. Lily's cleverness.
    c. Mariette's money.
    d. Venetian gondolas.

22. In the film, Lily pretends to be
    a. A perfume heiress.
    b. A countess.
    c. A wealthy dowager.
    d. Monescu's partner.

Focus: Students must make revising and editing decisions in the context of a passage on a humanities-related topic.

### Buddhism, Western Society, and the Self

In Western society, the individual self is generally prioritized over the collective self. This is evidenced in such things as the privatization of medicine and conceptions of ownership. In recent decades, however, there has been an increased tension in Western societies between institutions and ideologies that prioritize the individual and those groups that prioritize the collective. This is evidenced in the struggles that Western Buddhists face.

Central to Buddhist belief is the idea of "egolessness." While this term may seem to imply the absence of the individual ego or selfhood, this is not the case; rather, "egolessness" is a prioritization of the relationships between and among people over selfish concerns. "Egolessness" may also be thought of as an antonym of "ego-toxicity," that condition where an individual places his or her concerns before any other person or group's concerns. In Western societies, ego-toxicity is the reigning condition. Buddhists who live in such societies often find themselves caught between their ideology of egolessness and environmental ego-toxicity.

While a Western perspective might find it difficult to **(23)** understand how a Buddhist can keep egolessness; in Western society, Buddhists are able to maintain such a perspective as a natural consequent of their beliefs. The Western perspective expects moral actions to be quid pro quo; to put it another way, a Westerner assumes that if he or she does something considered "good," then he or she should and will be rewarded. Buddhists, on the other hand, believe that good should be done out of compassion for all beings, and to do good is to do good for all beings, including the self. Approaching society and social action in an egoless manner has begun to become more prevalent in secular institutions and movements, such as the transition to a more socialized form of medical treatment in some Western countries. The struggle between the ego and the collective continues, however.

Buddhist practitioners show through their actions that it is possible to do good in the world without giving up one's personhood. **(24)** When ego-toxicity is abandoned, is it possible to care for one's self and the rest of the world through compassionate, egoless behavior.

23.
    a. No Change
    b. understand how a Buddhist could maintain egolessness,
    c. understand how a Buddhist could stay egolessness
    d. believe what a Buddhist could maintain egolessness

24.
    a. No Change
    b. When ego-toxicity can be abandoned it is possible for one's self to care for the rest of the world through compassionate, egoless behavior.
    c. When ego-toxicity is abandoned it could be possible to care for one's self and the rest of the world through compassionate, egoless behavior.
    d. When ego-toxicity is abandoned, it is possible to care for one's self and the rest of the world through compassionate, egoless behavior.

25. What is the purpose of the first paragraph?
    a. To criticize Buddhist notions of the self.
    b. To criticize contemporary Western notions of the self.
    c. To introduce the tension between individuality and collectivity in Western society.
    d. To introduce the idea of "egolessness."

26. According to the passage, what is "egolessness?"
    a. The complete denial of the self.
    b. The rejection of psychoanalytic notions of ego, superego, and id.
    c. The prioritization of self over others.
    d. The prioritization of relationships between and among people.

27. Which of the following best describes the purpose of the second paragraph?
    a. It introduces the distinction between "egolessness" and "ego-toxicity."
    b. It makes light of the conflicts that Buddhists in Western societies experience.
    c. It praises egolessness as the only moral way of living.
    d. It harshly denounces ego-toxicity.

28. Based on the passage, "quid pro quo" most likely means:
    a. "something for nothing."
    b. "good merits money."
    c. "to each his own."
    d. "something for something."

29. According to the passage, why do Buddhists do good deeds?
    a. Doing good brings direct, personal benefits to the person doing the action.
    b. They do good so that they may go to heaven when they die.
    c. If they do not do good, they will be reincarnated again.
    d. Doing good for one person is doing good for all beings.

30. In this passage, which sentence in the first paragraph states a main idea that is developed in subsequent paragraphs?
    a. The second sentence
    b. The fourth sentence
    c. The third sentence
    d. The first sentence

31. This sentence appears in the second paragraph: "In Western societies, ego-toxicity is the reigning condition." Which of the following would be the most logical organization?
    a. No change
    b. Move it to the end of the paragraph
    c. Move it to the paragraph's beginning
    d. Move it out of the paragraph entirely

32. Which of these accurately describes a pattern in the first and/or last sentences of all the paragraphs in this passage?
    a. The last sentence of each paragraph identifies half a main conflict; the final sentence completes it.
    b. The first sentence of each paragraph identifies a main conflict, with the final sentence reiterating.
    c. The first sentence of each paragraph identifies a main conflict, with the final sentence resolving it.
    d. The last sentence of each paragraph identifies a main conflict, with the final sentence resolving it.

33. The style, mode, or type of text in this passage is best characterized as which of these?
    a. Description
    b. Persuasion
    c. Exposition
    d. Narration

Focus: Students must make revising and editing decisions in the context of a passage on a science-related topic.

## How are Hypotheses Confirmed?

Most scientists agree that while the scientific method is an invaluable methodological tool, it is not a failsafe method for arriving at objective truth. It is debatable, for example, whether a hypothesis can actually be confirmed by evidence.

When the hypothesis is of a form, "All x are y," which is commonly believed that a piece of evidence that is both x and y confirms the hypothesis. For example, for the hypothesis "All monkeys are hairy," a particular monkey that is hairy is thought to be a confirming piece of evidence for the hypothesis. A problem arises when one encounters evidence that disproves a hypothesis: while no scientist would argue that one piece of evidence proves a hypothesis, it is possible for one piece of evidence to disprove a hypothesis. To return to the monkey example, one hairless monkey out of one billion hairy monkeys disproves the hypothesis "All monkeys are hairy." Single pieces of evidence, then, seem to affect a given hypothesis in radically different ways. For this reason, the confirmation of hypotheses is better described as probabilistic.

Hypotheses that can only be proven or disproven based on evidence need to be based on probability because sample sets for such hypotheses are too large. In the monkey example, every single monkey in the history of monkeys would need to be examined before the hypothesis could be proven. By making confirmation a function of probability, one may make provisional or working conclusions that allow for the possibility of a given hypothesis being **(34)** <u>dissipated</u> in the future. In the monkey case, then, encountering a hairy monkey would slightly raise the probability that "all monkeys are hairy," while encountering a hairless monkey would slightly decrease the probability that "all monkeys are hairy." This method of confirming hypotheses is both counterintuitive and controversial, **(35)** <u>but it allowed for evidence to equitably effect hypotheses</u> and it does not require infinite sample sets for confirmation or disconfirmation.

34.
   a. No Change
   b. distilled
   c. disconfirmed
   d. destroyed

35.
   a. No Change
   b. but it allows for evidence to equitably effect hypotheses
   c. but it allowed for evidence to equitably affect hypotheses
   d. but it allows for evidence to equitably affect hypotheses

36. Which of the following best states the main idea of the second paragraph?
   a. One hairy monkey proves the hypothesis "All monkeys are hairy."
   b. The same piece of evidence can both confirm and disconfirm a hypothesis.
   c. Confirming and disconfirming evidence affect hypotheses differently.
   d. The scientific method is not a failsafe method for arriving at objective truth.

37. Which of the following is true of hypotheses of the form "All x are y"?
    a. Something that is neither x nor y disproves the hypothesis.
    b. Something that is both x and y disproves the hypothesis.
    c. Something that is x but not y disproves the hypothesis.
    d. Something that is y but not x disproves the hypothesis.

38. In the third paragraph, why does the author discuss the "sample set" of monkeys?
    a. To show that there are significant differences between monkey species.
    b. To show that all monkeys are hairy.
    c. To show that just a few monkeys can prove the hypothesis "all monkeys are hairy."
    d. To show that practical concerns make confirmation or disconfirmation a function of probability.

39. Using the same reasoning as that in the passage, an automobile with eighteen wheels does what to the following hypothesis: "All automobiles have only four wheels"?
    a. It proves the hypothesis.
    b. It raises the hypothesis's probability.
    c. It disproves the hypothesis.
    d. It decreases the hypothesis's probability.

40. Which of the following best describes this passage?
    a. The main idea of this entire passage is in the first sentence.
    b. The main idea of the first paragraph is in the first sentence.
    c. The main passage idea is both the first paragraph sentences.
    d. This passage's main idea is not in first paragraph sentences.

41. According to the passage, which of the following is true?
    a. It is possible to prove a hypothesis by simply giving only one piece of evidence.
    b. It is possible to prove but not disprove a hypothesis with one piece of evidence.
    c. It is possible to disprove but not prove a hypothesis with one piece of evidence.
    d. It is not possible to prove or disprove a hypothesis using one piece of evidence.

42. The last sentence of the second paragraph reads, "For this reason, the confirmation of hypotheses is better described as probabilistic." Which of the following is most accurate about this sentence?
    a. This sentence is not relevant to the passage topic and should be deleted.
    b. This sentence is not relevant to this paragraph and should be relocated.
    c. This sentence draws an inference related to the topic but not to purpose.
    d. This sentence draws a logical conclusion, based on preceding sentences.

43. This passage ends with, "...it does not require infinite sample sets for confirmation or disconfirmation." This statement refers to information found where in the passage?
    a. Most specifically in the initial sentence in this same paragraph
    b. Most specifically in the second sentence of the same paragraph
    c. Most specifically the fourth sentence of the previous paragraph
    d. Most specifically the information is not found in any paragraph

44. Which of these is correct regarding the sentence boundaries in this passage?
    a. This passage contains a sentence fragment.
    b. This passage contains one run-on sentence.
    c. This passage contains neither type of error.
    d. This passage contains both types of errors.

# Math - Calculator

*Questions 1-4 pertain to the following information:*

Elli wants to plant a flower garden that contains only roses and tulips. However, she has a limited amount of space for the garden, and she can only afford to buy a specific number of each plant. Elli has enough space to plant a total of 20 flowers, and she wants to spend a total of $100 to purchase the flowers. Roses cost $14 per plant and tulips cost $4 per plant. Let R represent the number of roses and let T represent the number of tulips Elli will plant in her garden.

1. Which system of linear equations can be used to solve for the number of roses and tulips Elli will plant in her garden?

a. $\begin{cases} 4R + 14T = 20 \\ R + T = 100 \end{cases}$

b. $\begin{cases} R + T = 20 \\ 14R + 4T = 100 \end{cases}$

c. $\begin{cases} R + T = 20 \\ 4R + 14T = 100 \end{cases}$

d. $\begin{cases} 14R + 4T = 20 \\ 14R + 4T = 100 \end{cases}$

2. How many roses will Elli plant in her flower garden?
   a. 4
   b. 16
   c. 18
   d. 2

3. How many tulips will Elli plant in her flower garden?
   a. 4
   b. 16
   c. 18
   d. 2

4. Based on the information provided, why might Elli plant more tulips than roses in her garden?
   a. Because tulips require less space than roses
   b. Because tulips are less expensive than roses
   c. Because tulips are prettier than roses
   d. Because tulips require less fertilizer than roses

5. Which of the following represents the solution of the following system of linear equations?
$$5x + 9y = -7$$
$$2x - 4y = 20$$

   a. $x = 3, y = 2$
   b. $x = 4, y = 3$
   c. $x = 4, y = -3$
   d. $x = 3, y = -2$

*Use the information below to answer question 6:*

José is participating in a school fundraiser by selling packages of cookie dough and soft pretzels. His order form is shown below.

| Customer name | Packages of cookie dough | Packages of pretzels | Total cost |
|---|---|---|---|
| Cedric | 1 | 4 | $42 |
| Madhavi | 3 | 2 | $51 |
| James | 2 | ? | $24 |
| Mei Ling | 2 | 1 | ? |

6. The cost per package of cookie dough is $_____. James ordered ____ packages of pretzels. The total cost of Mei Ling's order is $_____.

7. If $\frac{1}{2x} + \frac{1}{x} = \frac{1}{6}$, then $x =$
   a. 2
   b. 4
   c. 9
   d. 12

8. Which of the following data sets could be represented by the histogram shown below?

a. 6,7, 7, 8, 12, 13, 18, 22, 26, 27, 28, 31, 36, 36, 36, 36, 37, 38, 38, 38, 39, 41, 41, 41, 42, 42, 43, 43, 48, 49

b. 2, 3, 4, 4, 8, 9, 10, 10, 11, 15, 19, 21, 21, 21, 21, 22, 24, 24, 25, 29, 31, 33, 40, 43, 45, 46, 48, 48, 49, 50

c. 1, 2, 8, 8, 9, 9, 12, 13, 15, 15, 16, 17, 18, 19, 19, 21, 29, 31, 31, 35, 36, 38, 41, 42, 42, 45, 46, 47, 47, 49

d. 1, 4, 4, 5, 10, 10, 10, 12, 12, 16, 20, 22, 23, 23, 25, 27, 31, 31, 37, 39, 40, 41, 41, 43, 45, 46, 48, 49, 49, 50

9. A taxi service charges $5.50 for the first 1/5 of a mile, $1.50 for each additional 1/5 of a mile, and 20¢ per minute of waiting time. Joan took a cab from her home to a flower shop 8 miles away, where she bought a bouquet, and then another 3.6 miles to her mother's house. The driver had to wait 9 minutes while she bought the bouquet. What was the fare?
   a. $101.80
   b. $120.20
   c. $92.80
   d. $91.20

141

10. Prizes are to be awarded to the best pupils in each class of an elementary school. The number of students in each grade is shown in the table, and the school principal wants the number of prizes awarded in each grade to be proportional to the number of students. If there are twenty prizes, how many should go to fifth-grade students?

| Grade | 1 | 2 | 3 | 4 | 5 |
|---|---|---|---|---|---|
| Students | 35 | 38 | 38 | 33 | 36 |

    a. 5
    b. 4
    c. 6
    d. 3

11. The probability that Bryan goes to the store is 0.18. The probability that he goes to the movies is 0.34. The probability that he goes to the store, given that he goes to the movies, is 0.46. What is the probability he goes to the store or to the movies?
    a. 32.38%
    b. 36.36%
    c. 40.28%
    d. 44.46%

12. Suppose Ashley will receive a $6,000 scholarship if she chooses University A, a $4,500 scholarship if she chooses University B, and a $5,500 scholarship if she chooses University C. The probabilities that she will attend each university are equal. Which of the following best represents the expected value for the scholarship amount she will receive?
    a. $4,833
    b. $5,155
    c. $5,333
    d. $5,525

13. Calculate the fifth term of the sequence defined as $f(0) = 2$, $f(n + 1) = 2f(n) - 1$ for $n \geq 1$.
    a. 9
    b. 17
    c. 32
    d. 33

14. The table below displays the value of $h(x)$ for nine different values of $x$.

| $x$ | −4 | −3 | −2 | −1 | 0 | 1 | 2 | 3 | 4 |
|---|---|---|---|---|---|---|---|---|---|
| $h(x)$ | −16 | −8 | −4 | −2 | −1 | −0.5 | 0 | 2 | 6 |

What is the value of $h^{-1}(-2)$?
    a. $h^{-1}(-2) = -4$
    b. $h^{-1}(-2) = -1$
    c. $h^{-1}(-2) = 1$
    d. $h^{-1}(-2) = 3$

15. Which frequency table is represented by the histogram shown below?

a.

| Interval | Frequency |
|----------|-----------|
| 1 – 10 | 3 |
| 11 – 20 | 9 |
| 21 – 30 | 8 |
| 31 – 40 | 6 |
| 41 – 50 | 4 |

c.

| Interval | Frequency |
|----------|-----------|
| 1 – 10 | 3 |
| 11 – 20 | 9 |
| 21 – 30 | 8 |
| 31 – 40 | 5 |
| 41 – 50 | 4 |

b.

| Interval | Frequency |
|----------|-----------|
| 1 – 10 | 3 |
| 11 – 20 | 8 |
| 21 – 30 | 8 |
| 31 – 40 | 6 |
| 41 – 50 | 3 |

d.

| Interval | Frequency |
|----------|-----------|
| 1 – 10 | 2 |
| 11 – 20 | 9 |
| 21 – 30 | 8 |
| 31 – 40 | 6 |
| 41 – 50 | 4 |

16. In an election in Kimball County, Candidate A obtained 36,800 votes. His opponent, Candidate B, obtained 32,100 votes. 2,100 votes went to write-in candidates. What percentage of the vote went to Candidate A?
    a. 51.8%
    b. 53.4%
    c. 52.6%
    d. 46.8%

17. Given the ordered pairs below, in the form, $(x, f(x))$, which represent values and their corresponding probabilities, what is the expected value?
$(0, 18), (1, 12), (2, 20), (3, 24), (4, 10), (5, 36), (6, 4)$
    a. 354
    b. 362
    c. 368
    d. 374

18. You draw two cards from a deck with cards labeled $1 - 6$ and then graph the probabilities of the expected value of picking a 3 after choosing 2 cards. Which of the following represents the probabilities that correspond to $x$-values of 0, 1, and 2 cards?

    a. $\frac{2}{3}, \frac{1}{3}, 0$

    b. $\frac{1}{3}, \frac{1}{6}, 0$

    c. $\frac{2}{3}, \frac{1}{3}, \frac{1}{5}$

    d. $\frac{1}{3}, \frac{1}{6}, \frac{1}{9}$

*For questions 19-20, consider the set of data below:*
38  49  22  36  45  27  38  47  20  21  19  38  17  28  15  18  42  17  25  33  31

19. Organize the data using a stem-and-leaf plot.

| 1
| 2
| 3
| 4

20. State the mean, median, and mode(s). If necessary, round to the nearest tenth.
Mean:  _____
Median:  _____
Mode:  _____

21. Given the equation, $\frac{2}{x+4} = \frac{3}{x}$, what is the value of $x$?
   a. 10
   b. 12
   c. −12
   d. −14

22. Which of the following represents the points of intersection of the line, $x + y = -6$ and a circle, given by the equation, $(x - 2)^2 + (y + 4)^2 = 16$?
   a. (2, −6) and (−2, 4)
   b. (−2, −4) and (2, −8)
   c. (2, 4) and (−2, 8)
   d. (−2, −6) and (2, −12)

23. What is the solution to the equation, $\frac{x}{x+4} - \frac{3}{4} = \frac{4}{x+4}$?
   a. $x = 22$
   b. $x = 24$
   c. $x = 26$
   d. $x = 28$

24. Which of the following represents the solutions of the system of equations, $\begin{matrix} y = x + 2 \\ y = x^2 + 2 \end{matrix}$?
   a. (1, 3) and (2, 0)
   b. (3, 1) and (0, 2)
   c. (1, 3) and (0, 2)
   d. (3, 1) and (2, 0)

25. The path of ball thrown into the air is modeled by the first quadrant graph of the equation $h = -16t^2 + 47t + 3$, where $h$ is the height of the ball in feet and $t$ is time in seconds after the ball is thrown. The maximum height of the ball occurs at $t =$ ____ seconds, and the ball hits the ground at $t =$ ___ seconds. If necessary, round answers to the nearest tenth.

26. What is the range of the function $g(x) = 2x^2 + 8x + 5$?
   a. $g(x) \geq -3$
   b. $g(x) > -2$
   c. $g(x) \leq -2$
   d. All real numbers

27. The area of a rectangular bedroom is 120 ft², and the perimeter of the room is 44 ft. On a house plan drawn to a $\frac{1}{24}$ scale, what is the length in inches of the longer side of the rectangle representing the room? _____

28. In the figure, $C$ is the center of the circle and $m\angle ACD = 110°$.

$A$

$B$

$C$

$D$

Calculate $m\angle ADB$.

$m\angle ACD =$ _____

29. A typical soda can is approximately 4.8 in tall with a diameter of about 2.2 in. Assuming that the can is a perfect cylinder, what is its volume? If necessary, round your answer to the nearest tenth.

Its volume is approximately _____ in³.

30. In isosceles triangle $ABC$, the length of each leg is 13 and the length of the base is 10. Calculate the area of $\triangle ABC$. Write an exact answer in simplest form.
   a. 60
   b. 65
   c. 130
   d. $\frac{25\sqrt{3}}{2}$

31. In the figure, $C$ is the center of the circle with radius 4. The length of minor arc $AB$ is $3\pi$. Calculate the area of sector $ACB$. Write your answer in terms of $\pi$.

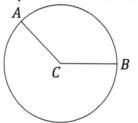

   a. $A = 3\pi$
   b. $A = 4\pi$
   c. $A = 6\pi$
   d. $A = 8\pi$

# Math - No-Calculator

1. Given the system of equations, $\begin{array}{l} 3x + 6y = 36 \\ 2x + 9y = 34 \end{array}$, which of the following equations may be added to produce the correct *y*-value solution?

a. $\begin{array}{l} 6x + 15y = 72 \\ -6x - 36y = -102 \end{array}$

b. $\begin{array}{l} 6x + 12y = 72 \\ -6x - 27y = -102 \end{array}$

c. $\begin{array}{l} 6x + 12y = 108 \\ -6x - 27y = -102 \end{array}$

d. $\begin{array}{l} 6x + 15y = 108 \\ -6x - 36y = -72 \end{array}$

2. Jonathan pays a $65 monthly flat rate for his cell phone. He is charged $0.12 per minute for each minute used, in a roaming area. Which of the following expressions represents his monthly cell phone bill for *x* roaming minutes?

a. $65 + 0.12x$
b. $65x + 0.12$
c. $65.12x$
d. $65.12 + 0.12x$

3. Which of the following equations is represented by the graph shown below?

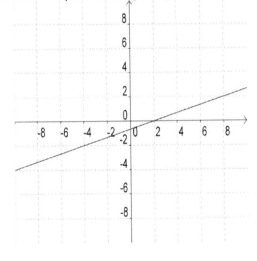

a. $14x - 21y = 7$
b. $12x - 6y = 16$
c. $7x - 21y = 14$
d. $16x - 18y = 12$

4. A taxi ride costs $4.25 for the first mile and $0.70 for each mile after the first. Which of the following functions $c(d)$ gives the total cost (in dollars) of traveling *d* miles (assuming that $d \geq 1$)?

a. $c(d) = 3.55 + 0.70(d + 1)$
b. $c(d) = 3.55 + 0.70(d - 1)$
c. $c(d) = 4.25 + 0.70d$
d. $c(d) = 4.25 + 0.70(d - 1)$

5. A pump fills a cylindrical tank with water at a constant rate. The function $L(g) = 0.3g$ represents the water level of the tank (in feet) after $g$ gallons are pumped into the tank. The function $w(t) = 1.2t$ represents the number of gallons that can be pumped into the tank in $t$ minutes. Write a function $L(t)$ for the water level of the tank after $t$ minutes.

 a. $L(t) = 0.25t$
 b. $L(t) = 0.36t$
 c. $L(t) = 0.9t$
 d. $L(t) = 3.6t$

6. Adam has $10 more than Betty. If Adam were to give $15 to Betty, then she would have twice as much money as Adam. Write this situation as a system of equations.

 a. $A = B + 10$
  $B + 15 = 2A$

 b. $B = A + 10$
  $B + 15 = 2A$

 c. $A = B + 10$
  $B + 15 = 2(A - 15)$

 d. $B = A + 10$
  $B + 15 = 2(A - 15)$

7. Linear functions grow by equal differences over equal intervals. By what amount does the linear function $f(x) = 4x - 8$ grow by over every interval whose length is 5?

 a. –40
 b. 12
 c. 20
 d. 40

8. The linear function $g(x)$ is graphed below.

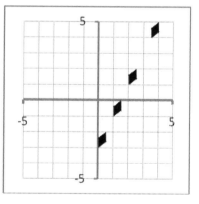

Write an explicit formula for $g(x)$.

 a. $g(x) = -2x - 3$
 b. $g(x) = -5x + 2$
 c. $g(x) = 2x - 3$
 d. $g(x) = 5x + 2$

9. What is the solution to the inequality, $3x + 18 > 6$?

    a. $x > -4$
    b. $x < -4$
    c. $x > -8$
    d. $x < -8$

10. What is the range of the function $g(x) = x - 2$?

    a. $g(x) \geq -8$
    b. $g(x) \geq 8$
    c. $g(x) > 0$
    d. All real numbers

11. Which of the following represents the difference of $(3x^3 - 9x^2 + 6x) - (8x^3 + 4x^2 - 3x)$?

    a. $-5x^3 - 13x^2 + 9x$
    b. $11x^3 - 13x^2 + 3x$
    c. $-5x^3 - 5x^2 + 3x$
    d. $5x^3 + 13x^2 + 9x$

12. Which of the following represents the sum of $(12x^3 - 8x + 6x^2 - 3)$ and $(8x^2 - 20x^3 + 6 - 2x)$?

    a. $-8x^3 + 14x^2 - 10x + 3$
    b. $20x^3 - 28x^2 + 12x - 5$
    c. $-8x^3 + 2x^2 + 6x + 3$
    d. $32x^2 + 14x^2 - 10x - 5$

13. The graph of $y = (x + 3)(x^2 - x - 2)$ has $x$-intercepts _____ and $y$-intercept _____.

14. Which of the following is the graph of $y = -2(x - 2)^2 + 1$.

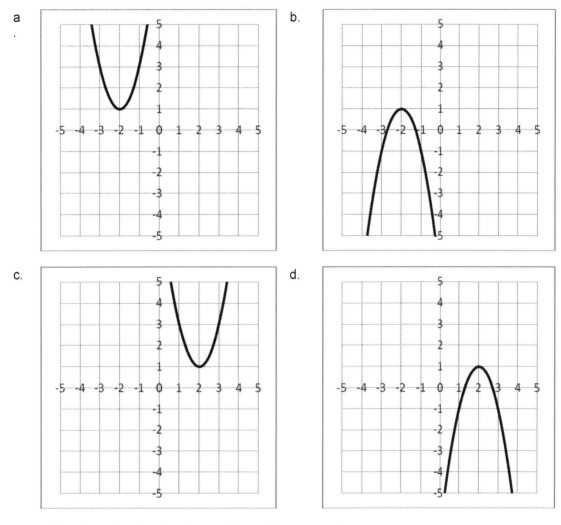

a.

b.

c.

d.

15. What is the domain of the function $f(x) = 2x^2 + 5x - 12$?
    a. $x \geq \frac{3}{2}$
    b. $x \leq -4$
    c. $-4 \leq x \leq \frac{3}{2}$
    d. All real numbers

16. What is the domain of the function $f(x) = \sqrt{x + 5}$?
    a. $x \geq -5$
    b. $x \geq 5$
    c. $x > 0$
    d. All real numbers

17. In the figure, *ABCD* is a rectangle. Lines *m* and *n* are parallel to $\overline{AB}$ and $\overline{BC}$, respectively, and intersect at point *P*. In addition, they each bisect rectangle. Which transformation of *ABCD* will NOT result in an image that coincides with the original rectangle?

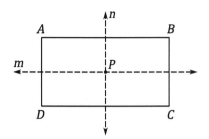

a. A reflection across *m*

b. A reflection across *n*

c. A 90° rotation about *P*

d. A 180° rotation about *P*

# Answers and Explanations

# Reading

**U.S. Literature**

1. C: The selection does not portray the themes offered in choices A, B, and D.

2. A: Choice B is incorrect because Mother did not forbid any presents. Choices C and D give some of the problems presented in the selection, but do not offer a complete summary.

3. D: The passage states: "'We haven't got Father, and shall not have him for a long time.' She didn't say 'perhaps never,' but each silently added it, thinking of Father far away, where the fighting was." The other choices may be true of Father, but they are not specified in this selection.

4. C: Although choices A and B may be true, they are not specified in this selection. Jo believes choice D to be true, but whether or not she is right is not stated: "'Mother didn't say anything about our money, and she won't wish us to give up everything. Let's each buy what we want, and have a little fun; I'm sure we work hard enough to earn it,' cried Jo."

5. D: The other sisters all specify what they want to buy. Choice A: "'I shall get a nice box of Faber's drawing pencils; I really need them,' said Amy decidedly." Choice B: "'I planned to spend mine in new music,' said Beth." Choice C: "'I do want to buy Undine and Sintran for myself. I've wanted it so long,' said Jo."

6. D: The presence of a hearth brush and kettle-holder indicate a fireplace, and the fact that the fireplace "hears" Beth's sigh when no one else does indicates that Beth is closest to it.

7. B: "Injured" in the context of this sentence means Amy feels that her sense of fairness, vanity, and pride have been injured—not that she has a physical injury (a) or hurt feelings at Meg's words (c), which were "'It's so dreadful to be poor!'"—basically more in agreement with Amy's subsequent sentiment than containing anything to hurt Amy's feelings. There is nothing in this passage indicating Amy has a cold (d); she sniffs to emphasize her sense of unfairness at being deprived of the pretty things some girls have.

8. A: Five paragraphs before this quotation, Beth says she planned to spend her dollar "in new music," so in the context of this entire passage alone we can assume she means practicing music. (We would know from reading the entire novel that Beth plays piano.) Drawing (b) is what Amy does: she says she will buy Faber's drawing pencils with her dollar. Teaching (c) is what Meg does; she complains about it in this passage. Schoolwork (d) is what Amy complains about following Beth's complaint about washing dishes and housecleaning.

9. D: (a) most explicitly shows there is a war going on by describing their father being "where the fighting was." (b) also alludes to war by mentioning "our" army men suffering. (c) only indicates that their father is not with his family and they may be separated for a long time, but it does not say where he is or why.

**Passage 1**

10. C: "Peculiar" can mean odd (a) or bizarre (b), but these make no sense in this context. "Peculiar" can also mean specific (c), unique, particular, distinctive, or characteristic, which is the meaning in this case, because Lincoln was referring to the specific and unique situation that, "One-eighth of the whole population were colored slaves, not distributed generally over the Union, but localized in the southern part of it," and the specific interest these slaves constituted. Appropriate (d) is another synonym offered by a thesaurus for the second (correct) meaning, but its denotation of suitable or fitting does not make sense in this context as specific, unique, particular, distinctive, etc. does.

11. B: The closest meaning is freedom for all citizens, which would include slaves. Lincoln issued the Emancipation Proclamation over nine months before the Gettysburg Address, but the Civil War was still being fought over the issue of slavery. He called for "us the living" to finish the "unfinished work" of soldier and "highly resolve that these dead shall not have died in vain" by giving the nation a "new birth of freedom". Without reaffirming the nation's bases of freedom and equality, the nation would "perish from the earth" and the soldiers would have died in vain. The entire paragraph leads up to this meaning. This does not indicate freedom from war (a): the speech does not say ending the war would bring freedom; but by restoring the nation's original foundations of freedom and equality for which soldiers fought, the dead would not die in vain—not that soldiers should be freed from fighting the war (c). Slavery violated the foundations of US democracy; hence (d) makes no sense in this context.

12. D: Lincoln's Biblical quotation established the subsequent supposition that the war is an example of the woe for causing offenses described in the quotation (just as previously in the same sentence he supposed American slavery was one of the offenses that must needs come). (a) does not support the supposition that God gave the war as woe; if anything, it supports his contention that despite their basic differences regarding slavery, "Both parties deprecated war" (second paragraph, last sentence). (b) reinforces the parallelism and comparison/contrast established in the second paragraph ("saving the Union without war/destroy it without war"; "make war rather than let the nation survive/accept war rather than let it perish") and continued in the third ("Neither...expected....Neither anticipated....Each looked for....") rather than supporting that war was God's giving both sides woe for offenses. (c) supports that even though everyone wanted the war to end soon ("Fondly...away", penultimate sentence), if it lasted longer it would be God's will.

13. A: Lincoln was reminding his audience that the nation was formed with the ideas of liberty and equality as foundations—seen symmetrically in the opening and closing sentences—and reasoning that upholding those ideals was the best way to honor the soldiers who fought for that nation. (b) is not the main idea as he explicitly stated in the third paragraph, first sentence, "we can not consecrate – we cannot hallow – this ground" because the soldiers had done so "far beyond our poor power to add or detract." He continues to say their deeds will never be forgotten even though his and others' words would—making (c) incorrect. Completing soldiers' unfinished work refers not to declaring a cease-fire (d) in particular, but to ensuring the nation's democratic government and its founding principles would not "perish from the earth."

14. D: By using the same syntactic structure in "what we say here" and "what they did here", Lincoln employed parallel structure to reinforce his message contrasting words vs. deeds. Epiphora (a), epistrophe, is repeating the same words/phrases at the *ends* of sentences/clauses. An example in Lincoln's Gettysburg Address is: "that government of the people, by the people, for the people..." in its final sentence. Anaphora (b) is repeating the same words/phrases at the *beginnings* of clauses/sentences, as Dickens did in the opening of *A Tale of Two Cities*: "It was the best of times, it was the worst of times, it was the age of wisdom, it was the age of foolishness..." etc. (he used "it was" 10 times in one sentence). Repetition (c) involves simply repeating the same word/phrase/clause multiple times. Parallelism/parallel structure does not

require exact word repetition, but symmetrical sentence/clause structure arranging the same parts of speech in the same word order.

15. C: In the Second Inaugural Address, Lincoln said in the final paragraph, "...let us strive on to finish the work we are in..." and in the Gettysburg Address, third paragraph, "...to be dedicated here to the unfinished work which they who fought here have thus far so nobly advanced." He spoke of (a), (b), and (d) in the former speech, but not overtly in the latter.

16. B: In the opening paragraph of his second inaugural address, Lincoln discusses his first address, describing how the first actions in the coming Civil War were just beginning to take place. The country had suffered much since then as the war got underway and continued throughout his first term as president. This change in the nation inspired the plea for an end to the hostilities that dominates his second inaugural address.

17. C: Lincoln believed that the South was wrong for making war by trying to secede from the union, and the North was right for trying to maintain the union by refusing to accept the hostile action. This quote shows he believed the actions of the North were more justifiable than those of the South.

18. A: Lincoln states that "if God wills that it [the war] continue ... until every drop of blood drawn with the lash shall be paid by another drawn with the sword, as was said three thousand years ago, so still it must be said 'the judgments of the Lord are true and righteous altogether.'" This statement indicates Lincoln's believe that the war was a product of God's will.

19. D: Lincoln delivered his Second Inaugural Address after a time of great hardship for the United States: the Civil War. His plea for the country's resolution of its severe problems must have been an emotional experience for the president, and his voice must have conveyed this emotionality as he read the speech. As a result, reading the document online could not have quite the same emotional impact as hearing it in person.

**Passage 2**
20. A: Since the beginning of our American history, we have been engaged in change—in a perpetual peaceful revolution—a revolution which goes on steadily, quietly adjusting itself to changing conditions—without the concentration camp or the quick-lime in the ditch.
This is the only statement listed here that directly supports the idea that FDR thought that America is constantly moving toward a better way of life.

21. A: It emphasizes the need for a social safety net for the aging populace. While the other ideas in Choices B and C are clearly mentioned in the blog, they are not derived from the speech. Choice A is the only one that discusses an idea that shows up in the speech.

22. B: The average citizen already feels overburdened by taxes and feels the money is not being well-spent by the government. The argument that needs to be evaluated is that people will be happy to give more money in taxes to the government. It would be safe to raise the counterargument that the general population may already believe they are paying enough in taxes and don't think the government is spending that money wisely. Not everyone will be happy to give more to the government to spend. Choices A and D do not address the question. Choice C actually agrees with FDR's premise.

23. D: There are four basic freedoms that are vital to the health of people: speech, worship, freedom from want, and freedom from fear. This speech is typically referred to as the "Four Freedoms" speech. In it, FDR articulates the basic freedoms he believes in. These freedoms are the central focus of the speech, since it supports the other ideas that he is focusing on (ie, social issues). Choice A is a detail in the speech, Choice B is not articulated, and Choice C is not in the speech.

24. C: FDR spoke of freedom, defining it in the previous paragraph as "the supremacy of human rights everywhere." This is the "high concept" he refers to in the following paragraph/sentence. In this context, the "end" of victory does not mean death (a). It does not precisely mean purpose (b), as in the common phrase "a means to an end" (a way of achieving a purpose): he was not saying victory was the only purpose of the concept, but rather that this concept could have no other outcome (c) or result than victory. "End" can also mean conclusion (d), i.e., the termination or finishing of something, which does not fit the meaning in this context quite as precisely as (c) because it does not imply cause and effect as "outcome" does.

25. D: After describing the four freedoms he identified, FDR said the vision of a world founded on those freedoms was "no vision of a distant millennium" but "a definite basis for a kind of world attainable in our own time and generation. That kind of world is the very antithesis of the so-called new order of tyranny..." referring to the "order" that dictators wanted to impose, to which "we oppose the greater conception—the moral order. He further described the "cooperation of free countries, working together in a friendly, civilized society" as the "world order which we seek". This context establishes that "order" more nearly means a system of societal and world politics (d) rather than a military leader's command (a); an authoritative decision or direction (b), e.g., a court order or a doctor's order; or an arrangement in sequence (c), e.g., alphabetical, numerical, or chronological order.

26. A: Following the paragraph beginning, "I have called for personal sacrifice", FDR said, "A part of the sacrifice means the payment of more money in taxes" for "a greater portion of this great defense program". While he called for taxpayers to support the military, in this passage he did not equate personal sacrifice with serving in the military (b). While he described worldwide arms reduction (c), he did not equate this with personal sacrifice, but with the fourth freedom: freedom from fear. The four freedoms (d) he identified were "essential human freedoms", i.e., things all human beings had rights to, not examples of personal sacrifice.

27. D: FDR implicitly referred to the American Revolutionary War (a) by contrasting it with the process of continual change which he characterized as America's ongoing "*perpetual peaceful revolution*". He continued a pattern of implicit contrast by further characterizing this peaceful revolution as adjusting to change "without the concentration camp or the quick-lime in the ditch." Concentration camps were established by the Nazis during World War II as part of the Holocaust; quicklime was used in trenches during World War I (b), when trench warfare was widely practiced. In World War II (c), soldiers dug more individual foxholes than trenches (though there were some); but quicklime was also used by Nazis in mass graves of people they murdered and on the floors of train cattle cars transporting people to concentration camps, labor camps, and death camps.

28. C: In this passage there is no mention of expanding the draft of citizens into military service. As examples of aspects of the social economy needing "immediate improvement", FDR cited, "We should bring more citizens under the coverage of old-age pensions...." (a); "We should widen the opportunities for adequate medical care" (b); and "We should plan a better system by which persons deserving or needing gainful employment may obtain it" (d).

29. B: Antistrophe is repeating a word/phrase at the end of each sentence/clause as FDR did in the successive sentences (which are also paragraphs) defining the four freedoms. Anastrophe (a) is inverting word order for emphasis, e.g., Longfellow's "the forest primeval" (*Evangeline*) or JFK's "**Ask not** what your country can do for you...." Apostrophe (c) is interrupting dialogue or narration to address the reader, audience, or a personification thereof directly ("Dear reader, what would you do in my place?" or an actor in a play speaking to the audience instead of other actors). Aposiopesis (d) is abruptly leaving a statement unfinished, e.g., "You do that once more and I'll—".

## Science

### Passage 1

30. C: The passage describes several distinctive features of annelid anatomy and tells how some of them differ from other worms.

31. A: The term is defined in the text as an organization of the anatomy into segments.

32. D: The term is defined in the text between commas.

33. C: The text gives the example of feet specializing into grasping organs to illustrate this evolutionary advantage of segmental plasticity.

34. D: The text gives the example of parapodia modified for grasping to illustrate evolutionary plasticity among metameres.

35. C: The text defines metemeres as segments, and discusses segmentation as the distinguishing feature of the phylum.

36. D: The paragraph tells us that annelids can live in salt or fresh water and on land, and then gives examples.

37. D: Stating that metameric segmentation is the distinguishing feature of the Annelid phylum (c) is stating a fact; though it is true, simply identifying this characteristic does not automatically inform the reader of the evolutionary flexibility it confers. The author establishes this flexibility by writing, "...certain segments can be modified and specialized to perform specific functions." To illustrate such modification and specialization, the author continues with (a) and (b), which are both actual examples of such modification and specialization.

38. D: The author compares (a) annelids and nematodes as both having a fluid-filled internal *coelum* or cavity separating the body wall and gut, and both having this cavity involved in their locomotion. The author also contrasts (b) the two phyla in that annelids develop this cavity much later during both embryonic growth and ("presumably") evolutionary progress. Hence both (d) relationships are established, meaning (c) [Neither] is incorrect.

### Passage 2

39. A: the movement of the Earth around the sun. Only this choice provides support for the idea of special relativity. Choice B. is used in the explanation, but does not provide support on its own. Choice C. is actually part of a counterargument to relativity. Choice D. only indicates that there are two sections, and does not provide any support.

40. B: If relativity is valid, then why can it not explain all parts of the natural world, including the rules of quantum mechanics? Only this choice deals closely with an argument against relativity. The classical laws of motion are in agreement with relativity. Choice C. does not pose an argument against relativity and Choice D. focuses on asking a detailed question about the thought experiment, not the entire theory.

41. C: validity regarding an understanding of the classical rules of motion. The word "truth" was quoted because Einstein was referring to the understanding of the laws of motion we had before relativity, which did indeed seem to provide the correct answers for a great deal of physics questions. However, according to the other sentences around this word, we can conclude that it does not refer to an absolute truth because relativity turns classical ideas on their heads.

42. B: Corresponding to the noun "delicacy", one meaning of the adjective "delicate" is fragile (a) or easily damaged. This meaning is not supported by the context. As it modifies "detail", delicacy here refers to how sensitively and specifically classical mechanics describes the movements of

stars, planets, etc. Another meaning of a delicacy is an expensive and/or rare delight (c), especially regarding food; e.g., caviar is considered a delicacy. This meaning makes no sense in this context. Delicacy can also refer to soft texture (d), e.g., the delicacy of a lace fabric. This meaning does not relate to the subject matter.

43. D: *A priori* is Latin, meaning literally "from the one before". In the context of Einstein's discussion, he means that because the principle of relativity can be generalized so broadly across domains, its applying so precisely in one domain predicts it would apply with comparable accuracy in another domain; and therefore, that its being valid for one domain but not another is not very likely. It is *a priori* not very likely when considering this application of a general principle to a specific domain, and this unlikeliness is logically true/valid independent of observation or experience.

44. A: Einstein used and defined this term in the same sentence: "However, the most careful observations have never revealed such anisotropic properties in terrestrial physical space, i.e., a physical non-equivalence of different directions." The latter boldfaced portion is the definition. Hence the meaning is explicit, not implicit; and physicists are not the only ones who would know the meaning (b) without the definition: it is also used in biology, botany, medicine, optics, and zoology, for example. Einstein did not coin this term (c); its origin is c. 1875-1880, and Einstein was born in 1879. He also had not defined it in an earlier paragraph (c) of this passage, but within the same sentence where he used it. Thus it is not true that he never defined it (d). Neither is it true that anyone can tell its meaning from context (d) here. If it were, he would not have defined it for his audience/readers.

45. C: As Einstein indicated in the sentence following this one, "This statement is called the principle of relativity (in the restricted sense)." The statements in (a), (b), and (d) are all conclusions predicated upon the condition that this principle were NOT true: (a) begins with "If the principle of relativity (in the restricted sense) does not hold," continuing with the "then" clause quoted. (b) continues from (a), saying, "In this case we should be constrained to believe that..." finishing with the clause quoted. (d) is prefaced by, "If the principle of relativity were not valid" and continues with the clause quoted.

46. A: The quoted phrase is most an example of understatement. To emphasize through reversal how exquisite he found the detail provided by classical mechanics, Einstein downplayed it by describing it as less than wonderful, but only a little less. He further qualified this by not writing "*nothing* short of wonderful", but "*little* short of wonderful", making it comparative rather than absolute. An example of overstatement (b) or hyperbole in this case would be something like "the most wonderful ever seen", "too wonderful to be believed", etc. Amplification (c) is repeating a word/phrase but with added details or expanded description for emphasis; e.g., "...it supplies us with the actual motions of the heavenly bodies with a delicacy of detail—a delicacy of detail so fine that it can only be perceived as wonderful." Metabasis (d) is a transitional summary that recapitulates what was said previously and predicts what will be said next, to clarify and organize discourse.

47. C: Of the first five paragraphs, the first four are completely positive in Einstein's assertions and explanations of his claims; the fifth is also mainly positive, with only a hint of counterclaim in its last sentence refuted to emphasize the claim's validity ("But that [this] principle...should hold...in one domain...and yet...be invalid for another, is a priori not very probable."). The last two paragraphs present counterclaims, introduced by "If the principle of relativity does not hold..." and similar clauses, followed by "then..." conclusions illustrating the logically necessary yet improbable results of such counterclaims.

# Writing and Language

## Careers

1. A: Paragraph 2 begins with a transition from paragraph 1 by referring to the same topic—what software developers do—as it further specifies this. Paragraph 3 begins with a transition from paragraph 2 by referring to information in both paragraphs 1 and 2 as it gives additional details about developers sometimes called IT project managers. The last sentence in paragraph 3 creates a transition by introducing the subtopics of paragraphs 4 and 5. This is the *only* place where the transition is explicitly at the end of the preceding paragraph (b) rather than introducing the next one. Since there are between-paragraph transitions in this passage, (c) is incorrect. Since there are multiple transitions, (d) is also incorrect.

2. D: The passage identifies systems software designers as those who design operating systems; Apple's iOS and Google's Android are operating systems. The late Steve Jobs (a) did not design any original Apple operating systems (OSs); he was not an engineer and did not write code. He did make changes and additions to others' designs. (Except for the Apple II "monitor" program which included Allen Baum's assistance, Steve Wozniak designed all of the Apple I and Apple II OSs by himself.) Bill Gates (a) co-founded the Microsoft Corporation with Paul Allen; he did not design Google's Android OS. Besides, this passage does not mention either name. Applications software designers (c) design games, programs, and other software applications rather than OSs; the passage makes this distinction. Hence (b) is incorrect.

3. B: The first paragraph of this passage gives a general description of what software developers do. The succeeding paragraphs all give more specific details about this topic. This passage does not introduce a problem and then provide a solution for it (a). Although it does describe the different types of software (applications and operating systems) designed by different types of software developers (applications software developers and systems software developers) respectively, it simply identifies what they each design without discussing their similarities and differences; and does not point out similarities and differences (c) otherwise or overall between aspects of software development. It does not explain how certain factors caused certain effects (d) regarding the topic.

4. C: The first paragraph of this passage states that software developers return to their design processes to improve their programs or solve problems if customers find the programs too hard to use or the programs do not work as expected; and that developers may conduct maintenance and upgrades for their programs after they become available to the public. This information is evidence that refutes the claim described in the question. Therefore (a) is incorrect. There is no evidence in the passage to support this claim (b); therefore, (d) is also incorrect.

5. A: This passage has an introduction(s): The first sentence introduces both the first paragraph and the entire passage topic; and the entire first paragraph can also be considered an introduction to the rest of the passage as it gives a more general summary of the topic, while the other paragraphs provide more specific details. There is no conclusion, which can be expected in a passage which could be excerpted from a longer work. Since there is an introduction but no conclusion, (b) is incorrect. Since there is no conclusion, (c) is incorrect. Since there is an introduction, (d) is incorrect.

6. B: To agree with the plural noun "(software) developers", "for software programs" should also be plural. The sentence as is (a) combines plural and singular nouns. Version (c) further specifies the singular by adding "one", but the singular object still disagrees with the plural subject; also, "one" changes the meaning. While (d) uses a plural object to agree with the plural subject, it also further specifies "programs" by adding "many", which changes the meaning.

7. A: This clause is correct as it is. Current convention dictates that "code", i.e., computer programming code, is a mass (collective or non-count) noun; and "writing code" is the conventional expression. Because the sense of "code" in this context is NOT as a count noun,

both using the plural "codes" (b) and specifying a singular count noun by using the article "a" (c) are incorrect. Although the word "coding" has become convention as a synonym for "*writing code*", this "-ing" progressive participle is only used that way—as a verb, but NOT as a noun or synonym for "code" (d).

8. B: Although in some cases it is preferable to keep the auxiliary verb ("are") and verb participle ("called") together, this depends on the individual instance. If placing a modifier outside the two reads or sounds awkward, placing it between them as in this case is better. "...are sometimes called" is not only smoother and less awkward than "sometimes are called"; the latter also is less clear: in that position, "sometimes" could modify either "supervise" before it or "called" after it. Placing the adverb at the end of the sentence (c) also reads awkwardly, plus detracts from the emphasis on the descriptor "information technology (IT) project managers" by following it with another word; and moreover interrupts the transition to the next sentence, "These workers...." Placing "sometimes" after "called" (d) is not only awkward but incorrect. To be correct and make sense, "sometimes" would need commas to signal its intervention between predicate and object to modify the verb (i.e., "are called, sometimes, information...."); but this would still be more awkward than (b).

9. C: By identifying both "the Internet" and "within a company's intranet" in the same sentence, the reader can infer that an intranet belongs to a single company, unlike the Internet. Company intranets have access restricted to the company's employees, owners, and other authorized users (a). Intranets are neither as large as the Internet, nor separate from it (b) because they use protocols and software developed for the Internet. An intranet does not refer to the Internet as used by one specific company (d), which does not make sense since any company with Internet access can use the Internet.

10. C: The context of the passage establishes that databases are software applications in the fourth paragraph by identifying applications software developers as designing computer applications and then stating, "Some applications software developers create complex databases for organizations." From the context, (a) is incorrect because the passage differentiates applications from operating systems, including databases in paragraph 4 about applications developers but not in paragraph 5 about systems developers. Paragraph 4 also specifies "databases for organizations"; it only identifies "commercial software to be sold to the general public", not databases (b). Paragraph 5 defines system interfaces (d) as enabling users to interact with operating systems and the computers running them. The passage never equates databases with interfaces and moreover differentiates them by identifying databases as applications developed by applications developers but interfaces as developed by systems developers.

11. D: The graph shows that all occupations are projected to increase in employment by 11% from 2012-2022; occupations in business and financial operations are projected to increase by 13% during the same period; and occupations as personal financial advisors are projected to increase by 27% during that time. Even without comparing these numbers, one can easily see by looking at the bars in the graph that the third category is projected to increase by far more than the first two. Therefore, if software developers are included in the total of all occupations, which is projected to increase by less the other two, (d) is true. The other choices are not true because the bar including software developers would have to be longer than the other two for software developer employment to be projected to increase by the same amount as (b), or more than either (c) or both of (a) the others.

**History/Social Studies**
12. A: *Imbued* in this context means *permeated* or *saturated*, which is the sense that this sentence is trying to convey.

13. D: The wording in this revision option is the only one that makes grammatical sense.

14. D: Choices A, B, and C all have similar meanings and match the text's description of Lubitsch's film style as elegant or sophisticated.

15. C: This phrase is used in the last sentence to describe the Lubitsch style.

16. B: Lubitsch's focus on seemingly irrelevant details as symbols is described in the text as his signature style. (Paragraph 2)

17. C: Lubitsch was invited in 1923 by Albert Zukor.

18. D: Made in 1912, the film could not have been a talkie, as it was not until 1923 that Lubitsch went to Hollywood to use sound technology. And the text tells us nothing of the film's content or cast.

19. A: Monescu and Lily were both thieves who posed as members of high society. Mariette was a real heiress, and Lubitsch, of course, was a director, not a character in the film.

20. C: This, indeed, is the underlying theme of the entire movie, as shown by the characters of Monescu and Lily, who appear to be elegant but are, in fact, thieves.

21. B: Lily has no wealth of her own, but Monescu finally chooses her over Mariette and her fortune. (Paragraph 5)

22. B: Lily passes herself off as a countess and Montescu poses as a baron (Paragraph 5).

**Humanities**
23. B: This is the only revision of the phrase that uses proper grammar and punctuation.

24. D Since the sentence ends with a period, it may not be phrased as a question, this is the correct revision.

25. C: In general, the first paragraph in an essay (of any length) introduces the discussion at hand or frames a particular debate. Most introductory paragraphs do not introduce extensive content. In this paragraph, there is no clear stance taken on either Buddhist or Western notions of the self, and so choices A and B are inappropriate. Choice C is a good answer because it stresses that the purpose of the first paragraph is to introduce a tension and not to make judgments one way or another. Choice D is inappropriate because "egolessness" is not discussed until the second paragraph. The best choice, then, is C.

26. D: Insofar as this is a definition question, the reader should look back to the passage for the exact wording of the definition. Doing so reveals that choice A is inappropriate because it is explicitly rejected as a valid definition within the passage. Choice B is inappropriate because superego and id are not mentioned within the passage. Choice C is inappropriate because it is the definition for "ego-toxicity." Choice D is a good choice because it is the definition of "egolessness" given in the passage.

27. A: This question is easy to over think. In the second paragraph "egolessness" and "ego-toxicity" are defined and contrasted. The purpose of this paragraph, then, should mention this in some form. Choice A is good because it captures the fact that these terms are distinguished in the paragraph. Choice B is inappropriate because the paragraph only mentions the conflict that Buddhists feel—there is no judgment made on the conflict. Choices C and D are inappropriate because the paragraph does not praise one perspective over another.

28. D: Looking to the passage, it seems as if "*quid pro quo*" means something like "if I do something, then I will be rewarded with something good." Choice A is not a good choice because it says "if I don't do anything, I will get something good." Choice B is inappropriate because money is not mentioned. While choice C might seem like a good choice, the passage does not really talk about what people deserve as much as it talks about what people should do or how they should behave. Choice D is a good choice because "something for something" implies the sort of exchange described in the passage.

29. D: This question asks for a detail from the passage, not for a larger, general idea. Choice A is inappropriate because this position describes ego-toxicity, not Buddhist egolessness. Choice B is inappropriate not only because Buddhists do not act out of expectation of reward, but also because the passage does not mention heaven. Choice C is inappropriate because the passage does not address the idea of reincarnation. Choice D is the best choice because in addition to doing good out of compassion, Buddhists do good because it is good for all beings.

30. C: In the first paragraph, the third sentence identifies increased tension in recent decades between individualism and collectivism in the West. This is developed in subsequent paragraphs by the discussion of ego-toxicity vs. egolessness reflecting individualism vs. collectivism. The second sentence (a) provides evidence supporting the first sentence, not a main idea. The fourth sentence (b) provides evidence supporting the third sentence. The first sentence (d) focuses only on Western emphasis of individualism over collectivism, not on the tension between the two that is a main idea on which the following paragraphs elaborate.

31. A: The sentence is in the best position for the most logical organization. Moving it to the end of the paragraph (a) would be illogical because as it is now, it precedes the sentence "Buddhists who live in such societies....", which refers back to "In Western societies..." so reversing their order would make no sense. Moving it to the beginning of the paragraph (c) would interrupt the transition between the previous paragraph's last sentence, "...the struggles that Western Buddhists face" and the second paragraph's first sentence, "Central to Buddhist belief is the idea of 'egolessness.'" The latter sentence logically follows the former one. Not only would moving the quoted sentence interrupt this logical progression; it would moreover mention ego-toxicity prematurely—before it is introduced in the second paragraph's third sentence. The quoted sentence should not be removed entirely from the paragraph (d) as it further specifies ego-toxicity, introduced and defined in the previous sentence, as prevalent in Western societies; hence it provides essential information.

32. D: The last sentence in each paragraph of this passage identifies "struggles", "caught between", "The struggle...continues"—all referring to a main conflict between individualism and collectivism—and the final sentence resolves it by stating that abandoning ego-toxicity enables compassionate caring for self and others. Hence none of these sentences identifies only half of this conflict, and the final sentence is not the only one to complete it (a). The first sentence of each paragraph does not identify this main conflict (b), (c); only the first sentence of the third paragraph does. In the first paragraph, the first sentence identifies Western emphasis of one over the other, not the conflict between them. In the second paragraph, the first sentence identifies the idea of "egolessness" central to Buddhist belief, not its conflict with ego-toxicity identified later in the paragraph. The final sentence does not simply reiterate the conflict (b) but resolves it.

33. B: This passage is best characterized as persuasive because the author is making a point, arguing in its favor, and providing evidence to support it. Descriptive (a) text paints a vivid picture of a person, place, thing, scene, or situation by providing many specific sensory details to help readers imagine they are really experiencing it. Expository (c) prose provides factual information objectively without adding the author's opinions or seeking to convince readers of anything. Narrative (d) text tells readers a story.

**Science**

34. C: In terms of determining their validity, hypotheses are confirmed or disconfirmed. None of the other options are meaningful.

35. D: Since the sentence begins in the present tense, it should continue in the present tense as well. The proper verb to be used in this clause is *affect*, meaning to have an impact, not *effect*, meaning to bring about.

36. C: With a complex passage like this one, main idea questions may require a re-reading of the relevant portion of the passage because some answer choices may not apply to the question. Answer choice D, for example, is the main idea of the first paragraph, not the second. Answer choices A and B on the other hand, are details that are directly contradicted by the passage. C is the only answer choice that is not contradicted by the passage and applies to the specified paragraph.

37. C: Even though this question seems like it requires logical operations, it actually asks for a detail from the passage. Choice A is inappropriate because something that is neither *x* nor *y* is irrelevant to the passage. Choice B is inappropriate because something that is both *x* and *y* proves the hypothesis. Choice C is a good choice because, using the monkey example, a monkey (*x*) that has no hair (*y*) disproves the hypothesis "all monkeys are hairy." Choice D is inappropriate because it is irrelevant to the passage. An example of something that is *y* but not *x* could be a hairy llama.

38. D: This is also a detail question. It asks why the author discusses "sample sets." A good answer to this question will say something about probability and/or the size of sample sets. Choice A is inappropriate because the passage does not discuss different monkey species. Choice B is inappropriate because the sample set example shows that it is practically impossible to prove that all monkeys are hairy. Choice C is inappropriate because the passage shows that neither large nor small sample sets can prove hypotheses. Choice D is the best choice because the passage shows that to prove a hypothesis about monkeys, the sample set needed would be functionally too large—every monkey past, present, and future, would have to be examined.

39. D: This question asks the reader to apply information learned in the passage to a new instance. In this case, an eighteen-wheel automobile will lower the probability of the hypothesis "all automobiles have only four wheels." Choices A and C are inappropriate because they refer to proving and disproving and not lowering probability. Choice B is inappropriate because it refers to raising and not lowering probability. Choice D is the best answer because an eighteen wheel automobile decreases the probability that all automobiles have only four wheels.

40. A: The main idea of the entire passage is found in the first sentence of the first paragraph. This is not the main idea of only the first paragraph (b) since the entire first paragraph itself is comprised of only two sentences. The second sentence of the first paragraph gives an example of the main idea stated in the first paragraph rather than being included with the first sentence as the main idea (c). Since (a) is correct, (d) is incorrect.

41. C: According to the second paragraph, third sentence, it is NOT possible to prove a hypothesis using only one single piece of evidence (a). However, it IS possible to disprove a hypothesis with just one piece of evidence (b), (c). Therefore, (d) is incorrect.

42. D: This paragraph uses examples to establish the idea that "Single pieces of evidence...seem to affect a given hypothesis in radically different ways." Based on the preceding sentences in this paragraph, which show how it can be impossible to prove a hypothesis using evidence if even one piece of evidence can disprove, the conclusion in the paragraph's last sentence that it is better to describe confirming hypotheses as probabilistic (i.e., rather than absolute) is a logical one. Since it is, this sentence is not irrelevant to the passage topic and should not be deleted (a). It is not irrelevant to this particular paragraph and should not be moved to another paragraph (b).

This sentence can be said to infer and is related to the topic, but it is not unrelated to the purpose (c), which apparently is to discuss hypothesis confirmation and propose one method, identifying its disadvantages and advantages.

43. B: The second sentence of the same last passage paragraph states, "In the monkey example, every single monkey in the history of monkeys would need to be examined before the hypothesis could be proven or disproven." In the last passage sentence, "...infinite sample sets for confirmation or disconfirmation" refers directly to that second sentence (quoted above here). The initial sentence of this paragraph (a) states that evidence-based hypotheses must use probability because sample sets are too large, which agrees with the sentence following it, but does not specifically identify infinite sample sets as that second sentence following it does. The fourth sentence of the previous paragraph (c) shows how even one piece of evidence out of a very large—but NOT infinite—sample size of one billion can disprove a hypothesis rather than showing how infinite sample sizes are required. Since (b) is correct, (d) is incorrect.

44. C: This passage does not contain any sentence fragments (a) as all sentences are complete, each having a subject and predicate and all necessary function words, etc. There are no run-on sentences in this passage (b) as all sentences are separated appropriately with capitalized first letters and periods at the ends and use correct internal punctuation. Since (c) is correct, (d) is incorrect.

# Math - Calculator

1. B: Since Elli will plant a total of 20 flowers, the number of roses plus the number of tulips is 20 or $R + T = 20$. Each rose costs $14; so multiply the number of roses by 14. Each tulip costs $4; so multiply the number of tulips by 4. Elli has a total of $100 to spend on roses and tulips. So $14R + 4T = 100$.

2. D: Use a linear system of equations to find the number of roses. See the explanation for question 36. In this case, the system of equations is $R + T = 20$ and $14R + 4T = 100$. Begin with $R + T = 20$ and solve for T.

$$R + T = 20$$
$$T = 20 - R$$

Now substitute the equation for T into the equation $14R + 4T = 100$.

$$14R + 4T = 100$$
$$14R + 4(20 - R) = 100$$
$$14R + 80 - 4R = 100$$
$$10R = 20$$
$$R = 2$$

Therefore, Elli will plant 2 roses in her garden.

3. C: The number of roses, R is 2 and $R + T = 20$. Therefore, $T = 20 - 2 = 18$. Hence, Elli will plant 18 tulips in her garden.

4. B: Based on the given information, roses cost $14 while tulips cost only $4. Therefore, tulips are less expensive than roses. No information is given about the amount of space or fertilizer tulips require or about which flower Elli thinks is prettier.

5. C: Using the method of elimination to solve the system of linear equations, each term in the top equation may be multiplied by −2, while each term in the bottom equation may be multiplied by 5. Doing so produces two new equations with $x$-terms that will add to 0. The sum of $-10x - 18y = 14$ and $10x - 20y = 100$ may be written as $-38y = 114$, where $y = -3$. Substituting the $y$-value of −3 into the top, original equation gives $5x + 9(-3) = -7$. Solving for $x$ gives $x = 4$. Thus, the solution is $= 4$, $y = -3$.

6. $12.00, 0, $31.50:
Writing and solving a system of equations is one way to determine the cost of a package of cookie dough. Let $c$ represent the cost of each package of cookie dough and $p$ the cost of each package of pretzels. An individual's order cost is equal the number of packages of cookie dough ordered times the cost per package of dough plus the number of packages of pretzels ordered times the cost per package of pretzels. Using the information from the order form for Cedric's and Madhavi's orders,

$$3c + 2p = 51$$
$$1c + 4p = 42$$

A system of linear equations can be solved using a variety of methods, including the elimination (or linear combination) method shown here. Since the question asks for the cost of cookie dough, eliminate the variable $p$ by multiplying the top equation by -2

$$-2(3c + 2p = 51) \rightarrow -6c - 4p = -102$$

and combining the result with the other equation. Then, solve the resulting equation for $c$.

$$-6c - 4p = -102$$
$$\underline{+ 1c + 4p = \quad 42}$$
$$-5c \qquad = -60$$
$$c = 12$$

James bought two packages of cookie dough for $12.00 each; since his order total was $24.00, he must not have purchased any packages of pretzels.

To determine Mei Ling's total order cost, first find the cost per package of pretzels. Madhavi bought one package of cookie dough for $12.00, and her order total was $42.00; it follows that she spent $42.00 − $12.00 = $30.00 on four packages of pretzels. Each package of pretzels therefore costs $\frac{\$30}{4}$=$7.50.

Mei Ling ordered two packages of cookies at $12.00 per package and one package of pretzels at $7.50 per package, so her order total was 2($12.00) + ($7.50) = $31.50.

7. C: Probably the simplest way to solve this equation is to first get rid of the fractions by multiplying each term by their lowest common denominator, which is $6x$: then we have $\frac{6x}{2x} + \frac{6x}{x} = \frac{6x}{6}$, which reduces to $3 + 6 = x$. So, $x = 3 + 6 = 9$.

8. A: The data set, shown in Choice A, correctly represents a frequency of 4 for the interval $1 - 10$, a frequency of 3 for $11 - 20$, a frequency of 4 for $21 - 30$, a frequency of 10 for $31 - 40$, and a frequency of 9 for $41 - 50$.

9. C: The total distance traveled was 8 + 3.6 = 11.6 miles. The first 1/5 of a mile is charged at the higher rate. Since 1/5 = 0.2, the remainder of the trip is 11.4 miles. Thus, the fare for the distance traveled is computed as $5.50 + 5(11.4)($1.50) = $91.00$. To this, the charge for waiting time must be added, which is simply $9($0.20) = $1.80$. Finally, add the two charges, $91 + $1.80 = $92.80.

10. B: First, determine the proportion of students in the fifth grade. Since the total number of students is 180, this proportion is $\frac{36}{180}$ = 0.2, or 20%. Next, determine the same proportion of the total prizes, which is 20% of 20, or $0.2(20) = 4$.

11. B: The probability of events, A or B, may be written as $P(A \text{ or } B) = P(A) + P(B) - P(A \text{ and } B)$. The probabilities of A and B are given, as is the probability of A, given B, so first use the formula $P(A \text{ and } B)$ $P(B) \cdot P(A|B)$. Thus, $P(A \text{ and } B) = 0.34 \cdot 0.46 = 0.1564$. Substituting all probabilities gives 0.18 + 0.34 − 0.1564, which equals 0.3636. Thus, the probability that he goes to the store or to the movies is 36.36%.

12. C: The expected value is equal to the sum of the products of the scholarship amounts and probability she will attend each college, or $\frac{1}{3}$. Thus, the expected value is $\left(6000 \cdot \frac{1}{3}\right) + \left(4500 \cdot \frac{1}{3}\right) + \left(5500 \cdot \frac{1}{3}\right)$, which equals 5,333. So, she can expect to receive $5,333.

13. A: The data set, shown in Choice A, correctly represents a frequency of 4 for the interval $1 - 10$, a frequency of 3 for $11 - 20$, a frequency of 4 for $21 - 30$, a frequency of 10 for $31 - 40$, and a frequency of 9 for $41 - 50$.

14. C: The probability of independent events, A and B, may be found using the formula,
$P(A \text{ and } B) =$
$P(A) \cdot$
$P(B)$. Thus, the probability she draws a jack, replaces it, and then draws an ace card may be represented as $P(A \text{ and } B)$
$\frac{4}{52} \cdot \frac{4}{52}$, which simplifies to $P(A \text{ and } B) = \frac{1}{169}$.

15. A: The frequency table for Choice A correctly shows the frequencies represented by the histogram. The frequencies of values, falling between 1 and 10 is 3, between 11 and 20 is 9, between 21 and 30 is 8, between 31 and 40 is 6, and between 41 and 50 is 4.

16. A: Candidate A's vote percentage is determined by the number of votes that he obtained, divided by the total number of votes cast, and then multiplied by 100 to convert the decimal into a percentage. Therefore,
Candidate A's vote percentage $= \frac{36,800}{36,800+32,100+2,100} = \frac{36,800}{71,000} = 51.8\%$.

17. C: The expected value is equal to the sum of the products of the probabilities and their x-values. Thus, the expected value is $(0 \cdot 18) + (1 \cdot 12) + (2 \cdot 20) + (3 \cdot 24) + (4 \cdot 10) + (5 \cdot 36) + (6 \cdot 4)$. The expected value equals 368.

18. A: The table below represents the probabilities:

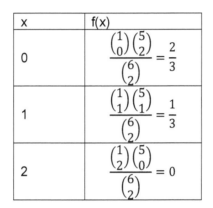

| x | f(x) |
|---|---|
| 0 | $\frac{\binom{1}{0}\binom{5}{2}}{\binom{6}{2}} = \frac{2}{3}$ |
| 1 | $\frac{\binom{1}{1}\binom{5}{1}}{\binom{6}{2}} = \frac{1}{3}$ |
| 2 | $\frac{\binom{1}{2}\binom{5}{0}}{\binom{6}{2}} = 0$ |

19. 1 | 5 = 15:

| 1 | 5, 7, 7, 8, 9 |
|---|---|
| 2 | 0, 1, 2, 5, 7, 8 |
| 3 | 1, 3, 6, 8, 8, 8 |
| 4 | 2, 5, 7, 9 |

20. Mean: 29.8; Median: 28; Mode: 38: The mean, or average, is equal to the sum of the data divided by the number of values in the data set.

Mean $= \frac{15+17+17+18+19+20+21+22+25+27+28+31+33+36+38+38+38+42+45+47+49}{21} = \frac{626}{21} = 29.8$

The median is the middle number or the average of the two middle numbers in the set of data organized from least to greatest. Since there are 21 numbers in the data set, the median is the eleventh number, below and above which there are ten numbers. The eleventh number is 28. The mode is the value that occurs with the greatest frequency in the set. If all values occur with equal frequency, there is no mode; if more than one value appears with the highest frequency, there is more than one mode. In this set, there is one mode, namely 38, which appears three times in the set of data.

21. C: The least common denominator of
$x(x + 4)$ may be multiplied by both rational expressions. Doing so gives $2x = 3(x + 4)$ or $2x = 3x + 12$. Solving for $x$ gives $x = -12$.

22. B: Graphing the linear equation and a circle, with a center at (2, −4) and radius of 4, shows points of intersection of (−2, −4) and (2, −8).

23. D: The equation may be solved by multiplying each term on each of the equation by the least common denominator, or $4(x + 4)$. Doing so gives $4(x + 4) \cdot \frac{x}{x+4} - 4(x + 4) \cdot \frac{3}{4} = 4(x + 4) \cdot \frac{4}{x+4}$, which simplifies to $4x - 3x - 12 = 16$, where $x = 28$.

24. C: When graphing the equations, the points of intersection represent the solutions of the system of equations. The line and parabola intersect at the points, (1, 3) and (0, 2). Thus, the solutions of the system include the points, (1, 3) and (0, 2). Substitution of the *x*- and *y*-values into each equation produces true statements.

25. 1.5, 3: The ball follows a parabolic path, and the ball's maximum height occurs at the vertex of the parabola. Since the equation of the parabola is given in the form $h = at^2 + bt + c$, the $t-$value of the vertex can be found using $\frac{-b}{2a} = \frac{-47}{2(-16)} \approx 1.5$. The ball reaches a maximum height about 1.5 seconds after having been thrown into the air.

When the ball hits the ground, its height is zero. Substitute 0 for $h$ into the equation and solve for $t$.
$$h = -16t^2 + 47t + 3$$
$$0 = -16t^2 + 47t + 3$$
Factor and use the zero-product property.
$$0 = (-16t - 1)(t - 3)$$
$$0 = -16t - 1 \quad 0 = t - 3$$
$$1 = -16t \quad \mathbf{3 = t}$$
$$-\frac{1}{16} = t$$
Since $t$ cannot be negative, $t = 3$. The ball hits the ground three seconds after having been thrown into the air.

26. A: The range of a function is the set of all possible output values for the function. In this case, the output for *g(x)* is the function itself, *g(x)*. To find the range, first graph the given function.

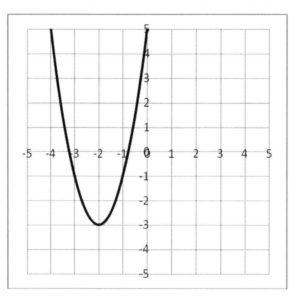

Notice that the graph is a U-shaped parabola, which means that its vertex is a minimum (rather than a maximum). Because of this, the range is the set of *y*-values above (and including) the minimum. In this case, the minimum is the point (-2,-3). Therefore, the range of $g(x)$ is $g(x) \geq -3$.

27. 6 inches: The area of a rectangle is equal to its length times its width, while the perimeter is the sum of the four sides, or the sum of twice the length and twice the width. So, to find the dimensions of the rectangle, set up and solve a system of equations. Here, the substitution method of solving is shown.

$$lw = 120 \rightarrow l = \frac{120}{w}$$
$$2l + 2w = 44$$
$$2\left(\frac{120}{w}\right) + 2w = 44$$
$$\frac{240}{w} + 2w = 44$$
$$w\left(\frac{240}{w} + 2w\right) = w(44)$$
$$240 + 2w^2 = 44w$$
$$2w^2 - 44w + 240 = 0$$
$$2(w^2 - 22w + 120) = 0$$
$$w^2 - 22w + 120 = 0$$
$$(w - 10)(w - 12) = 0$$
$$w = 10 \text{ or } w = 12$$

If the width is 10 ft, the length is 12 ft, or if the width is 12 ft, the length is 10 ft.

On the house plan, the scale is $\frac{1}{24}$, which means that a 1 ft length is represented as 1/24$^{th}$ of a foot on the plan. 1/24$^{th}$ of a foot is $\left(\frac{1}{24}\right)(12") = \frac{12"}{24} = \frac{1"}{2}$. So, the 12' side of the room is represented as a 6" side of a rectangle on the house plan.

28. 55: Since $m\angle ACD = 110°$, the measure of $\overset{\frown}{AB}$ is 110°. In a circle, the measure of an inscribed angle is equal to one half of the measure of the intercepted arc. Since $\angle ADB$ is an inscribed angle, its measure is half of $m\overset{\frown}{AB}$, or $110° \div 2 = 55°$.

29. 18.2: The formula for the volume of a cylinder is $V = \pi r^2 h$, where $r$ is the radius of the cylinder and $h$ is its height. The diameter of the soda can is 2.2 in, so its radius is $2.2 \div 2 = 1.1$ in. Thus, the volume of the can is

$$V = \pi(1.1)^2(4.8)$$
$$\approx 18.2 \text{ in}^3$$

30. A: An isosceles triangle is a triangle with two congruent sides called its *legs*. The other side is called the *base* of the triangle. First draw isosceles triangle *ABC*.

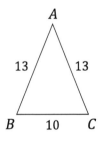

To calculate its area, we must find the height $h$ of the triangle, so draw an altitude from $A$.

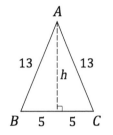

Use the Pythagorean Theorem to calculate $h$.

$$a^2 + b^2 = c^2$$
$$h^2 + 5^2 = 13^2$$
$$h^2 + 25 = 169$$
$$h^2 = 144$$
$$h = 12$$

The formula for the area of a triangle is $A = \frac{1}{2}Bh$, where $B$ is the length of the base and $h$ is the height. The base of $\triangle ABC$ is 10 and its height is 12. Use these values to calculate the triangle's area.

$$A = \frac{1}{2}(10)(12)$$
$$= 60$$

31. C: The circumference of a circle is given by the formula $C = 2\pi r$, where $r$ is the length of the radius. One section of a circle is called an *arc*, and it is proportional to the central angle that defines the arc. Thus, the length of an arc with central angle $\theta$ (in degrees) is given by the formula
$$L = 2\pi r \cdot \frac{\theta}{360}$$

Calculate the measure of the central angle.
$$3\pi = 2\pi(4) \cdot \frac{\theta}{360}$$
$$3\pi = 8\pi \cdot \frac{\theta}{360}$$
$$\frac{3}{8} = \frac{\theta}{360}$$
$$135 = \theta$$

Thus, $\mathrm{m}\angle ACB = 135°$. A sector is a slice of a circle bounded by two radii. The area of a sector with angle $\theta$ (in degrees) is given by the formula
$$A = \pi r^2 \cdot \frac{\theta}{360}$$

Substitute the value of the radius and angle into this formula and simplify the result.
$$A = \pi(4)^2 \cdot \frac{135}{360}$$
$$= 16\pi \cdot \frac{135}{360}$$
$$= 6\pi$$

# Math - No-Calculator

1. B: Using the method of elimination to solve the system of equations, each term in the top equation may be multiplied by 2, while each term in the bottom equation may be multiplied by −3. Doing so produces two new equations with $x$-terms that will add to 0; $2(3x + 6y) = 2(36)$ can be written as $6x + 12y = 72$; $-3(2x + 9y) = -3(34)$ can be written as $-6x - 27y = -102$. Thus, the equations, $\begin{array}{l} 6x + 12y = 72 \\ -6x - 27y = -102 \end{array}$, may be added to find the correct $y$-value solution.

2. A: The flat rate of $65 represents the $y$-intercept, and the charge of $0.12 per roaming minute used represents the slope. Therefore, the expression representing his monthly phone bill is $65 + 0.12x$.

3. C: The slope of the line may be determined by calculating the ratio of the change in $y$-values per change in corresponding $x$-values. Using the points, (2, 0) and (8, 2), the slope may be written as $\frac{2-0}{8-2}$, which equals $\frac{1}{3}$. Substituting the slope into the slope-intercept form of an equation gives $y = \frac{1}{3}x + b$. Substituting a pair of corresponding $x$- and $y$-values into the equation will reveal the $y$-intercept. Substituting the $x$- and $y$-values from the point, (2, 0), gives: $0 = \frac{1}{3}(2) + b$, where $b = -\frac{2}{3}$. Thus, the equation of the line is $y = \frac{1}{3}x - \frac{2}{3}$. The equation, $7x - 21y = 14$, may be written as the same equation, when solved for $y$.

4. D: The cost of the taxi ride is the sum of two functions, a constant function for the first mile and a linear function for the rest of the ride. The constant function is $c_1(d) = 4.25$ since the cost of the first mile is $4.25. For the linear part, subtract 1 from $d$ to exclude the first mile, and then multiply the result by 0.70 since it costs $0.70 per mile. The result is $c_2(d) = 0.70(d - 1)$. Finally, write the function for the total cost of the taxi ride by adding the two functions.

$$c(d) = c_1(d) + c_2(d)$$
$$= 4.25 + 0.70(d-1)$$

5. B: The first function $L(g)$ gives the water level after $g$ gallons are pumped into the tank. The second function $w(t)$ gives the number of gallons pumped into the tank after $t$ minutes, which the first function calls $g$. Consequently, we can have $L$ act on $w$: the composition of the functions $L(w(t))$ is the water level of the tank after $t$ minutes. Calculate $L(w(t))$.

$$L(w(t)) = 0.3 \cdot w(t)$$
$$= 0.3 \cdot 1.2t$$
$$= 0.36t$$

Thus, the function $L(t) = 0.36t$ represents the water level of the tank after $t$ minutes.

6. C: T the first sentence, "Adam has $10 more than Betty," can be written as $A = B + 10$, where $A$ represents the amount of money Adam has and $B$ represents the amount of money Betty has.

Next translate the second sentence "If Adam were to give $15 to Betty, then she would have twice as much money as Adam." This means that if Adam had $15 less (represented by the expression $A - 15$) and Betty had $15 more ($B + 15$), then Betty would have two times what Adam would have. So, the correct equation is $B + 15 = 2(A - 15)$.

7. C: The length of an interval is the difference between its endpoints. For example, the length of the interval [2, 4] is 2. To determine how the given function grows over an interval of length 5, determine the value of $f$ at each endpoint of that interval. Since linear functions grow by equal differences over equal intervals, you can use any interval of length 5, and your answer will apply to all such intervals. For example, you can use the interval [0, 5]:

$f(0) = 4(0) - 8$
$= 0 - 8$
$= -8$

$f(5) = 4(5) - 8$
$= 20 - 8$
$= 12$

Since $f(0) = -8$ and $f(3) = 12$, the function increases by $12 - (-8) = 20$ over this interval, and over any interval of length 5.

8. C: Linear functions can be written in the form $g(x) = ax + b$. To determine the value of $a$, notice that $g(x)$ increases by 2 every time $x$ increases by 1. For instance, when $x$ goes from 0 to 1, the value of $y$ goes from $-3$ to $-1$; and when $x$ goes from 1 to 2, the value of $y$ increases from $-1$ to 1. Since $g(x)$ increases by 2, the value of $a$ is 2, so the function is $g(x) = 2x + b$. Next calculate the value of $b$. From the graph, you can tell that $g(0) = -3$. Use this to calculate $b$:

$g(0) = -3$
$2(0) + b = -3$
$0 + b = -3$
$b = -3$

Thus, the function is $g(x) = 2x - 3$.

Alternatively, writing an explicit formula in the form $g(x) = ax + b$ means solving for two variables, $a$ and $b$. Use the information given in the graph to write two equations relating these two variables in terms of $x$ and $g(x)$:

$-3 = a(0) + b$
$1 = a(2) + b$

The first readily solves to $b = -3$, which you can substitute into the second to solve for $a$:

$1 = a(2) - 3$
$4 = a(2) = 2a$
$a = 2$

Thus, the function is $g(x) = 2x - 3$.

9. A: The inequality may be solved by first subtracting 18 from both sides. Doing so gives $3x > -12$. Dividing both sides of the inequality by 3 gives $x > -4$.

10. D: The range of a function is the set of all possible output values for the function. In this case, the output for $g(x)$ is the function itself, $g(x)$. Examine the given function. Let's say you choose some particular real number for $g(x)$. For any choice you make, you can find an $x$-value that will result in that choice by simply adding 2 to it. For example, say you choose $g(x) = -3$. Then you can use $x = -3 + 2 = -1$ to get your original value because $g(-1) = -1 - 2 = -3$. Since this will work for any real value for $g(x)$, the range of $g(x)$ is all real numbers.

You can see this visually by graphing the function. In the graph below, notice that the function can go up and down without end.

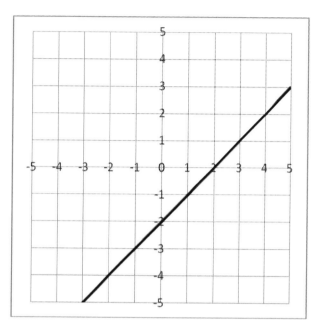

11. A: After distributing the minus sign across the second trinomial, the expression can be rewritten as $3x^3 - 9x^2 + 6x - 8x^3 - 4x^2 + 3x$. Combining like terms gives $-5x^3 - 13x^2 + 9x$.

12. A: The sum can be written as $12x^3 - 8x + 6x^2 - 3 + 8x^2 - 20x^3 + 6 - 2x$. Combining like terms and writing the expression in standard form gives: $-8x^3 + 14x^2 - 10x + 3$.

13. $x = -3, 2, -1; y = -6$: $y = (x + 3)(x^2 - x - 2)$ is a cubic equation written as a product of a linear and quadratic factor, $x - 3$ and $x^2 - x - 2$, respectively. The quadratic expression can be further factored to $(x - 2)(x + 1)$, so $y = (x + 3)(x^2 - x - 2) = (x + 3)(x - 2)(x + 1)$. The $x$-intercepts of the graph of $y$ occur when $y = 0$, so to find the $x$-intercepts, solve $0 = (x + 3)(x - 2)(x + 1)$ using the zero-product property.

$$x + 3 = 0 \qquad x - 2 = 0 \qquad x + 1 = 0$$
$$x = -3 \qquad x = 2 \qquad x = -1$$

The $y$-intercept of the graph of the equation occurs when $x = 0$, so solve $y = (0 + 3)(0^2 - 0 - 2 = 3 - 2 = -6$.

14. D: Since the equation is in the form $y = a(x - h)^2 + k$, the graph is a parabola. For an equation in this form, the vertex is $(h,k)$, and the parabola either opens up (is U-shaped) or opens down (is an upside-down U) depending on the value of A: If $a$ is positive, the parabola opens up, and if $a$ is negative, it opens down. Moreover, if $|a|$ is greater than one, the graph is wider than the parent function $y = x^2$, and if $|a|$ is smaller than one, the graph is skinnier than the parent function.

15. D: The domain of a function is the set of all possible input values for the function. In this case, the input for $f(x)$ is $x$. The easiest way to find the domain of $f(x)$ is to determine for which values of $x$ the function is undefined. Then you can exclude those values from the domain.

Examine the given function. Notice that it does not contain a square root sign, a logarithm, or a fraction with $x$ in the denominator. Therefore, the function will be defined for all real numbers. You can see this visually by graphing the function. In the graph below, notice that the function can go to the left and right without end.

16. A: The domain of a function is the set of all possible input values for the function. In this case, the input for $f(x)$ is $x$. The easiest way to find the domain of $f(x)$ is to determine for which $x$-values the function is undefined. Then, you can exclude those values from the domain.

Examine the given function. Notice that $f(x)$ has a square-root sign. Since negative numbers do not have real square roots, we need to exclude all the $x$-values that will make the expression under the square root negative. The expression $x + 5$ is negative only when $x$ is strictly less than $-5$. Therefore, the domain is all values greater than or equal to $-5$, or $x \geq -5$.

17. C: Since $ABCD$ is a rectangle, opposite sides are equal and all the angles are right angles. Moreover, $m$ and $n$ are parallel to the sides of the rectangle and bisect the rectangle, so they are both perpendicular to the sides of the rectangle. Consider the four given choices:

- If you reflect $ABCD$ across $m$, then $\overline{AB}$ and $\overline{BC}$ will switch places, so the image $A'B'C'D'$ will look like the original rectangle.
- Similarly, if you reflect $ABCD$ across $n$, then $\overline{BC}$ and $\overline{AD}$ will switch places, so the image will look like the original as well.
- However, if you rotate the rectangle $90°$ about point $P$, the image will be a "tall" rectangle, rather than a "long" (or "wide") rectangle, so the image will not look like the original.
- Finally, if you rotate the rectangle $180°$ about point $P$, then both pairs of opposite sides of the rectangle will switch places.

# What Your PSAT Score Means for National Merit Qualification

In 2012, more than 1,550,000 juniors took the PSAT. In the following chart, the column on the left is the score range, and the three columns to the right show what percentage of juniors taking the test scored within that range.

| Score range | Reading | Math | Writing |
|:---:|:---:|:---:|:---:|
| 76 - 80 | 1 | 1 | 1 |
| 71 - 75 | 2 | 2 | 1 |
| 66 - 70 | 4 | 4 | 4 |
| 61 - 65 | 6 | 9 | 7 |
| 56 - 60 | 10 | 12 | 9 |
| 51 - 55 | 14 | 15 | 13 |
| 46 - 50 | 17 | 16 | 13 |
| 41 - 45 | 19 | 17 | 19 |
| 36 - 40 | 14 | 12 | 17 |
| 31 - 35 | 9 | 7 | 9 |
| 26 - 30 | 3 | 3 | 4 |
| 20 - 25 | 1 | 2 | 3 |

As you're probably aware, the PSAT is no longer scored as three separate sections. Instead, student performances on the Reading and Writing sections are combined to give a single score for both areas: a Reading and Writing score. Also, the range of possible scores has changed from 20-80 on each section to 160-760 on each section. Here is what the previous chart would look like if it were displayed using the new scoring convention.

| Score range | Reading and Writing | Math |
|:---:|:---:|:---:|
| 711 – 760 | 1 | 1 |
| 661 – 710 | 2 | 2 |
| 611 – 660 | 4 | 4 |
| 561 – 610 | 6 | 9 |
| 511 – 560 | 10 | 12 |
| 461 – 510 | 13 | 15 |
| 411 – 460 | 15 | 16 |
| 361 – 410 | 19 | 17 |
| 311 – 360 | 16 | 12 |
| 261 – 310 | 9 | 7 |
| 211 – 260 | 3 | 3 |
| 160 – 210 | 2 | 2 |

Most of these changes were made to make it clearer that the PSAT score is supposed to predict or at least correlate with the SAT score. The maximum possible score on the PSAT is now 1520, which is less than the maximum possible score of 1600 on the new SAT, to account for the fact that the SAT is a more difficult test.

Based on this information, your scores should be close to 700 or higher in both categories to guarantee qualification. However, since semi-finalist status is awarded to students in approximately the top 1.5% of composite scores (the sum of your two individual scores), you can have a lower score in one subject as long as your scores in the other is high enough to bring up your composite total. The following chart shows a breakdown of the percentage of juniors receiving given ranges of composite scores.

| Composite Range | Percentage Receiving |
| --- | --- |
| 1446 - 1520 | <1 |
| 1371 - 1445 | 1 |
| 1296 - 1370 | 2 |
| 1221 - 1295 | 4 |
| 1146 - 1220 | 6 |
| 1071 - 1145 | 8 |
| 996 - 1070 | 9 |
| 921 - 995 | 10 |
| 846 - 920 | 12 |
| 771 - 845 | 13 |
| 696 - 770 | 12 |
| 621 - 695 | 10 |
| 546 - 620 | 7 |
| 471 - 545 | 4 |
| 320 - 470 | 1 |

Scoring a 1400 or higher should be enough to ensure that you qualify for semi-finalist status. If you live in a very competitive state (the highest cutoff scores were from California, DC, Massachusetts, New Jersey, and Virginia), you may need another 10 or 20 points to guarantee qualification.

Unless you plan to graduate from high school a year early, only your junior year PSAT scores will be used. You must also be a US citizen or a permanent resident in the process of becoming a US citizen. Although taking the PSAT at one of the October administrations is the easiest way to qualify for the National Merit Program, the NMSC does provide alternatives to students who miss these dates. Contact the NMSC at 1-847-866-5100 for more information.

The initial stages of the Merit Program are judged entirely based on a student's selection index. The selection index is simply the sum of your component scores. In April, 50,000 students with the highest selection indices will be notified and made eligible for NMSC referral service. In September, about 34,000 of these students will be named Commended Students and the remaining 16,000 will be named Semifinalists. Only Semifinalists are eligible to advance further in the competition for Merit Scholarships.

Semifinalists are determined on a state-by-state basis, and the selection index cut-off varies by state and by year. Each state's allotment of semifinalists is determined based on its percentage of the national total of high school graduating seniors.

Semifinalists who meet eligibility standards (students must submit an application, high school record, and SAT I scores among other requirements) will be among the 14,000 National Merit Finalists named in February.

In March and April the NMSC awards 7,600 scholarships to students based upon their abilities, skills, and accomplishments. The three types of scholarships awarded are National Merit Scholarships (2,400), corporate-sponsored scholarships (1,200), and college-sponsored scholarships (4,000).

Some corporations offer a number of scholarships to eligible students (for example, the children of employees) that are not filled entirely by Finalists. These 1,500 scholarships are called Special Scholarships and are chosen from applicants from among the qualified pool that the company has designated.

You can find out more detailed information about the National Merit Program in the PSAT/NMSQT Student Bulletin available in your college counseling office. The College Board maintains information on the PSAT/NMSQT at their website, or you can contact the NMSC directly:

> National Merit Scholarship Corporation
> 1560 Sherman Avenue, Suite 200
> Evanston, IL 60201-4897
> (847) 866-5100

# FREE Test Taking Tips DVD Offer

To help us better serve you, we have developed a Test Taking Tips DVD that we would like to give you for FREE. **This DVD covers world-class test taking tips that you can use to be even more successful when you are taking your test.**

All that we ask is that you email us your feedback about your study guide. Please let us know what you thought about it – whether that is good, bad or indifferent.

To get your **FREE Test Taking Tips DVD**, email freedvd@studyguideteam.com with "FREE DVD" in the subject line and the following information in the body of the email:

    a.   The title of your study guide.

    b.   Your product rating on a scale of 1-5, with 5 being the highest rating.

    c.   Your feedback about the study guide. What did you think of it?

    d.   Your full name and shipping address to send your free DVD.

If you have any questions or concerns, please don't hesitate to contact us at freedvd@studyguideteam.com.

Thanks again!